W0263896

Informatik – Fachberichte

Band 1: Programmiersprachen. GI-Fachtagung 1976. Herausgegeben von H.-J. Schneider und M. Nagl. (vergriffen)

Band 2: Betrieb von Rechenzentren. Workshop der Gesellschaft für Informatik 1975. Herausgegeben von A. Schreiner. (vergriffen)

Band 3: Rechnernetze und Datenfernverarbeitung. Fachtagung der GI und NTG 1976. Herausgegeben von D. Haupt und H. Petersen. VI, 309 Seiten. 1976.

Band 4: Computer Architecture. Workshop of the Gesellschaft für Informatik 1975. Edited by W. Händler. VIII, 382 pages. 1976.

Band 5: GI – 6. Jahrestagung. Proceedings 1976. Herausgegeben von E. J. Neuhold. (vergriffen)

Band 6: B. Schmidt, GPSS-FORTRAN, Version II. Einführung in die Simulation diskreter Systeme mit Hilfe eines FORTRAN-Programmpaketes, 2. Auflage. XIII, 535 Seiten. 1978.

Band 7: GMR–GI–GfK. Fachtagung Prozessrechner 1977. Herausgegeben von G. Schmidt. (vergriffen)

Band 8: Digitale Bildverarbeitung/Digital Image Processing. GI/NTG Fachtagung, München, März 1977. Herausgegeben von H.-H. Nagel. (vergriffen)

Band 9: Modelle für Rechensysteme. Workshop 1977. Herausgegeben von P. P. Spies. VI, 297 Seiten. 1977.

Band 10: GI – 7. Jahrestagung. Proceedings 1977. Herausgegeben von H. J. Schneider. IX, 214 Seiten. 1977.

Band 11: Methoden der Informatik für Rechnerunterstütztes Entwerfen und Konstruieren, GI-Fachtagung, München, 1977. Herausgegeben von R. Gnatz und K. Samelson. VIII, 327 Seiten. 1977.

Band 12: Programmiersprachen. 5. Fachtagung der GI, Braunschweig, 1978. Herausgegeben von K. Alber. VI, 179 Seiten. 1978.

Band 13: W. Steinmüller, L. Ermer, W. Schimmel: Datenschutz bei riskanten Systemen. Eine Konzeption entwickelt am Beispiel eines medizinischen Informationssystems. X, 244 Seiten. 1978.

Band 14: Datenbanken in Rechnernetzen mit Kleinrechnern. Fachtagung der GI, Karlsruhe, 1978. Herausgegeben von W. Stucky und E. Holler. (vergriffen)

Band 15: Organisation von Rechenzentren. Workshop der Gesellschaft für Informatik, Göttingen, 1977. Herausgegeben von D. Wall. X, 310 Seiten. 1978.

Band 16: GI – 8. Jahrestagung, Proceedings 1978. Herausgegeben von S. Schindler und W. K. Giloi. VI, 394 Seiten. 1978.

Band 17: Bildverarbeitung und Mustererkennung. DAGM Symposium, Oberpfaffenhofen, 1978. Herausgegeben von E. Triendl. XIII, 385 Seiten. 1978.

Band 18: Virtuelle Maschinen. Nachbildung und Vervielfachung maschinenorientierter Schnittstellen. GI-Arbeitsseminar. München 1979. Herausgegeben von H. J. Siegert. X, 230 Seiten. 1979.

Band 19: GI – 9. Jahrestagung. Herausgegeben von K. H. Böhling und P. P. Spies. (vergriffen)

Band 20: Angewandte Szenenanalyse. DAGM Symposium, Karlsruhe 1979. Herausgegeben von J. P. Foith. XIII, 362 Seiten. 1979.

Band 21: Formale Modelle für Informationssysteme. Fachtagung der GI, Tutzing 1979. Herausgegeben von H. C. Mayr und B. E. Meyer. VI, 265 Seiten. 1979.

Band 22: Kommunikation in verteilten Systemen. Workshop der Gesellschaft für Informatik e.V.. Herausgegeben von S. Schindler und J. C. W. Schröder. VIII, 338 Seiten. 1979.

Band 23: K.-H. Hauer, Portable Methodenmonitoren. Dialogsysteme zur Steuerung von Methodenbanken: Softwaretechnischer Aufbau und Effizienzanalyse. XI, 209 Seiten. 1980.

Band 24: N. Ryska, S. Herda, Kryptographische Verfahren in der Datenverarbeitung. V, 401 Seiten. 1980.

Band 25: Programmsprachen und Programmierentwicklung. 6. Fachtagung, Darmstadt, 1980. Herausgegeben von H.-J. Hoffmann. VI. 236 Seiten. 1980

Band 26: F. Gaffal, Datenverarbeitung im Hochschulbereich der USA. Stand und Entwicklungstendenzen. IX, 199 Seiten. 1980.

Band 27: GI-NTG Fachtagung, Struktur und Betrieb von Rechensystemen. Kiel, März 1980. Herausgegeben von G. Zimmermann. IX, 286 Seiten. 1980.

Band 28: Online-Systeme im Finanz- und Rechnungswesen. Anwendergespräch, Berlin, April 1980. Herausgegeben von P. Stahlknecht. X, 547 Seiten, 1980.

Band 29: Erzeugung und Analyse von Bildern und Strukturen. DGaO – DAGM Tagung, Essen, Mai 1980. Herausgegeben von S. J. Pöppl und H. Platzer. VII, 215 Seiten. 1980.

Band 30: Textverarbeitung und Informatik. Fachtagung der GI, Bayreuth, Mai 1980. Herausgegeben von P. R. Wossidlo. VIII, 362 Seiten. 1980.

Band 31: Firmware Engineering. Seminar veranstaltet von der gemeinsamen Fachgruppe „Mikroprogrammierung" des GI Fachausschusses 3/4 und des NTG-Fachausschusses 6 vom 12. – 14. März 1980 in Berlin. Herausgegeben von W. K. Giloi. VII, 289 Seiten. 1980.

Band 32: M. Kühn, CAD Arbeitssituation. Untersuchungen zu den Auswirkungen von CAD sowie zur menschengerechten Gestaltung von CAD-Systemen. VII, 215 Seiten. 1980.

Band 33: GI – 10. Jahrestagung. Herausgegeben von R. Wilhelm. XV, 563 Seiten. 1980.

Band 34: CAD-Fachgespräch. GI - 10. Jahrestagung. Herausgegeben von R. Wilhelm. VI, 184 Seiten. 1980.

Band 35: B. Buchberger, F. Lichtenberger: Mathematik für Informatiker I. Die Methode der Mathematik. XI, 315 Seiten. 1980.

Band 36: The Use of Formal Specification of Software. Berlin, Juni 1979. Edited by H. K. Berg and W. K. Giloi. V, 388 pages. 1980.

Band 37: Entwicklungstendenzen wissenschaftlicher Rechenzentren. Kolloquium, Göttingen, Juni 1980. Herausgegeben von D. Wall. VII, 163 Seiten. 1980.

Band 38: Datenverarbeitung im Marketing. Herausgegeben von R. Thome. VIII, 377 pages. 1981.

Band 39: Fachtagung Prozeßrechner 1981. München, März 1981. Herausgegeben von R. Baumann. XVI, 476 Seiten. 1981.

Band 40: Kommunikation in verteilten Systemen. Herausgegeben von S. Schindler und J.C.W. Schröder. IX, 459 Seiten. 1981.

Band 41: Messung, Modellierung und Bewertung von Rechensystemen. GI-NTG Fachtagung. Jülich, Februar 1981. Herausgegeben von B. Mertens. VIII, 368 Seiten. 1981.

Band 42: W. Kilian, Personalinformationssysteme in deutschen Großunternehmen. XV, 352 Seiten. 1981.

Band 43: G. Goos, Werkzeuge der Programmiertechnik. GI-Arbeitstagung. Proceedings, Karlsruhe, März 1981. VI, 262 Seiten. 1981.

Informatik-Fachberichte

Herausgegeben von W. Brauer
im Auftrag der Gesellschaft für Informatik (GI)

53

Programmiersprachen und Programmentwicklung

7. Fachtagung, veranstaltet vom Fachausschuß 2 der GI
München, 9./10. März 1982

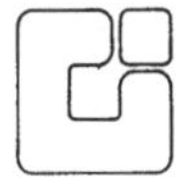

Herausgegeben von Hans Wössner

Springer-Verlag
Berlin Heidelberg New York 1982

Herausgeber

Hans Wössner
Institut für Informatik, Technische Universität München
Postfach 20 24 20, 8000 München 2

CR Subject Classifications (1981): 4.0, 4.1, 4.2, 4.6, 5.23, 5.24, 6.21

ISBN-13:978-3-540-11204-4   e-ISBN-13:978-3-642-68355-8
DOI:10.1007/978-3-642-68355-8

CIP-Kurztitelaufnahme der Deutschen Bibliothek

Programmiersprachen und Programmentwicklung:
Fachtagung d. Fachausschusses 2 d. GI. – Berlin; Heidelberg; New York: Springer
    Bis 5 u.d.T.: Programmiersprachen

7. München, 9./10. März 1982. – 1982. – 243 S. (Informatik-Fachberichte; 53)

NE: Gesellschaft für Informatik / Fachausschuss Programmiersprachen; GT

2145/3140 – 5 4 3 2 1 0

<u>Vorwort</u>

Dieser Band enthält die Beiträge zur Fachtagung "Programmiersprachen
und Programmentwicklung", 9. und 10. März 1982 in München. Die Tagung
ist die siebte in der Reihe der Fachtagungen, die der Fachausschuß 2
"Programmiersprachen und Programmentwicklung" der Gesellschaft für Informatik veranstaltet und deren erste 1971 ebenfalls in München stattgefunden hat. Dazwischen liegen Saarbrücken (1972), Kiel (1974), Erlangen (1976), Braunschweig (1978) und Darmstadt (1980). Ziel dieser
Fachtagungen war und ist es, den jeweils aktuellen Stand des Fachgebiets darzustellen, neuere Entwicklungen aufzuzeigen und den Erfahrungs-
austausch zwischen Forschern und Anwendern zu fördern.

Die Erweiterung der früheren Bezeichnung "Programmiersprachen" des
Fachausschusses (und seiner ersten fünf Fachtagungen) trägt der in den
letzten Jahren gewachsenen Einsicht Rechnung, daß sprachliche und me-
thodische Fortschritte in der Programmierung nur gemeinsam erzielt werden können. Dieses umfassendere Selbstverständnis des Fachgebiets, wie
auch die zunehmende Annäherung von Forschung und Anwendung kommen gerade in der Gesamtheit der vorliegenden Beiträge deutlich zum Ausdruck.

Auf eine thematische Untergruppierung wurde deshalb verzichtet. Die Anordnung der Vorträge entspricht ihrer Reihenfolge im Tagungsprogramm.
Vorgezogen wurden lediglich die Hauptvorträge, in denen anerkannte Experten richtungweisend über neuere Entwicklungen in Theorie und Praxis
berichten. Während von einem der Hauptvorträge bei Drucklegung leider
nur die Zusammenfassung vorlag, traf das Manuskript von Professor Turski,
Universität Warschau, - in der gegenwärtigen Krise eigentlich wider Erwarten - noch rechtzeitig ein.

Das aus den Mitgliedern des Fachausschusses 2 bestehende Programmkomitee,

      K. Alber, TU Braunschweig

      U. Ammann, Contraves, Zürich

      H. Gerstmann, IBM, Böblingen

      P. Gorny, U Oldenburg

      C. Haenel, Siemens, München

      W. Henhapl, TH Darmstadt

      H.-J. Hoffmann, TH Darmstadt

      G. Mußtopf, SCS, Hamburg

      J. Nehmer, U Kaiserslautern

      H. J. Schneider, U Erlangen-Nürnberg

C. v. Urach, Daimler-Benz, Stuttgart
H. Wössner, TU München   (Vorsitz),

hat es sich nicht leicht gemacht, aus insgesamt 41 eingegangenen Vortragsanmeldungen die hier abgedruckten 13 Beiträge auszuwählen. Es hat sich dabei auch auf zusätzliche Gutachten jeweils ausgewählter Spezialisten außerhalb des Programmkomitees (siehe unten) gestützt.

Der Dank der Veranstalter gilt zunächst der Technischen Universität München und den Direktoren des Instituts für Informatik, die als Gastgeber die Durchführung der Tagung wesentlich unterstützen. Er gilt sodann den Vortragenden, den Gutachtern und allen übrigen, die sich um das Gelingen der Tagung bemüht haben. Schließlich danken wir dem Springer-Verlag für die gute Zusammenarbeit bei der kurzfristigen Herstellung dieses Tagungsbands.

München, im Januar 1982   Hans Wössner

Gutachter

Das Programmkomitee dankt den folgenden Damen und Herren für ihre Unterstützung bei der Begutachtung der eingereichten Arbeiten:

B. Austermühl, Darmstadt
G. Barth, Kaiserslautern
J. Bergmann, Darmstadt
M. Broy, München
W. Dosch, München
J. Eickel, München
A. Endres, Böblingen
F. Geiselbrechtinger, Dublin
L. Geissmann, Zürich
G. Goos, Karlsruhe
Ch. Herzog, München
U. Hill-Samelson, München
Ch. Jacobi, Zürich
J.L. Keedy, Clayton, Victoria (Australien)
H. Klaeren, Aachen
S.E. Knudsen, Zürich
B. Krieg-Brückner, München
H.H. Kron, Darmstadt
I. Kupka, Hamburg
A. Laut, München
J. Ludewig, Baden (Schweiz)
R. Lutze, Darmstadt
E. Marmier, Zürich
T.A. Matzner, München
O. Mayer, Kaiserslautern
B. Möller, München
F. Muheim, Zürich
M. Nagl, Osnabrück
H. Oberquelle, Hamburg
A. Reiser, München
W. Rüb, München
H. Sandmayr, Dättwil (Schweiz)
R. Schild, Zug
R. Steinbrüggen, München
M. Tienari, Helsinki
R. Wilhelm, Saarbrücken
G. Winkler, Darmstadt
G. Winterstein, Karlsruhe
M. Wirsing, München

Inhaltsverzeichnis

A View of Current Concerns in Software Engineering

Władysław M. Turski

Institute of Informatics

Warsaw University

> By puttin' two and two together, you get
> an answer, and it don't seem to be the
> right one.
>
> Earle Stanley Gardner, <u>The Clue of the
> Runaway Blonde</u>.

A Retrospective

When the term "software engineering" was launched over a decade ago, the software
scene was dominated by concerns with (what I would like to call) <u>static problems</u>
of computer programming. The main characteristics of these concerns is the explicit or implicit assumption that a program (or a suit of programs, ie. a system)
is always being written for a clearly defined purpose which can be considered as
an immutable frame of reference for the process of programming, as well as for
"measuring" the qualities of its results, ie. of finished programs.

Most of the static problems of programming have been satisfactorily resolved.
This is not to say that the discovered solutions are as widely applied as they
could be, nor that they necessarily provide ready-to-use universal tools making
the day-to-day programming effortless. The nature of these solutions -- as, of
course, of the problems themselves -- is methodological rather than technical,
a distinction often overlooked, sometimes, one suspects, quite intensionally (as
when, eg., complaints are being voiced that the application of the stepwise refinement method to a single programming task may result in several quite different end-products, or, indeed, that the very steps through which the program

development progresses could vary from case to case, depending on idiosyncrasies of persons engaged in programming).

Perhaps the most significant methodological breakthrough in static problems of programming occurred when it was realized that the notion of program correctness could be made sufficiently precise to allow replacing qualitative correctness arguments based on (necessarily incomplete) empirical evidence by calculable correctness analyses based on (verifiably consistent and complete) set of simple rules. It is with the Floyd-Naur-Hoare notion of program correctness that the definitive statement of the program's purpose, i.e. its static specification, gained the central place in software engineering.

As soon as the sentence "a program is considered correct if it meets its specification" assumes an analytic meaning we can start playing a number of interesting intellectual games, all of them improving our understanding of what is going on in programming.

Indeed, let us assume that the specification is given as a pair of predicates, IN and OUT, defined on certain spaces X and Y. Elements of X are referred to as initial states, elements of Y -- as final states. No assumption with respect to the intersection $X \cap Y$ is made, in particular, it is explicitly not excluded that $X \cap Y \neq \emptyset$. In order to include some theoretically interesting cases in our considerations, let us formally extend Y by a special element 8, called the transfinal state, and denote $\overline{Y} = Y \cup \{8\}$. A program is considered to be a (perhaps partial) function $p: X \rightarrow \overline{Y}$. A program is said to meet the specification (IN,OUT) iff

$$(A\,x)\,(IN(x) \supset p(x) \text{ is defined } \underline{\text{and}}\ OUT(p(x)) \tag{1}$$

(Throughout this paper, wherever we write $P(x) \supset Q(x)$ we restrict our considerations to such x only that both sides of the implication are defined; exceptions to this convention shall be explicitly mentioned.)

For most practical applications $OUT(y) = y \neq 8$ $\underline{\text{cand}}$ $FOUT(y)$, where $\underline{\text{cand}}$ stands for the "conditional and" (ie. P $\underline{\text{cand}}$ Q = $\underline{\text{true}}$ if both P and Q are defined and $\underline{\text{true}}$, P $\underline{\text{cand}}$ Q is undefined if P is undefined or when P is $\underline{\text{true}}$ but Q is undefined, P $\underline{\text{cand}}$ Q = $\underline{\text{false}}$ in all other cases). The predicate IN is often called the precondition, predicate OUT -- postcondition, and FOUT -- finite postcondition.

Note that if $OUT(y) \equiv y \neq 8$ <u>cand</u> <u>true</u> (ie. $FOUT(y) \equiv true$) the specification requires that the set of final states that are the range of the specified program exclude the transfinal state but imposes no other constraint on this set. This corresponds to the requirement that the execution of the specified program terminate. On the other hand $OUT(y) \equiv y = 8$ satisfies a program whose execution "loops forever".

With such an interpretation of the OUT part of the specification, the "aborting" programs, ie. those whose execution sooner or later becomes "illegal", must be somehow "detected" by the IN part of the specification. It is useful to adopt the convention that the abortion (eventual illegality) property is expressed by the undefinedness of the IN predicate. In particular, if $IN(x) \equiv true$, ie. the precondition is trivially satisfied by any state, no program that can abort would be able to meet the specification.

Hence we get the following interpretation table:

	OUT	(IN,OUT) specifies a program that
$IN \equiv true$	$y \neq 8$ <u>cand</u> <u>true</u>	neither aborts nor loops forever, but otherwise is arbitrary.
	$y = 8$	loops forever (without aborting).
	$y \neq 8$ <u>cand</u> $FOUT(y)$	terminates without aborting, the final state satisfies FOUT.
$(Ex)(IN(x) \equiv false)$	$y \neq 8$ <u>cand</u> <u>true</u>	either aborts or terminates in an arbitrary final state.
	$y = 8$	either aborts or loops forever.
	$y \neq 8$ <u>cand</u> $FOUT(y)$	either aborts or terminates in a finite state satisfying FOUT.

(In all above formulae x (y) stands for an element of the initial (extended final) space.)

Omitting for short the arguments, we may interpret the familiar formula

$$\{IN\} \ p \ \{OUT\} \tag{2}$$

as a semantic function. (Another version of (2) is: "program p meets the specification (IN,OUT)" with (1) as the interpretation of the verb part of this version.) Given an (IN, OUT) specification and a program p we may consider the semantic function (2) as a theorem that needs to be established: it is required to prove that upon substitution of concrete program and predicates for p, IN and OUT formula (2) becomes a sentence that evaluates to <u>true</u>. If only IN and OUT are given, the semantic function (2) -- this time with a single variable p -- turns into an equation defining a program p.

<u>Example 1</u>

$$\{\underline{true}\}\ p\ \{y = 8\} \tag{E1}$$

is an equation that in Dijkstra's programming mini-language /2/ admits a solution: p = DO <u>true</u> → skip OD . Indeed, DO <u>true</u> → skip OD is a non-aborting non-terminating program. Similarly, p1 = DO <u>true</u> → S OD with any statement S that cannot "turn illegal" would also be a solution of (E1), but if S were such that it could abort, program p1 would not be a proper solution of (E1). (End of Example 1)

Since (2) as the equation for p admits a class of solutions, a variety of meaningful problems can be formulated with respect to the family of programs satisfying given (IN,OUT) specification, such as looking for the simplest or least expensive one.

If IN and p are given, (2) may be viewed as an equation for the predicate OUT, and, symmetrically, given p and OUT -- as an equation for the predicate IN. With both these interpretations of (2) the solutions are, of course, classes of predicates. Indeed, let INO be a solution of (2) for given p and OUT. This means that INO is such a predicate that for any initial state x satisfying INO program p is defined and the p-corresponding final state satisfies OUT. Clearly, if we take a predicate IN1 satisfying $(A\,x)\,(IN1(x) \supset INO(x))$ we also get a solution of (2), although by taking IN1 instead of INO we may be restricting the admissible set of initial states. In other words, it is meaningful to consider a problem of the weakest precondition, ie. of such a solution of (2) with p and OUT given that is the least restrictive.

All the above problems bear upon practical issues of software engineering; in a less formal way they may be restated as follows:

1. How to make sure that a program is a "right" one?
2. How to get a "right" program, and how to select the "best one" among those that are right?

3. How to determine the most relaxed constraints on input to a given program so as to guarantee the desired properties of the computation and/or of its output?

4. Given a program and properties of its input data, what are the guaranteed properties of the computation and/or of its output?

In order to solve these (and similar) static problems of software engineering the mere ability to write and interprete formulae like (1) and (2) is not sufficient even if they concisely capture a large variety of issues. What is needed to carry out the solutions of thus stated problems -- with the precision granted by the gained ability to phrase them -- is a way in which all pertinent program properties could be treated in a calculable fashion. This need is answered by the emergence of formalized semantics of programming languages, which was the second major break-through in software engineering during the last decade or so.

Briefly said, a calculable semantics of a programming language is given in seve-ral steps.

First, the elementary statements are identified with solutions of certain equations of the form (2).

Example 2

Consider a predicate $P(x)$ containing a free variable x and an equiform predicate $P(e)$, differing from the former only in that each free occurence of x is replaced by the expression e ("variable" and "expression" being here understood as purely syntactic notions). The solution of the equation

$$\{P(e)\} \text{ s } \{P(x)\}$$

for any predicate P is known as the assignement statement and denoted by $x := e$. (End of Example 2)

Then, the composition rules are introduced by means of which compound statements are identified with solutions of certain special sets of equations of the form (2).

Example 3

Consider predicates P, Q and R, and let S1 (S2) be the solution of the first (se-cond) equation of the set

$$\{P\} \; sl \; \{Q\}$$
$$\{Q\} \; s2 \; \{R\} \tag{E3.1}$$

Then the solution of the equation

$$\{P\} \; s \; \{R\} \tag{E3.2}$$

is known as the sequential composition (sequence) of statements S1 and S2, and is denoted by S1; S2. (End of Example 3)

Example 4

Consider predicates P, B and Q, and let S1 (S2) be the solution of the first (second) of the set of equations

$$\{P \; \underline{and} \; B\} \; sl \; \{Q\}$$
$$\{P \; \underline{and} \; \underline{nonB}\} \; s2 \; \{Q\} \tag{E4.1}$$

Then the solution of the equation.

$$\{P\} \; s \; \{Q\} \tag{E4.2}$$

is known as the (deterministic) alternative (choice) of statements S1 and S2 with guard B and is denoted by $\underline{if}$ B $\underline{then}$ S1 $\underline{else}$ S2 $\underline{fi}$ or by IF B $\rightarrow$ S1 $\Box$ $\underline{nonB}$ $\rightarrow$ S2 FI (End of Example 4)

Finally, programming language statements are (recursively) defined by means of elementary statements and compound statements.

The particular form in which we have presented the development of calculable semantics of programming languages has been chosen with the most important of the listed practical issues of software engineering in mind. Indeed, the problem of constructing a correct program, ie. the problem of solving a specification equation (2) in a programming language, can now be seen as the problem of interpolation in the space of predicates: Given an (IN, OUT) specification and assuming the composition rule of Example 3, we construct a suitable sequence of predicates P1, ... , Pn so that equations

$$\{IN\} \; sl \; \{Pl\}$$
$$\{Pl\} \; s2 \; \{P2\} \tag{3}$$
$$\cdots \cdots \cdots$$
$$\{Pn\} \; s(n+1) \; \{OUT\}$$

can each be solved by a statement of our programming language. Let these solu-

tions be S1, ..., S(n+1), respectively. Then the program p = S1; S2; ... ; S(n+1)
is a solution of (2), i.e. a correct program specified by the pair (IN, OUT).

Of course, it is not to be expected that the actual cases of equation (2) can be
transformed into (3) by mechanical application of the interpolation rule (E3.1).
Yet, the most general methodical approach to program design and construction --
the method of stepwise refinement -- is firmly based on the recursive application
of this principle.

That the actual progress in program design depends on human inventiveness can be
clearly seen from the analysis of the interpolation principle of Example 4. If we
restrict our attention to the (P, Q) specification pair (as the equation (E4.2)
seems to tell us) it is very unlikely that we shall discover statements S1 and S2
that, along with the predicate-guard B, are needed to construct the solution of
(E4.2). It requires certain inventiveness, or, at the very least, a lot of practice and considerable perceptiveness, to notice that by splitting P in two: P´=
P and B and P´´= P and nonB , we may obtain a set of equations (E4.1), each of
which is --hopefully -- easier to solve than the original equation (E4.2).

Observe that in general strengthening of the precondition P into P´ such that
P´⊃ P simplifies the solution of equation {P} s {Q} , but may make the global interpolation more difficult. Indeed, consider

   {IN} p {OUT}

interpolated as

   {IN} s {P}
   {P} t {OUT}

If we strengthen P by choosing P´⊃ P, we get

   {IN} s {P´}
   {P´} t {OUT}

where the second equation is (hopefully) easier to solve (because its precondition
is stronger), but almost invariably the first equation will be more difficult to
solve as its postcondition is stronger than the corresponding postcondition of the
first set of equations. The advantage of the interpolation by alternative statements consists in replacing one equation by two, each of which has a stronger pre-

condition than the original one, but whose union -- due to the dychotomy of B and nonB -- is exactly equivalent to the original precondition.

Many similar metodological observations of direct practical value can be made, explaining the "tricks" of programming art (craft) in terms of calculable semantics, which not only provides a scientific foundation for programming activity, thus making it both more reliable and easier to learn, but also shifts the emphasis in good programming practice away from serendipity towards calculations.

The methodological advances caused by the two great discoveries in the field of static problems of programming, ie. by the introduction of a meaningful notion of program correctness and by the invention of calculable semantics of programming languages, are quite remarkable. In addition to providing direct means for program verification and a calculus for program design and construction, they played a crucial rôle in the development of many important auxiliary programming techniques.

We have already mentioned the stepwise refinement and its relation to the calculable semantics via the interpolating equations. It is, perhaps, necessary to add that this technique is equally strongly related to the dual interpretation of equation (2), ie. to its interpretation as both: the theorem (hypothesis) to be proven and an equation to be solved. If it can be proven that the equation (2) can be solved then -- even without having written down the actual solution -- we are entitled to rely on the formula (2) as on a statement of a fact and use the name of the program p as if it were a program having the desired (IN, OUT) properties. Even more importantly, we are entitled to assume the existence of such a program and apply its name wherever the program itself will be eventually needed, provided we do so salva conditione of eventually supplying the proof of the existence, and, ultimately, the program-solution itself. Thus, whenever we have isolated a program component by writing down its (IN, OUT) specification, we may advance the program design process as if the component existed, leaving for later the actual construction of this component.

This methodological observation can be readily generalized into a full-scale method of modular programming, whereby the software design progresses not so much by a gradual, more or less uniform, breaking of the specification pairs into ever denser interpolation grid (stepwise refinement), as by dividing the state-space into clusters and collecting together properties of transformations acting on a cluster, thus forming as it were a subspecification. The subspecification defines the global properties of a module, ie. all such properties that may be relevant to state transformations pertaining to state-space elements outside the particular cluster. Thus, as soon as the specification of a module is written, the module may be used in developing "outside" parts of the program. Since, on the other hand, the local cluster of state-space elements cannot be manipulated by any outside transformations, the development of the module itself may proceed quite independently.

Thus, modular programming can be seen as approximating the program-solution by a combination of subprograms defined on disjoint parts of the state-space.

Up to now we were discussing the state-space in which the desired transformation is to be described by the program-solution of the given specification equation as an a priori given entity. Usually, this is far from true. The program design progresses just as much by developing the transformations as by imposing (or discovering) a structure of the state-space and by introducing auxiliary state-space elements. Thus it is perfectly reasonable to approach the software design issues from the point of view of the state-space structure and specify properties of various structures.

Just as the transformational approach was put on a sound basis by the formalization of the correctness problem and by invention of calculable semantics of programming languages, the state-space structural approach has been made workable by the introduction of algebraic specifications of abstract data types. The space limitations of this paper prevent even the sketchiest exposition of this approach; let us just observe that the modular programming method can be seen as a practical embodiment of either of the two mentioned approaches and that both can be -- in the most fundamental terms -- described as consisting in two steps:

(i) formulation of equations expressing the desired properties,
(ii) solving the equations by combinations of a priori given constructs.

In both approaches the second step is formally verifiable by the application of a suitable calculus.

Before we finish the discussion of the advances in the domain of static software problems, we should like to stress several points:

1. Whatever "tools" are provided for easing the clerical tasks of programming (in all its stages) they must reflect the most important aspect of the rational approach to software engineering, ie. it must be possible to use them in a calculable way. In practical terms this means, for instance, that programming languages ought to posses not only a well-defined syntax, but also a formalized semantics.

2. The formalization of the software development is not a goal in itself, but a means by which the programming process gains its only unambiguous interpretation. The foremost purpose of all formalizations is to get rid of silent assumptions and loose connotations; this goal is achieved first of all by an explicit semantics.

3. The human aspects of programming, including the ergonomics of programmer's tools (programming language, documentation standards, support systems, etc.) are extremly important, but since per se they do not provide the backbone of the framework in which programming is carried out, they should always be considered in context of the main issues discussed above.

A Prospect

The phenomenon of software evolution, identified as one of the most significant attributes of "large programs" as early as 1970 (cf./3/), remains the most troublesome aspect of software engineering. Its thorough phenomenological studies, carried out by M.M. Lehman and his associates, clearly indicate that the managerial disregard of this phenomenon has catastrophic consequences for the quality of software products in use, as well as for the whole sphere of software economics. It seems, therefore, that a rational approach to software engineering cannot avoid treating the dynamic problems of computer programming as seriously and thoroughly as its static ones. Moreover, it is natural to expect that just as the static problems were put on a sound basis (and eventually resolved) by a relatively simple expedient of suitable formalization, the solutions of the dynamic problems will be facilitated by a formal treatment. In the sequel we shall describe a possible framework for a formalization of the dynamic problems of computer programming, which seems both natural and promising as far as the possibility to introduce a calculable means of investigations is concerned. It should be noted that the view taken in this part of the paper strongly differs from the emerging near-consensus of software technicians who see remedies againts growing pains of software evolution in assorted technical support systems, such as "improved programming environment", "software development data bases", etc. Without denigrating the rôle of such tools, indeed, fully appreciating their labour-saving potential, one cannot help observing that just as the static problems of computer programming were not solved by "improved" programming languages, the dynamic ones shall not be removed by "improved programming environments"; quite the contrary: the realization of the significance of calculable semantics helped to design better programming languages and -- one hopes -- the appreciation of formal treatment of software evolution will eventually assist in designing suitable technical means of support.

An existing software product -- a program or a suit of programs -- evolves because its current version is found unsatisfactory. The dissatisfaction with an existing and correct piece of software may arise from several different, but often related, reasons:

- it lacks certain facilities which are deemed useful,
- it performs certain functions less efficiently than expected or hoped for,
- it does not fully (or even at all) exploit certain hardware facilities.

It is not true that causes of dissatisfaction, such as these listed above, can always be traced to an imperfect specification. Indeed, hardware facilities are likely to be changed ("upgraded") during the life-time of a program, the emphasis on performance efficiency is likely to change (e.g. when cheaper store becomes available), the opinion on which facilities provided by the system are most valuable is apt to change with time, sometimes as a (direct or indirect) consequence of the system application. In all these instances we might have had a "perfect" specification and a program meeting this specification, and yet, after some time, the feeling of dissatisfaction may become too strong to resist the temptation to change the software.

The widespread practice to actually change (parts of) existing programs whenever the dissatisfaction with their current version is detected, ie. the so-called software maintenance activity, is responsible for an uncontrolled, cancerous growth of software systems and for all its disastrous consequences. (That the consequences are disastrous -- we all know, that the growth is uncontrolled, indeed, seems uncontrollable in the sense of not responding to managerial controls -- we have learned from many convincing case studies.)

Even the most cursory analysis of the software evolution (as it is) shows that the first victim of tinkering with the existing programs is likely to be their correctness: whatever relationship there existed between the specification and the corresponding program is usually destroyed by software maintenance, without slightest attention being paid to the consequences. Perhaps the only exception to this sad rule is provided by these cases where programs are replaced by more efficient ones; such improvements often do not violate the relation that existed between the specification and corresponding software. We shall use the expression "software changes under the invariance of specification" to describe just such instances, and shall not be concerned with them -- they do not cause big troubles, indeed, as long as software evolves under the invariance of its specification one does not expect to encounter issues much different from those of static software problems. This leaves us with software changes likely to violate the specification/program relationship as our primary object of interest.

In approaching this problem we shall impose upon ourselves one basic condition: any rational treatment of evolving software cannot invalidate the fundamental achievement of static software design. Thus, whatever means we will be inclined to propose for coping with problems of evolving software, they must be consistent with the principles captured by the notion of program correctness and proof obligations, as developed for static software.

One way of progressing, fully respecting the just stated condition, would be to restrict software evolution to the following process:

Given a specification S0 and a program p0 that satisfies it, the only changes to be considered fall in two categories:

    (i) program changes under invariance of S0,

    (ii) specification changes, followed by construction of the new program.

Symbolically, if we write p $\underline{sat}$ S to express the fact that program p satisfies specification S, and denote a change by a wavy arrow leading from "old" to "new" object, category (i) can be represented by

    1. p0 <u>sat</u> S0

    2. p0 $\leadsto$ p1, such that p1 <u>sat</u> S0

$$(4)$$

and category (ii) by

    1. p0 <u>sat</u> S0

    2. S0 $\leadsto$ S1

    3. construct p1 such that p1 <u>sat</u> S1

$$(5)$$

Two objections may be raised to such a simpleminded treatment of evolving software:
first, the fact that there exists a program satisfying S0 does not necessarily en-
tail the existance of a program satisfying S1; second, it is expected that the cost
(complexity, effort etc.) of constructing a program <u>ab ovo</u> -- given its specification -- could be far greater than the cost of <u>modifying</u> the program so as to meet
modified specifications.

At the first glance it transpires that the first objection imposes a restriction
on the scope of admissible specification changes, whereas the second one indicates
that there could be a better scheme:

    1. p0 <u>sat</u> S0

    2. S0 $\leadsto$ S1

    3. p0 $\leadsto$ p1, such that p1 <u>sat</u> S1

$$(5')$$

where the change displayed in line 3 is somehow "directed" by the change displayed
in line 2.

A moment's reflection is sufficient to link these two observations: if some restrictions are imposed on specification changes, then should we not to select them
in such a way as to make scheme (5') workable? Accepting this approach, we are
in fact expressing our willingness to allow only such specification changes that
<u>are guaranteed</u> to lead to specifications satisfiable by a program obtainable from
the original one by means of well-defined operations directed by the requested
specification changes. Presently we are going to argue that this quite compelling
approach is not only feasible, but also, perhaps, the only viable one, given present understanding of the specification/program relationships. Our argument runs
as follows.

First, we can safely leave aside all software modifications that neither are made under the invariance of specification, nor start with an explicit change in specification. (We shall not be concerned with the specification-preserving program modifications because , as already noted, they are quite manageable with well-developed static techniques, and we refuse to consider direct program-changes violating the specification/program relationships because they either are contrary to the accepted basic condition or imply establishing a specification after a program is written, which is sufficiently unnatural to be left out from our discussion. The refusal to consider specification-unrelated tinkering with a program is not a purely academic point: it is also a practical advice, perhaps the most important one in this whole paper.)

Secondly, because we are concerned with a controlled evolution of software, we need to impose a stability requirement on this process. (Intuitively, we speak of a stable dynamic process if a small variation of initial conditions is guaranteed not to lead to disproportionally large variations in results. Sometimes it is required that small variations of initial conditions lead to small variations in results; asking that the latter merely be not disproportionally large we accept a more liberal attitude: translating back into software development terms, we are simply requesting that a smallchange of specifications does not result in a disastrously large change of the program.)

In order to meaningfully interpret the stability requirement in context of software development we need some way to tell a "small" change of specification from a "non-small" one. (We also need to define what is meant by a non-disproportionally large change of a program. This, however, seems a little bit easier because we can at least limit it from above by defining the total re-programming to be the "maximal change" of a program.) It very well may be that the practice of specification writing will eventually progress to a stage at which the space of specification changes will become measurable; at the present, however, such prospect seems quite remote and even somewhat doubtful. With current treatment of specifications, even a weaker requirement of a meaningful ordering relation on specification changes seems pretty hard to meet in sufficient generality, although by no means impossible in a limited sense.

Thus, the key to any progress in controlled (stable) software evolution is to be found in the ability to meaningfully consider a specification as an object in a space of objects of the same type. This can be achieved, for instance, by considering specifications as formal theories, a view that has interesting methodological consequences for dynamic as well as for static issues of software engineering Since these consequences were discussed at some length elsewhere (cf., eg. /4/), let us just mention here that considering a specification as a formal theory and the corresponding program as its model, we can interpret the specification/program relationship as the satisfaction relationship from the mathematical theory of models and apply this interpretation recursively to all stages of software development, from an early specification down to the program implementation in microcodes.

One of the most important consequences of the specification-as-a-formal-theory view consists in providing a well-defined meaning to such notions as "consistency" and "completness" of specifications. It is, for example, quite easy to explain (and justify) an intuitive belief that the specification must be (formally) consistent , whereas the requirement of completness can be -- at the very best -- interpreted only "in a sense".

On the other hand, considering specifications as formal theories encourages such design of specification systems in which operations on specifiactions (such as forming a union of specifications, extending and restricting a specification) assume a well-defined, algebraic (theory-of-cathegoric) sense (cf.eg. /1/).

From the particular vantage point of this paper, however, the most interesting consequence of the suggested view of specifications is the ability to relate the the specification changes and similarities.

Assuming that we start with a specification SO which is correctly met by a program (and thus is consistent), we may say that another specification, S1, is similar to SO if S1 is also consistent (and thus can be met by a program) and may be obtained form SO by the application of a legitimate specification-modifying operation. If we consider specifications similarity to be a transitive property, we get a specifications chain SO, S1, S2, ... and may call any pair Si, Sj on such a chain a pair of similar specifications. Thus a specification S´ is considered similar to a consistent specification S if it is consistent and can be obtained from S by application of a finite number of legitimate specification-

-modifying operations (in some order). In this definition the (yet undefined) term "legitimate specification-modifying operation" carries the largest semantic load, the remainder of the definition is purely technical.

Our argument is concluded by observing that we may legitimize the use of such specification-modifying operations only for which explicit rules for corresponding program changes are known. Thus, we shall consider a set of partial operations $M1, \ldots, Mk$ in the specification space $\mathbb{S}$:

$$Mi: \mathbb{S} \to \mathbb{S}, \quad i = 1, \ldots, k$$

with following properties

(i) if $S \in \mathbb{S}$ is a consistent specification and Mi is defined for S then
$S' = Mi(S)$ is also a consistent specification,

(ii) if p <u>sat</u> S then the change $p \rightsquigarrow p'$ is known and p' <u>sat</u> S'.

The partiality of Mi's reflects the obvious fact that not all Mi's need to be defined for all specifications. In fact, it seems that apart from some very special cases most Mi's will be defined for a concrete specification or for a class of specifications.

<u>Example 5</u>

Let the specification SL be that of a compiler for a programming language L, and let the corresponding program, the compiler cL, be such that cL <u>sat</u> SL. Consider a change of specification consisting in consistently replacing the alphabet of L, AL, in SL by another alphabet AL'. Thus we get a specification SL' of a compiler for "another" language L'. Obviously, a compiler cL' such that cL' <u>satSL'</u> can be obtained from a well-designed cL by a simple expedient of replacing the "left-hand columns" of a symbol-table in cL. (End of Example 5)

<u>Example 6</u>

Let the specification SL be that of a compiler for a progarmming language L. Consider a class of languages $\mathbf{L}$, $L \in \mathbf{L}$, and let mcL be a metacompiler accepting specifications of compilers for languages of this class and producing suitable compilers. Thus we may write symbolically

$$(AL \in \mathbf{L})\,((mcL(SL) = cL)\ \underline{and}\ (cL\ \underline{sat}\ SL))$$

as an easy to interpret description of our assumptions.

Let now M be any modification of L such that $L' = M(L)$ **L** . Denoting by **M** such modification of SL that $SL' = $ **M**(SL) specifies a compiler for L', we can write

$$(mc\textbf{L}(SL') = cL') \underline{\textbf{and}} (cL'\underline{\textbf{sat}} SL')$$

Thus -- as long as the changes in specification reflect only such changes of the language (ie. of our goal in the real world) which do not take it out of the class for which the metacompiler is guaranteed to produce correct compilers -- we can safely cope with these changes. (End of Example 6)

<u>Note 1</u>

In Example 6 the original specification SL was for a compiler. Construction of the metacompiler and delineation of the class **L** are to be considered as a means of solving the original problem. If only static software problems are admitted this means is clearly excessive. On the other hand, if dynamic problems are to be expected, ie. if the specification is likely to evolve, the solution by means of a metacompiler defines the upper limit on legitimate specification-modifying operations.

<u>Note 2</u>

For the specification change of Example 5 the use of full procedure outlined in Example 6 though certainly effective is -- in general -- very inefficient. It has, however, a significant advantage: because cL is constructed by the metacompiler its design follows well-defined rules and therefore we may expect that indeed the change of alphabet can be taken care of quite simply by replacing a well-defined part of auxiliary tables in the lexical pre-processor. If the metacompiler is designed smartly enough, no further changes in cL would be needed. (End of notes)

We have devoted so much space to these two rather simple examples because they well serve to illustrate a basic pragmatic approach to dynamic problems of software.

Given a specification, it is prudent to expect that eventually it will be changed. It is, therefore, adviseable to consider as large a class of specifications (of which the given one is a member) as possible under the constraint of being able to design a generally applicable solution. The software resulting from such ge-

neral design needs not to be the most efficient one in each individual case. Then
we analyse factors which make the given specification unique in the class and design a recognizer (not necessarily automatic!) of these features. Finally, we
design and compose a correct (and perhaps "optimal" -- whatever that may mean)
program for the given specification, carefully noting in its development where
and which of the unique factors are exploited.

When faced with a new, modified specification, we first of all check if it is of
the considered class. If not, the only prudent course of action is to start a new
project. If, however, the new specification happens to be of the considered class,
we may take the cost of applying the general solution as the maximum non-disproportionally large "program change" and consider how large a part of the "old"
program can be salvaged. Of course, all design steps not vitally dependent on
specific factors of either old or new specification can be accepted without change
If well-established practice of stepwise refinement has been adhered to, it is
quite probable that only parts of the design are influenced by specific factors,
and thus the cost of producing a program satisfying the new specification by following as much as possible the old design will be considerably smaller than the
established upper limit.

The outlined pragmatic strategy becomes particularly appealing when we force ourselves to design programs in well-defined steps, establishing at each step the
formal relationships between the current specification and program (cf. the interpolation calculus described in the first part of this paper). It goes without
saying that a suitable programming support systems that perform clerical tasks
of keeping track of alternatives and options can be of immense assistance in this
process.

Finally, let us observe that both, a calculus of specification approach, in which
specification changes are expressed explicitly as operations on specification-type
objects, and a pragmatic procedure, recognizing the dynamic evolution of specifications, heavily depend on the use of a formalism in which specifications can
be written so as to allow calculable manipulations on them with a well-defined
meaning.

References

/1/ Burstall, R.M. and Gougen, J.A.: Putting theories together to make specifications. Proc. 5th Intnl. Joint Conf. on Artificial Intelligence, MIT, Cambridge, Mass., pp. 1045 - 1058 (1977).

/2/ Dijkstra, E.W.: A Discipline of Programming. Englewood Cliffs: Prentice-Hall
Inc., 1976.

/3/ Efficient Production of Large Programs. Proc. Intnl. Workshop, Comp. Centre
Polish Acad. of Scie. (1971).

/4/ Turski, W.M.: Specification as a theory with models in the computer world
and in the real world. In: System Design (P. Henderson, Ed.), Infotech State
of the Art Report, Ser. 9, No. 6, pp. 363 - 378 (1981).

Towards a Decentralised General-Purpose Computer

Philip C. Treleaven

Computing Laboratory
University of Newcastle upon Tyne

Abstract

Research into novel decentralised computer architectures may be broadly classified in terms of the computer's program organisation as: control flow, data flow, reduction, actor and logic. Each of these program organisations supports efficiently a single category of programming language: control flow - conventional languages, data flow - single assignment languages, reduction - applicative languages, actor - object-oriented languages, and logic - predicate logic languages. However general-purpose computers are required ideally to support a number of categories of language efficiently.

Our approach to the design of general-purpose computers, in particular a future decentralised architecture, is to develop computers that embody more than one traditional program organisation. In this paper we describe a computer providing both control flow and data flow. We are working on a computer design that also includes reduction. And our target is a computer providing control flow, data flow, reduction and other styles of programming.

1. Introduction

Computing is moving from a sequential, centralised world to a parallel, decentralised one in which large numbers of computers are to be programmed to work together in computer systems [11]. These computer systems range from main-frame computers that are geographically distributed, to miniature microcomputers on a single VLSI chip. To allow all these component computers to co-operate in the execution of a program and to be used as building blocks for larger computer systems it is necessary for them to conform to a common (decentralised) system architecture. Separate strands of research are coming together to form this new generation of decentralised computer [2]. These strands are expert systems, very high level programming languages, data driven and demand driven computer architectures, and very large scale integration (VLSI).

Expert or knowledge-based systems [14] embody knowledge bases (modules of organised knowledge concerning specific areas of human expertise) which support sophisticated problem-solving and inference functions. These systems are predicted by the Japanese Government to be the application area of the 1990's [2]. Closely associated with this application area is the categories of very high level programming languages such as functional languages [7] and logic languages [12]. In turn, these languages are suitable for programming new data driven and demand driven architectures [19] such as data flow and reduction computers. Lastly, these parallel, decentralised computers provide a means of exploiting the rapid developments in VLSI [13] through the use of replicated general-purpose and special-purpose microcomputers in their construction. Our discussion of decentralised computers will centre on the relationship of high level programming languages with computer architectures.

Research into novel decentralised computer architectures may be broadly classified as: control flow, data flow, reduction, actor and logic. Each of these program organisations corresponds to, and hence supports efficiently, a single category of programming languages: control flow - conventional languages, data flow - single assignment languages, reduction - applicative languages, actor - object-oriented languages, and logic - predicate logic languages. At present only conventional languages are supported efficiently by todays general-purpose computers, which is acceptable because almost all programming is done in conventional languages. In the future, however, it is probable that all of these categories of language will achieve a significant level of usage and may be considered "main-stream" programming languages. Thus the new generation of decentralised computer, to be considered general-purpose, must support efficiently a number of these categories of language.

We believe such a decentralised general-purpose computer is possible to obtain. Our approach is to develop computers that embody more than one traditional program organisation. In this paper we describe the organisation of a computer providing both control flow and data flow. For this computer, a compiler for a conventional language may generate a control flow style of code, one for a single assignment language may generate a data flow style, or more interestingly a compiler could use a mixed style of code.

2. Spectrum of Considerations

Figure 1 illustrates various important considerations that need to be reviewed for the design of the new generation of decentralised computer. These considerations are arranged in three groups: programming language, program organisation, and machine organisation.

```
programming   |conventional|single         |applicative |object-  |predicate
language      |            |assignment     |            |oriented |logic
--------------|------------|---------------|------------|---------|----------
program       |control     |data           |reduction   |actor    |logic
organisation  |flow        |flow           |            |         |
--------------|------------|---------------|------------|---------|----------
machine       |centralised |packet         |expression  |   ?     |   ?
organisation  |            |communication  |manipulation|         |
```

Figure 1: Spectrum of Considerations.

Programming language covers the categories of high level languages that are likely to be used extensively for programming in the future. The most well developed categories are: conventional languages (e.g. Fortran, PL/1), single assignment languages (e.g. Id [3], VAL [1]), applicative languages (e.g. Lisp, SASL [20], FP [4]), object-oriented languages (e.g. Smalltalk [6]),and logic languages (e.g. PROLOG [12]). Single assignment and applicative languages are collectively known as functional languages.

Program organisation covers the way machine code programs are represented and executed in a computer architecture. The major categories are: control flow, data flow, reduction, actor and logic. In control flow organisations explicit flows of control cause the execution of instructions. In data flow organisations [8] the availability of input operands triggers the execution of the instruction which consumes the inputs. In reduction organisations [5] the requirement for a result triggers the execution of the instruction that will generate the value. In actor organisations [22] the arrival of a message for an instruction causes the instruction to execute. In logic organisations [12] an instruction is executed when it matches a target pattern and backtracking is used to execute alternatives to the instruction.

Machine organisation covers the way a machine's resources are configured and allocated to support a program organisation. The major categories we have termed [19]: centralised, packet communications, and expression manipulation. (The "?" symbols represent, as yet, undefined categories.) A centralised organisation consists of a single computer that sequentially executes instructions. A packet communications organisation consists of a circular pipeline of processing and memory resources that process the instructions to be executed as packets of work. Lastly, an expression manipulation organisation consists of a tree structure of identical computers which process logically adjacent parts of the program structure.

It may be apparent from the above brief descriptions that each category of programming language, program organisation and machine organisation has its own operational model of program execution. And as shown by the columns in Figure 1 specific categories of programmming language, program organisation and machine organisation have a natural affinity because of the similarities of their operational models. Although, as we might expect, research into novel computer architectures usually groups in columns, various research groups are showing [19] that other combinations of program and machine organisations are viable. Thus for a decentralized computer architecture the choice of program organisation and machine organisation can be made independently. The choice of program organisation depends on how efficient it is for program representation and execution, whereas the choice of machine organisation depends on issues such as resource allocation and communication. We have made a detailed study of program organisations and found that each has advantages and disadvantages for computation [19]. In addition we have identified certain underlying data mechanisms and control mechanisms [19] that seem to be shared by these program organisations. Using this information we are attempting to synthesise two or more program organisations. A program organisation combining control flow and data flow is described in the next section.

3. Combining Control Flow and Data Flow

Program organisations are distinguished by the way in which data is communicated between instructions, and by the way in which the execution of instructions is initiated. In a control flow organisation a result is passed indirectly between instructions via a shared memory cell. Once a result is stored, it may be read an unspecified number of times. Execution of an instruction in a sequential control flow organisation is caused by the flow of control which we will view as the availability of a control token. In a parallel control flow organisation execution is caused by the availability of a number of flows of control – a complete set of control tokens. In a data flow orgranisation, when an instruction generates a result, the result is passed directly to an instruction that consumes the value. If the result is required as input to more than one instruction then separate copies are generated and dispatched. The availability of a complete set of inputs – known as data tokens – for an instruction causes the instruction to execute. When an instruction executes, it consumes the set of data tokens, after which these tokens disappear and are no longer available as inputs to this or any other instruction.

Figures 2 and 3 show how the assignment statement "a=(b+1)*(b-c)" would be represented by a parallel control flow and a pure data flow organisation.

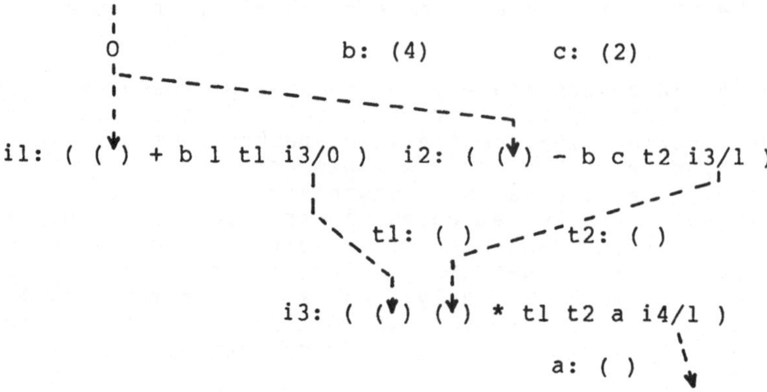

Figure 2: Control Flow Representation of a=(b+1)*(b-c).

In Figure 2 each instruction "i:(...)" consist of an operator followed by one or more operands which are literals or references. Each operator is preceded by one or more "( )" symbols defining the number of control tokens that are required before the instruction can execute. For instance instruction "i1" requires one control token and consists of the dyadic operator "+" followed by four operands. The first two operands "b" and "1" provide the input data, the second "t1" is the memory cell for the result, and the last "i3/0" is a reference for a control token. This token is passed to instruction "i3" at argument position "0". Instruction "i3" requires both this control token and another from instruction "i2" to be available before it can execute.

In the pure data flow organisation the data mechanism and control mechanism are supported by a single scheme - data tokens are used to pass data from one instruction to another and they are also used to cause the execution of instructions.

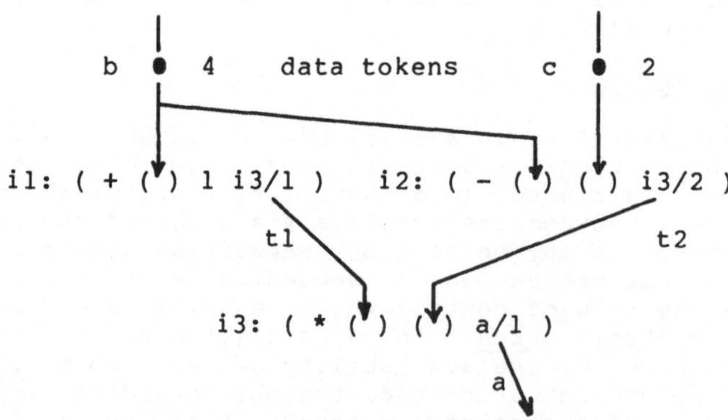

Figure 3: Data Flow Representation of a=(b+1)*(b-c).

In Figure 3 each data flow instruction consists of an operator, two input operands which are either literals or required data tokens defined by "( )" symbols, and a reference such as "i3/1" defining a consumer instruction and argument position for the result data token. An instruction is enabled for execution when all its input arguments are available, i.e. when all its data tokens have arrived. The operator then consumes the data tokens, performs the required operation, and using the embedded reference stores a copy of the result data token into the consumer instruction(s). In Figures 2 and 3 the flows of control and data are shown as directed graphs. A dotted arc defines a flow of control, with a "O" symbol specifying a control token, and a solid arc defines a flow of both control and data, with a "●" symbol specifying a data token.

Having examined the control flow and data flow program organisations, the question to be asked is which organisation is the most general-purpose; suitable for efficiently modelling a variety of algorithm structures. Each organisation has particular advantages and disavantages [19]. For example control flow is efficient for manipulating data structures that are to be shared in place, while data flow is efficient for evaluating expressions. Rather than being competitive, the attributes of control flow and data flow program organisations appear complementary. Thus we believe that the two forms of program organisation can be usefully combined. For instance a compiler writer might take advantage of this "Combined" program organisation to generate part control flow and part data flow code for the assignment statement, as shown in Figure 4.

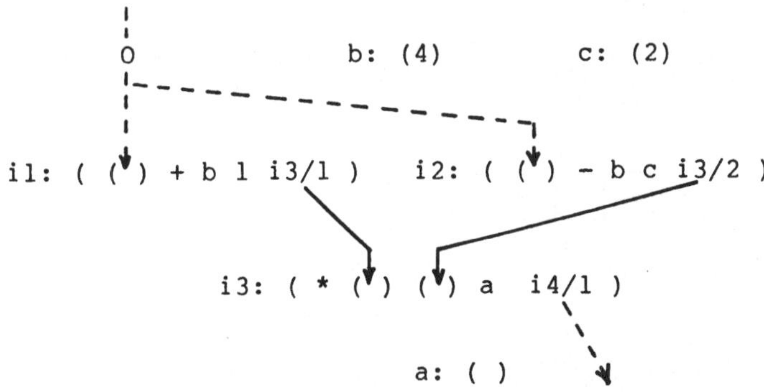

Figure 4: Combined Representation of a=(b+1)*(b-c).

In Figure 4 instructions "i1" and "i2" are each activated by the arrival of a single control token. These instructions access their inputs by de-referencing "b" and "c". Then each instruction passes on its result as a data token to instruction "i3", which is executed when these two data tokens are available. Instruction "i3" consumes these two data tokens, stores its result in memory cell "a", and releases a control token to the succeeding instruction "i4/1".

In the control mechanism of the Combined program organisation an instruction is activated by the availability of a complete set of tokens — when some specific number of tokens are available. A set of tokens may consist of control tokens, or data tokens, or a mixture of control and data tokens. Once a set of tokens is complete the data tokens are passed to the data mechanism. In the data mechanism of the Combined organisation there are two ways in which an instruction may obtain its iputs, namely (i) by receiving data tokens which may carry either a literal or a reference to a memory cell, or (ii) by means of embedded arguments stored in the instruction which may also be literals or references.

When an instruction is activated the data token arguments and embedded arguments are merged to produce a set of literals and references. Certain of these references, for instance those supplying inputs, are next de-referenced and replaced by their corresponding values from memory. The instruction then has a complete set of arguments from which to compute the results. When the results have been obtained the outputs of the instruction are generated. Three types of output are provided by the organisation, namely (i) control tokens, (ii) data tokens, and (iii) data to be stored in memory.

4. Program Organisation

The instruction execution cycle of the Combined program organisation is illustrated by Figure 5.

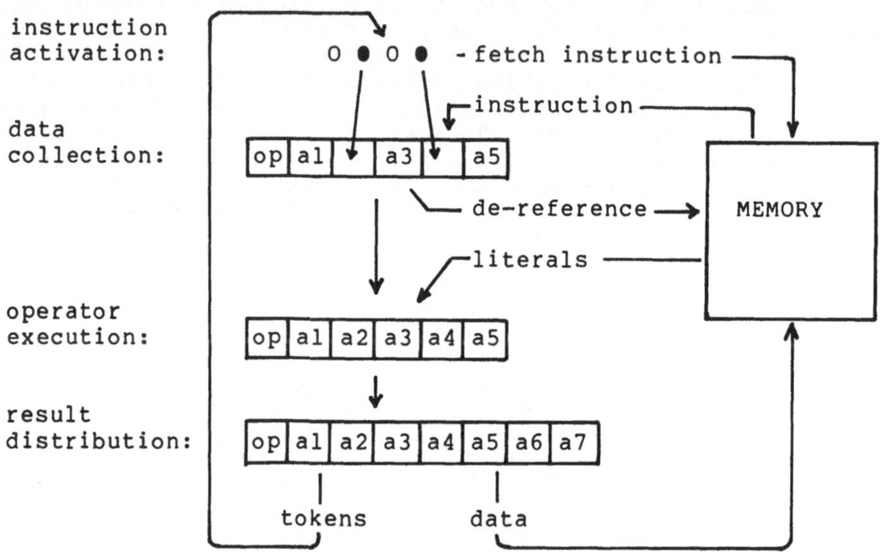

Figure 5: Instruction Execution Cycle.

This instruction execution cycle consists of four stages, referred to as: (i) instruction activation, (ii) data collection, (iii) operator execution and (iv) result destribution. The instruction activation stage handles the control mechanism. Here individual tokens are formed into sets for particular destination instructions and a set of tokens is released when complete. The data collection stage handles the data mechanism. Here a copy of an activated instruction is taken from memory and any data tokens from the instruction activation stage are inserted. Next certain specified arguments are de-referenced and replaced by their corresponding values form memory to produce an executable instruction. The operator execution stage processes an executable instruction by applying the operator to certain of the arguments and appending the results to the instruction. Lastly, the result distribution stage generates the outputs by combining certain of the arguments and results. The three types of output are control tokens, data tokens and data to be stored in memory.

In the computer instructions, tokens and stored data may be viewed as name:value pairs, as illustrated by Figures 6-8. A name consists of two parts: the process name identifies a specific process containing three sets of, respectively, instructions, tokens and stored data; and the relative name identifies a specific instruction, token or item of stored data.

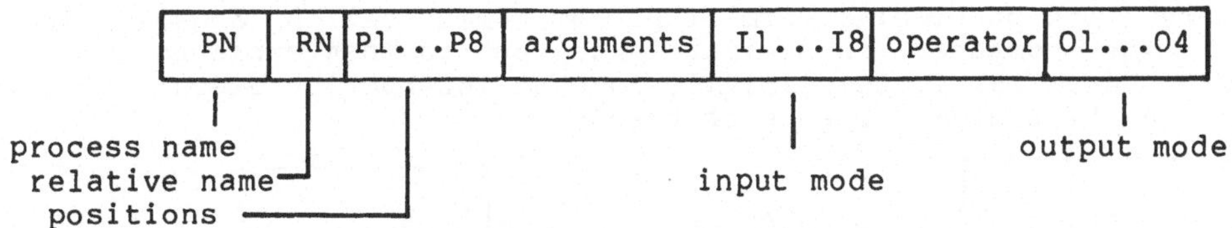

Figure 6:   Instruction Format.

Figure 6 illustrates the instruction format whose value part consists of: a position field - a bit vector - defining which of upto 8 following arguments are present; the arguments; an input mode - a bit vector - defining which arguments are to be de-referenced; an operator to be applied to arguments in specific positions; and an output mode containing a field for each output specifying its type and construction.

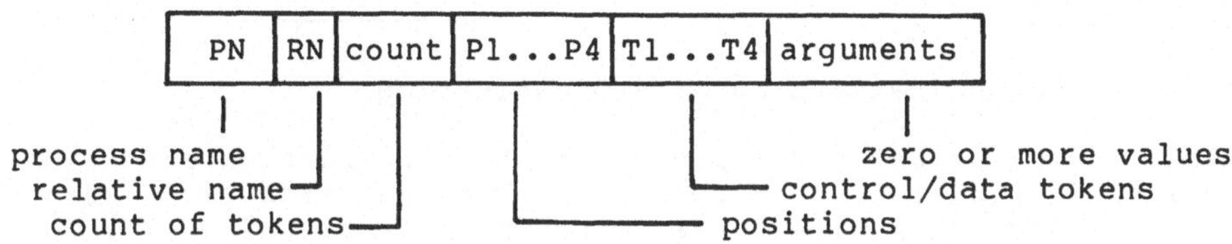

Figure 7:   Token Format.

Figure 7 shows the format of a token. Its value part consists of a count of the number of tokens in the complete set; a position field bit vector defining which arguments (i.e. tokens) are present; another bit vector defining the types of the arguments (i.e. tokens) that are present; and the actual arguments - the values from data tokens.

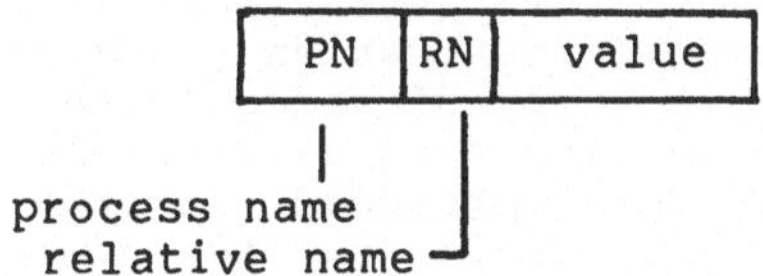

Figure 8:   Stored Data Formats.

Figure 8 shows the stored data format whose value part consists of a single value - this form was adopted for consistency with the traditional control flow view of a variable.

5.   Machine Organisation

Having presented the machine's program organisation we will now briefly examine its machine organisation, which is based on a packet communication organisation as illustrated by Figure 9. Packet communication is a simple strategy for allocating work to resources in a parallel computer. A packet communications organisation consists of a circular instruction execution pipeline of resources in which processors, communications and memories are interspersed with "pools of work". The organisation views an executing program as a number of independent information packets. Each packet to be processed is placed with similar packets in one of the "pools of work". When a resource becomes idle it take a packet from its input pool, processes it, places a modified packet in an output pool and then returns to the idle state. The particular form of packet communication organisation used in the computer is similar in concept to that employed in the Manchester Data Flow system [15,21], in that instruction execution is based on the "matching" of sets of tokens.

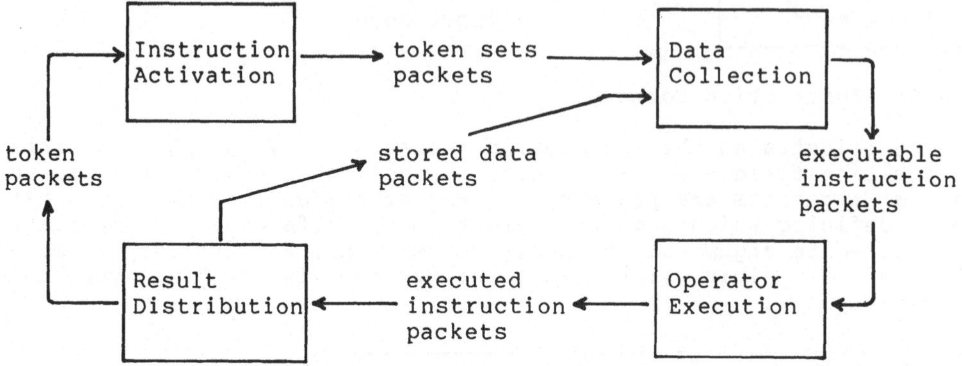

Figure 9: Packet Communications Machine Organisation.

The machine organisation corresponds to the instruction execution cycle described in Figure 5. A group of resources supports each stage in the cycle, and they are interspersed with "pools of work". The machine operates as follows:

1. instruction activation – takes individual token packets from the token packets pool and forms them into token sets for a particular destination instruction. When the set is complete a token set packet is released. This token set packet consists of the instruction name and any data from the tokens.

2. data collection – provides a memory for the instructions and stored data, and generates an executable instruction packet by inserting the arguments into a copy of an activated instruction. These arguments come from two sources, namely (i) data tokens and (ii) arguments embedded in the instruction, both of which may supply literals or references to memory cells.

3. operator execution – applies the operator to certain of the arguments and appends the results to produce an executed instruction packet.

4. result distribution – generates outputs by combining certain of the arguments and results. The three types of output packet are (i) control tokens, (ii) data tokens, and (iii) stored data for memory.

The actual implementation of this machine organisation is based on Motorola M6800 microcomputers that support the four groups of resources. These microcomputers are interconnected by hardware first-in-first-out queues that support the pools of work. For further details of the Combined control flow – data flow computer the interested reader should consult the references [10,18].

6. Conclusions

The work reported here forms part of a larger project investigating the design of decentralised, general-purpose computer architectures. This project has involved the investigation of control flow [9], data flow [15] and reduction [16] computers and is thus representative of the spectrum of research into novel computer architectures. Traditionally such research has been compartmentalised, concentrating on a single category of programming language, program organisation and machine organisation. For example data flow research usually involves single assignment languages and packet communication machine organisations.

The theme of our project is the synthesis of a number of traditional program organisations into a single "general-purpose" organisation. We wish to obtain the program organisation and the machine organisation for a decentralised computer architecture that is able to efficiently support at least conventional and functional categories of programming language. In this paper we have described the program organisation and machine organisation of a computer supporting control flow and data flow. For this computer, a compiler for a conventional language can generate a control flow style of code, one for a single assignment language can generate a data flow style, or more interestingly a compiler could use a mixed style of code. We are currently working on the next stage of the overall project which is the design of a computer supporting control flow, data flow and reduction [17].

Acknowledgements

The ideas and computer design presented in this document are the work of Richard Hopkins, Paul Rautenbach and the author. This work owes much to the support and encouragement of our colleagues at the University of Newcastle upon Tyne, in particular David Brownbridge and Simon Jones. The Computer Architecture Group has also been greatly aided by the Distributed Computing Systems Panel of the UK Science and Engineering Research Council, which funds this research.

References

[1] Ackerman W.B. and Dennis J.B.: "VAL – A Value Oriented Algorithmic Language (preliminary reference manual)". Tech. Report MIT/LCS/TR-218, Laboratory for Computer Science, MIT (June 1979).

[2] Anon.: "Proceedings of International Conference on Fifth Generation Computer Systems". Japan Information Processing Development Center (October 1981) to be publishied by North Holland Press.

[3] Arvind et al: "The Id Report: An Asynchronous Programming Language and Computing Machine". Tech. Report 114a, Dept. of Information and Computer Science, University of California, Irvine (May 1978).

[4] Backus J.: "Can Programming be Liberated from the von Neumann Style? A Functional Style and Its Algebra of Programs". Comm. ACM vol. 21, no. 8 (August 1978) pp. 613-641.

[5] Berkling   K.J.:   "Reduction   languages   for   Reduction
     Machines". Proc. Second Int. Symp. on Computer Architecture
     (April 1975) pp. 133-140.

[6] Byte: "A special issue on the Smalltalk-80 Programming
     Language". Byte (August 1981).

[7] Darlington J. et al: "Functional Programming and Its
     Applications". Cambridge University Press (1982).

[8] Dennis J.B.:   "Data Flow Supercomputers". IEEE Computer
     Magazine vol. 13, no. 11 (November 1980) pp. 48-56.

[9] Farrell E.P. et al: "A Concurrent Computer Architecture and
     a Ring Based Implementation". Proc. Sixth Int. Symp. on
     Computer Architecture (April 1979) pp. 1-11.

[10] Hopkins R.P. et al: "A Computer supporting Data Flow,
     Control Flow and Updateable Memory". Tech. Report 144,
     Computing Laboratory, University of Newcastle upon Tyne
     (September 1979).

[11] Kobayashi K.:   "Computer, Commuincations and Man: The
     Integration of Computer and Commuincations with Man as an
     Axis". Computer Networks vol. 5, no. 4 (July 1981) pp.
     237-250.

[12] Kowalski R.A.: "Logic for Problem Solving". North Holland
     Press (1980).

[13] Mead C. and Conway L.:   "Introduction to VLSI Systems".
     Addison-Wesley Press (1980).

[14] Michie D. (ed.), "Expert Systems in the Micro Electronic
     Age". Edinburgh University Press (1979).

[15] Treleaven P.C.:   "Principle Components of a Data Flow
     Computer".   Proc. 1978 Euromicro Symp. (October 1978) pp.
     366-374.

[16] Treleaven P.C. and Mole G.F.: "A Multi-processor Reduction
     Machine for User-defined Reduction Languages".   Proc.
     Seventh Int. Symp. on Computer Architecture (April 1980) pp.
     121-129.

[17] Treleaven P.C. and Hopkins R.P.:   "A Recursive (VLSI)
     Computer Architecture".   Tech. Report 161, Computing
     Laboratory, University of Newcastle upon Tyne (March 1981).

[18] Treleaven P.C. et al: "Combining Data Flow and Control Flow
     Computing". The Computer Journal vol. 25, no. 1 (January
     1982).

[19] Treleaven P.C. et al: "Data Driven and Demend Driven
     Computer Architecture". ACM Computing Surveys vol. 14, no.
     1 (March 1982).

[20] Turner D.: "A New Implementation Technique for Applicative
     Languages". Software - Practice and Experience vol. 9,
     (1979) pp. 31-49.

[21] Watson I. and Gurd J.: "A Prototype Data Flow Computer with
     Token Labelling". Proc. AFIPS vol. 48 (1979) pp. 623-628.

[22] Wilner W.T.: "Recursive Machines". Internal Report, Xerox
     Palo Alto Research Center, Palo Alto, California (1980).

<u>Directions and Trends in FORTRAN</u>
(Abstract) *

George Paul

Computer Sciences Department
IBM T.J. Watson Research Center

Work is currently underway by the X3J3 Committee of the American
National Standards Institute to draft new proposals for the future ANSI FORTRAN Standard. These proposals include a model architecture for the language containing: a core language module, a
language extension module and an obsolete features module as well
as application area support modules. In addition new extensions
are being provided in the language for data structures, array
processing, name management and internal procedures among other
extensions. This paper reports on the current status of these
draft proposals and the expected trends and directions these proposals are taking.

----

* Manuskript nicht rechtzeitig eingegangen

FINDET ADA ZURÜCK NACH EUROPA ?

Horst Hünke
Kommission der Europäischen Gemeinschaften
DG III/B/1

Die europäische Software-Industrie braucht Normen für eine
bessere Marktdurchdringung und fortgeschrittene Software-
Entwicklungsmethoden zum Erhalt ihrer Konkurrenzfähigkeit.
Die ESL-Studie (European Systems Language) kam zu dem
Ergebnis, dass Ada für einen wichtigen Marktbereich brauch-
bare Basis für die Erreichung beider Ziele ist.

Im Rahmen des Mehrjahresprogramms für Datenverarbeitung der
Europäischen Gemeinschaft wird die Entwicklung der grundlegenden Software-Werkzeuge für Ada gefördert. Hierzu
gehören eine Familie portabler Kompilierer und eine
portable Programmierumgebung.

Kleinere Studien beschäftigen sich mit Themen wie denen
eines europäischen Ada-Kompilierer-Validationsdienstes,
Konversionsproblemen, Anwendbarkeit von Ada in der
Fertigungssteuerung, Regelwerke für Programmbibliotheken
in Ada, benutzerfreundliche Kommandoschnittstelle für Ada-
Entwicklungsumgebungen, der Koexistenz von Chill und Ada in
einer Ada-Umgebung, Ada-Maschinen und den Voraussetzungen
für eine volle Ada-Programmierumgebung.

Informationsaustausch und Meinungsbildung - derzeit der
Entwickler - wird gefördert durch die Unterstützung von
Ada Europe, deren Arbeitsgruppen auch zur Beratung heran-
gezogen werden.

Die Darstellung zeichnet die Entwicklung nach und gibt
Perspektiven für die Rolle von Ada in der Zukunft.

DAS DV-PROGRAMM DER GEMEINSCHAFT

Das Mehrjahresprogramm der Gemeinschaft für eine Politik

auf dem Gebiet der Datenverarbeitung (1) will einen Beitrag

zur systematischen Unterstützung von Forschung, industrieller

Entwicklung und Anwendung der Datenverarbeitung in der

Gemeinschaft leisten. Zwei Typen von Massnahmen werden

unterschieden :

- Massnahmen auf dem Gebiet der Normung, des öffentlichen
  Beschaffungswesens, der Zusammenarbeit der Forschungs-
  zentren, Organisationen zur Förderung des Einsatzes der
  Datenverarbeitung, rechtliche Studien und Studien über
  Beschäftigungsfragen, Datensicherung und Datenschutz und
  rechtlicher Schutz von Software;

- Unterstützungsmassnahmen für Software und Anwendungen und
  für Arbeiten auf Gebieten, die der Rat aufgrund von
  Studien genehmigt.

Im Vorlauf zur Aufstellung des Mehrjahresprogramms hatte
sich die Kommission seit 1974 mit Industrie, Anwendern und
Forschungsstellen beraten. Zersplitterung des Marktes und
fehlende Normen waren als eine wichtige Ursache für die
Probleme der europäischen Software-Industrie erkannt worden.
Für Anwender war der Wechsel von einem Hersteller zum
anderen, für den Hersteller die Adaption des Produktes für
die Maschine oder das Betriebssystem eines anderen Kunden
zu teuer. Vertreter der Software-Industrie forderten eine
einheitliche algorithmische Sprache zur Systementwicklung
mit Eignung für Datenbank- und Datenkommunikations-Anwendungen.

Die zweite Tranche von Prioritätsmassnahmen sah eine Studie
zur Grobdefinition einer Systemimplementierungssprache für
die europäische Software-Industrie (2),(3) vor.

Die Notwendigkeit zur Kostenreduktion, zur Öffnung des Marktes,
zur Erleichterung der Konversion von Software zum Gebrauch
auf verschiedenen Anlagen führten zur starken Betonung der
Portabilität in dem Vorschlag der Kommission (2). Andere
Ziele in diesem Vorschlag betrafen eine genormte Sprache
für Realzeitprogrammierung und eine engere Verbindung von
Nachrichtenübertragung und Datenverarbeitung. Eine starke
Betonung erfuhr auch die Normung.

Das HOL Programm

Im Jahre 1975 richtete das amerikanische Verteidigungsministerium eine Arbeitsgruppe ein, die Anforderungen an
allgemein anwendbare höhere Programmiersprachen definieren
sollte. Besonders betont wurde der Anwendungsbereich -
abstrakt beschrieben - der in technische Systeme inte-
grierten - eingebetteten - DV-Systeme. Weitere wichtige
Ziele waren

- Portabilität von Software durch Einsatz einer maschinenunabhängigen Sprache;

- Kostenreduktion und Qualitätsverbesserung von Software;

- erhöhter Wettbewerb zwischen Anbietern und freiere Auswahl
  der Behörde bei der Vergabe von Anschlussaufträgen;

- die Einführung effektiverer Software-Entwicklungsmethoden.

Die Anforderungsdefinition wurde in ständiger öffentlich ge-
führter Diskussion verfeinert, bis sie ihre Endfassung im
Jahre 1978 im "Steelman"-Dokument erreichte (4). Zwei sehr
globale Gesichtspunkte hatten hohes Gewicht: Qualität der
Sprache und breite Anwendbarkeit und Akzeptanz auch ausser-
halb des militärischen Bereichs (5).

In einer internationalen Ausschreibung wurden vier Angebote
ausgewählt, die zwischen 1977 und 1978 zu Grobentwürfen führten.
1978 - 1979 wurden zwei Entwürfe weiter verfeinert. Die
Entscheidung für den Entwurf des Teams unter Leitung von
Jean D. Ichbiah von Honeywell Bull fiel im Mai 1979.

Der Ansatz der HOLWG war von Beginn an gewesen, dass nicht
nur ein wissenschaftliches Problem zu lösen war - die Definition
einer Sprache - oder ein technisches - die Bereitstellung von
Kompilierern in Industriequalität. Man war sich bewusst, dass
auch ein sozialer Prozess in Gang zu bringen war (7), der
allerdings nicht bei allen Beteiligten gänzlich Erfolg
hatte (6). Dennoch stellt Ada unter den Gesichtspunkten Eignung

und Akzeptanz den realisierbaren, den realistischen Kompromiss dar.

Ergänzend zum Programm der Entwicklung der Sprache begann - manche meinen verspätet - die Anforderungsdefinition für Software-Werkzeuge für Ada (8). Inzwischen hierzu vorliegende Entwürfe werden wiederum öffentlicher Diskussion unterzogen.

Zur Sicherung der Normeneinhaltung wird ein Validationsdienst vorbereitet (9). Nur solche Kompilierer, die die Validation erfolgreich durchlaufen, sollen den Namen Ada tragen dürfen. Hierzu hat das amerikanische Verteidigungsministerium "Ada" in den USA als Warenzeichen eintragen lassen und in verschiedenen anderen Ländern als Warenzeichen angemeldet.

Die Normungsberatungen zu Ada im Rahmen der US-Normen-organisation sind weit fortgeschritten; bei ISO haben sie begonnen.

In verschiedenen Vorhaben wird versucht, zu einer formalen Beschreibung der Semantik von Ada zu gelangen, die sowohl höhere Präzision der Beschreibung wie auch direktere Brauch-barkeit für die Entwicklung von Ada-Kompilierern verspricht (10 .. 13).

Zur Koordinierung seiner Aktivitäten hat das US-Verteidigungs-ministerium ein Ada Joint Project Office eingerichtet. Von hier aus werden auch die Normungsarbeiten im Rahmen von ANSI und, soweit angelaufen, von ISO unterstützt.

<u>ESL und Ada</u>

Das Vorhaben für die Grobdefinition der europäischen Implementierungssprache ESL wurde 1978 ausgeschrieben. Die Ausschreibung wurde von einem Konsortium bestehend aus der Siemens AG und CII-Honeywell Bull gewonnen. Die im Jahre 1978 und 1979 durchgeführten Arbeiten führten zu einem Bedarfsprofil und einem Grobentwurf von ESL. Dieser war der von

CII-HB und Honeywell Information Systems entwickelten Definition
von "Green" sehr ähnlich.

Im Jahre 1979 wurde "Green" als zukünftige Sprache ausgewählt - "Green" wurde Ada.

Die Kommission beriet sich mit von den Mitgliedsländern be-
nannten Experten und hörte den die Portabilitätsprojekte
begleitenden technischen Ausschuss an.

Zur Wahl standen zwei - in unterschiedlichem Detaillierungsgrad vorliegende, sich aus anderem Anwendungsbedarf be-
gründende - sehr ähnliche Sprachentwürfe. Einer konnte für
den europäischen Markt von Bedeutung sein. Der andere würde
auf dem Weltmarkt Bedeutung erringen - falls COBOL als Beispiel
dienen konnte.

Die Wahl von Ada versprach einen weitaus grösseren Markt zu
öffnen. Die Normungsziele für ESL und Ada waren die gleichen.
Gleiches galt für die Bedingungen für Portabilität. Kostenreduktion und Qualitätserhöhung von Software sind allgemein
angestrebte Ziele jeder Massnahmen zur Verbesserung der Software-
Produktion. Die Ziele des HOL-Programms nach Unabhängigkeit von
speziellen Anbietern und erhöhter Flexibilität bei der Auftrags-
vergabe decken sich mit den Zielen der Erhöhung der Unabhängigkeit der Benutzer. Ada war ausserdem im Anwendungsbereich der
in (2) beschriebenen Realzeitprogrammiersprache einsetzbar.

Ada wurde ESL.

<u>Ada als Ziel</u>

Das Mehrjahresprogramm für Datenverabeitung hat eine Reihe
von Teilzielen: Unterstützung kollaborativer Grundsoftware-
und Anwendungsvorhaben, die einen Beitrag zur Normung und der
Erhöhung der Portabilität von Software leisten, die zum ver-
stärkten Einsatz der Datenverarbeitung im gemeinsamen Markt
beitragen und einen homogenen gemeinschaftsweiten Hardware-

und Software-Markt zu schaffen helfen, die die europäische
DV-Industrie durch Kooperation stärken und die durch Bereitstellung hochwertiger Informationstechnik die Wettbewerbs-
fähigkeit der europäischen Industrie allgemein verbessern.

In der Durchführung des Mehrjahresprogramms wird versucht, einen
Beitrag dazu zu leisten, dass in der Durchführung zwar risiko-
reiche, im Falle des Erfolgs jedoch eine grosse Wirkung ent-
faltende, gute Projekte mit den genannten Zielen früher als
ohne die Unterstützung aus Mitteln der Gemeinschaft in Angriff
genommen oder überhaupt erst ermöglicht werden.

Aufbauend auf den Arbeiten zu ESL suchte die Kommission im
Jahre 1980 Kontakte bezüglich der Entwicklung von Ada Kompilierern. Es sollte mit den geplanten Aktionen auch erreicht
werden, dass das weitgehend in Europa angesiedelte Entwurfs-
team für Ada dort verbleiben und einen Beitrag zur Weiterentwicklung der europäischen DV-Industrie leisten würde. Auf
eine allgemeine Ausschreibung(16) hin wurden ebenfalls einige
Ada-orientierte Vorhaben vorgeschlagen.

Im Jahre 1980 wurden zwei grosse und ein kleineres Vorhaben
verabschiedet. Hierzu bedarf die Kommission der qualifizierten
Zustimmung des Beratenden Ausschusses für die Durchführung und
Koordinierung der Programme auf dem Gebiet der Datenverarbeitung (1).

Alsys, CII-Honeywell Bull und die Siemens AG entwickeln eine
Familie portabler Ada-Kompilierer. Die Projektlaufzeit ist
von Januar 1981 bis Mitte 1983.

Olivetti, Dansk Datamatik Center und Christian Rovsing A/S
entwickeln eine portable Programmierumgebung. Es ist vorgesehen, auch den Alsys/CII-HB/Siemens-Kompilierer, beziehungs-
weise seinen maschinenunabhängigen Teil, in diese Umgebung
zu integrieren.

Mit der Unterstützung soll ein Beitrag geleistet werden, dass
sowohl der Technologiestand auf dem Ada-Gebiet vorangetrieben

wird wie auch dass Grundsoftware für Ada in Industriequalität
und für europäische DV-Anlagen möglichst früh in Europa verfügbar ist.

Eine kleinere Studie, durchgeführt von Olivetti und SPL behandelt technische Aspekte und Marktaussichten von Konversions-
hilfen zwischen Pascal und Ada. Ein Zwischenbericht hierzu
liegt vor.

Im Jahre 1981 wurden zwei Studien vergeben. Das französische
Normenbüro BNI, das National Physical Laboratory (NPL),
Teddington, und die Gesellschaft für Mathematik und Datenver-
arbeitung mbH untersuchen die technischen, organisatorischen
und vertragsrechtlichen Voraussetzungen für die Einrichtung
eines europäischen Validationsdienstes für Ada-Kompilierer.
Ziel ist, dass die von diesem Zentrum durchgeführten
Validationen auch in den Vereinigten Staaten anerkannt werden.

Die zweite Ausschreibung im Jahre 1981 brachte weitere Vor-
schläge, die meist in Form von Vorstudien durchgeführt werden.
Die Unterstützungsverträge stehen Ende 1981 kurz vor der
Unterzeichnung.

Eine Studie von SDL (Camberley) und TECSI (Paris) soll den
Rahmen einer vollen Ada-Umgebung (APSE), die alle Aktivitäten
des Software-Lebenszyklus unterstützt, abstecken. Die Existenz
einer MAPSE wird vorausgesetzt; es sollen ein Methodenbündel
und die zugehörigen Werkzeuge identifiziert werden. Das
Ergebnis wird für Anbieter und Anwender von Ada gleicher-
massen von Nutzen sein.

Für den Bereich der industriellen Anwendung verteilter Multi-
Mikroprozessoren untersuchen Zeltron (Mailand) und SPL
(Abingdon) die Eignung von Ada und einiger der konkret in
Entwicklung befindlichen APSEs. Dazu soll ein Vergleich mit
der speziell für diesen Anwendungsbereich unter Förderung des
Italienischen Forschungsrates CNR entwickelten Sprache MML
angestellt werden. Die Studie soll die Wahl des geeigneten
Ansatzes ermöglichen.

NPL und das Mathematische Zentrum (Amsterdam) erarbeiten ein
Regelwerk für die Entwicklung grosser modularer wissenschaftlicher Programmbibliotheken in Ada. Damit soll die Kompatibilität und Portabilität zukünftig zu entwickelnder Programmbibliotheken, ähnlich bestehenden wie NAG, IMSL oder NUMAL,
verbessert werden.

Die Probleme der Koexistenz eines Chill-Kompilierers und
seiner zugehörigen Werkzeuge mit Ada-Werkzeugen in einer APSE
wollen GEC Telecommunications Ltd und DDC untersuchen. Dieses
Vorhaben könnte zur Überbrückung der möglicherweise marktzer-
splitternd wirkenden Kluft zwischen Ada und Chill beitragen.

Für den Bereich Kommandosprachen ist von einer Gruppe von
Universitäten (Dublin, Leeds, Hagen) der auf UNCLE (Universal
Nice Command Language Environment) basierende Vorschlag zu
einer fortschrittlichen Benutzerschnittstelle gemacht worden.
Aus diesem Projekt werden wichtige Anstösse für laufende und
zukünftige MAPSE- und APSE-Entwicklungen und für mögliche
Normungsdiskussionen erwartet.

Zum Thema Konversion von RTL/2 nach Ada untersuchen SPL und
Hollandse Signaalapparaten (Hengelo) die wirtschaftlichsten
Möglichkeiten für RTL/2-Anwender, ihre in RTL/2-Systeme ge-
tätigten Investitionen in eine Ada-Zukunft zu übertragen.
Ada hat den selben Anwendungsbereich wie RTL/2. Es soll eine
Teilmenge von RTL/2 identifiziert werden, die leicht nach Ada
übersetzt werden kann. Die Koexistenz von bestehender RTL/2-
Software und neuer Ada-Software soll untersucht werden. Der
Bericht soll exemplarischen Charakter haben und über den
direkten Nutzen für RTL/2-Benutzer hinaus als Modell dienen
können, wie Anwender ihre Software-Produktionstechnik um-
stellen können.

Neben der Förderung von Projekten und der Vergabe von Studien
allgemeiner Bedeutung unterstützt die Kommission die Arbeit
von Ada Europe. Mit neun Untergruppen, wie "Environment",
"Compiler Implementation", "Language Review" oder "Portability"

dient Ada Europe dem Informationsaustausch zwischen Entwicklern,
der Meinungsbildung zu technischen und entwicklungspolitischen
Fragen und der Beratung der Kommission in wissenschaftlichen,
technischen und Normungsfragen. Derzeit stehen die meisten
Beratungen im Zusammenhang mit Software für Ada. Eine Er-
gänzung in Richtung Anwendung von Ada wäre durchaus wünschens-
wert.

<u>Ada als Mittel</u>

Die Entwicklung einer Programmiersprache, oder auch von
Kompilierern hierfür und weiterer Software-Werkzeuge, ist nicht
nur Selbstzweck. Sie ist auch Hilfsmittel.

Ada ist eine der Sprachen, die auf der Basis von Wissen, zum
Teil Meinung, über wünschenswerte Programmiertechniken und
wirkungsvolle Software-Entwicklungsmethoden entworfen worden
ist. Der software-technologische Hintergrund von Ada (15)
gibt die Möglichkeit, die Sprache im Zusammenhang mit zu ihr
passenden Methoden und Werkzeugen zur Software-Produktion zu
sehen. Legt man eines der verschiedenen Modelle über den
Software-Entwicklungsprozess zugrunde, so kann man in Umrissen
eine Software-Produktionstechnik erkennen, in der Verfahren,
Methoden und Werkzeuge integriert und aufeinander abgestimmt
sind. Das Ziel der Mondfahrt hat der US-Raumfahrtindustrie
eine Aufgabe gegeben, die zu lösen zwangsläufig zu einem
höheren technischen und organisatorischen Entwicklungsstand
dieser Industrie führen musste. Anhand eines Beitrags zur
Zielerreichung, der Erreichung eines gemeinsamen Ziels, konnten
einzelne Vorhaben beurteilt werden. Auf ähnliche Weise kann
Ada wirken. Die Sprache kann als Leitfaden dienen, welche
Werkzeuge und Verfahren zu entwickeln sind. Die Wahrschein-
lichkeit der Konsistenz des Ergebnisses und seiner Wirkung
wird erhöht gegenüber dem Versuch, "gezielt" Einzelmassnahmen
zu ergreifen, die jeweils für sich allein beurteilt besonders
förderungswürdig erscheinen mögen, deren Ergebnisse sich
aber nicht kombinieren lassen.

Das oben zitierte Beispiel der Mondfahrt hat allerdings einen
erheblichen Vorteil: seine unvergleichlich bessere Eignung,
das Interesse der öffentlichen Meinung zu erwecken und über
Jahre zu halten. Ziele wie die Entwicklung der "nächsten
Rechnergeneration" eignen sich schon besser für diesen Zweck;
ihre Rolle als Basis für planungstechnische Leitlinien ist die
gleiche.

Als Beispiel für die Leitfunktion kann man, in Anlehnung an den
Meinungsbildungsprozess zu Programmiertechniken, die Notwendigkeit einer adäquaten Entwurfssprache und dazugehöriger Werkzeuge erläutern. IBM-FSD (14) geht zum Beispiel diesen Weg.
Es folgen Spezifikationssprache, Anforderungsanalyse samt der
erforderlichen, rechnerunterstützten Arbeitsweise. Die Notwendigkeit der Vermittelbarkeit der verschiedenen Darstellungen
untereinander wird leichter einsichtig. Man gewinnt leichter
ein konsistentes Modell. Als PL/1 eingeführt wurde, wurden
seinen Nutzern   als Fehlerdiagnose-"Hilfen" hexadezimale
Speicherauszüge und betriebssystemorientierte Fehlermeldungen
angeboten. Syntax-orientierte Editoren sind noch heute selten.
Die angebotenen Editoren haben als Modell das Universum der
Zeichen und Zeilen. Der Benutzer einer Sprache aber denkt in
syntaktischen und semantischen Kategorien über sein Programm.

Die hier beschriebene Blickrichtung ist "bottom up". Die
Rationale (15) vermittelt Erklärungen auch zu Aspekten wie
"Programmierung im Grossen". Ein Ausgangspunkt für die Entwicklung von Ada war die Verringerung der Kosten von Software
über den gesamten Lebenszyklus eines Software-Systems, im
Gegensatz zu suboptimalen Lösungen, die nur einzelne Phasen
oder Entwicklungsaktivitäten betrachteten.

Ada kann didaktisches und methodisches Hilfsmittel zur schritt-
weisen Entwicklung einer rechnergestützten Software-Produktionstechnik sein.

Schluss

Eines der grundlegenden Ziele der Europäischen Wirtschafts-
gemeinschaft - offene Märkte und freier Austausch von Dienst-
leistungen - erfordert breit anerkannte Normen. Ada verspricht
diese Rolle für einen wichtigen Bereich der Datenverarbeitung
- Softwareentwicklung unter Verwendung einer algorithmischen
Sprache - erfüllen zu können.

Wenngleich in ihren technischen Merkmalen nicht unumstritten
stützt sich Ada auf einen breiten Konsens in der Fachwelt.
Eine breite Verwendung von Ada und die Entwicklung weiterer
Normen und Standards auf der Basis einer genau kontrollierten
Sprachnorm können einen erheblichen Beitrag zum Aufbau einer
industrialisierten Software-Produktion leisten.

Die im Rahmen des Mehrjahresprogramms gewährten Finanzhilfen
und geleisteten Koordinierungsmassnahmen zeigen erste er-
mutigende Ergebnisse. Über die direkte Wirkung der vergebenen
Mittel hinaus können mehr und mehr katalytische Wirkungen
dieser Mittel beobachtet werden. Firmen investieren in
für die bisherige Praxis in der Softwarebranche und die derzeitige Wirtschaftslage erstaunlicher Weise Eigenmittel in
Nachfolgeaktivitäten ursprünglich geförderter Projekte.

Das Bewusstsein der zukünftigen Bedeutung von Ada steigt. Die
Einsicht in die Notwendigkeit und Bereitschaft zur Kooperation
wächst. Eine Fortführung der Unterstützungsmassnahmen kann für
diesen Prozess nur förderlich sein und erscheint notwendig im
Vergleich zu den in anderen Ländern vergleichbarer Industria-
lisierung mit dem gleichen Ziel, zum Teil auf anderen Wegen
durchgeführten Massnahmen.

Ada ist Ziel und Mittel zugleich. Die Bedeutung dieser Sprache
kann für einen weiten Bereich der Systementwicklung und wissen-
schaftlich-technische Anwendungen die Bedeutung erlangen wie
Cobol - vor etwa zwanzig Jahren wurde seine Entwicklung begonnen - für kommerzielle DV-Anwendungen erlangt hat.

Referenzen

(1) Amtsblatt der Europäischen Gemeinschaften No. L 231 vom 13.9.1979

(2) Community Policy for data-processing Document COM(75) 467 final, Sept. 1975

(3) Beschluss des Rates, Amtsblatt No. L 255 vom 6.10.1977

(4) Requirements for High Order Computer Programming Languages, "Steelman", US Department of Defense, 1978

(5) Carlson W.E., L.E. Druffel, D.A. Fisher, W.A. Whitaker: Introducing Ada. Proceedings ACM 1980 Annual Conference

(6) Hoare C.A.R.: The Emperor's Old Clothes, CACM Vol. 24 No. 2, Feb. 1981

(7) D. Fisher , Schlussvortrag beim ACM SIGPLAN Symposium on Ada, Dec. 1980. (Nicht in den Proceedings ACM SIGPLAN Notices, Vol. No. 1980 enthalten)

(8) Requirements for Ada Programming Support Environments "Stoneman", US Department of Defense, February 1980

(9) Goodenough J.B.: The Ada Compiler Validation Capability, IEEE Computer, June 1981

(10) Bjørner D., O.N. Oest, Editors, Towards a Formal Description of Ada, Lecture Notes in Computer Science Vol. 98, 1981

(11) Formal Definition of the Ada Programming Language, INRIA, November 1980

(12) Belz F.C., E.K. Blum, D. Heimbigner, A Multi-Processing Implementation-Oriented Formal Definition of Ada in SEMANOL, ACM SIGPLAN Notices Vol. 15, Number 11, November 1980

(13) Dewar R.B.K., G.A. Fisher, E. Schonberg, R. Froehlich, S. Bryant, C.F. Goss, M. Burke, The NYU Ada Translator and Interpreter, ACM SIGPLAN Notices Vol. 15, Number 11, November 1980

(14) IBM Software Engineering Exchange, Vol. 3 No. 1, October 1980

(15) Ichbiah, J.D., J.G.P. Barnes, J.C. Heliard, B. Krieg-Brückner, O. Roubine, B.A. Wichman, Rationale for the Design of the Ada Programming Language. ACM SIGPLAN Notices Vol. 14 Number 5, June 1979, Part B

(16) Amtsblatt der Europäischen Gemeinschaften C46 vom 23. Februar 1980

Funktionelle Spezifikation interaktiver Systeme
und ihre Zerlegung in Teilsysteme *

Rupert Gnatz

Institut für Informatik
Technische Universität München

Zusammenfassung

Interaktive Systeme realisieren Schnittstellen zwischen einem Anwenderprogramm und Dialogpartnern. Operationen an gewissen systeminternen Programmvariablen können technisch als Spezifikation von Ausgabeoperationen und mehrdeutige Ausdrücke bzw. nichtdeterministische Anweisungen als Spezifikation von Eingabeoperationen aufgefaßt werden. Bei der Zerlegung eines Systems in eine Hierarchie von Teilsystemen werden diese Spezifikationen in untergeordnete Teilsysteme verdrängt. Diese Betrachtungsweise führt zu einer Vereinheitlichung der Spezifikation für nicht-interaktive und interaktive Software.

1. Vorbemerkung

Die Benutzung abstrakter Datentypen zur Definition von Programmiersprachen (vgl. /CIP-L-Sprachreport 81/) bietet eine Reihe von Vorteilen. Die Definition von interaktiven Systemen mit ihren Dialogsprachen läßt sich im Prinzip ähnlich auf abstrakte Datentypen abstützen, wodurch sich ein direkter Zusammenhang zu den algebraisch-automatentheoretischen Beschreibungsmethoden wie etwa in /Kupka, Wilsing 74 und 80/ ergibt (vgl. Abschnitt 5). Dies erlaubt es, dem zentralen Anliegen bei interaktiven Systemen gerecht zu werden, nämlich die Verflechtung von Ein- und Ausgabe in ihrer Semantik global zu spezifizieren (zur allgemeinen Problematik vgl. auch /Seillac II/).

Während z.B. in /Riethmayer 81/ das Spezifikationsproblem für ein umfangreiches System unter Abstützung auf den klassischen Funktionsbegriff behandelt wird, wird hier das *Konzept der mehrdeutigen Funktionen* (vgl. z.B. McCarthy 63/) bzw. der *nicht-deterministischen Anweisungen* benutzt. Diese Konzepte erlauben es aus der Sicht des interaktiven Systems, die "Breite" (vgl. /Broy, Gnatz, Wirsing 79/) der möglichen, aber im einzelnen nicht kalkulierbaren oder vorhersehbaren Reaktionen der Dialogpartner exakt zu modellieren. Ein interaktives System stellt sich damit als ein System von Algorithmen dar, welchen neben der mathematischen Semantik eine zusätzliche Interpretation für die Auswertung der nicht-deterministischen Konstruktionen beigegeben ist: Es wird unterstellt, daß der Dialogpartner, dem die jeweilige Konstruktion zugeordnet ist, eine

---

* Diese Arbeit ist im Sonderforschungsbereich 49, Programmiertechnik, München, entstande

Auswahl aus der Breite der möglichen Reaktionen vornimmt. Das interaktive System kann
zwar diese Reaktionsbreite definieren bzw. vorschreiben; welche Wahl der Partner jedoch innerhalb dieser Breite trifft, bleibt seinem *freien Willen* überlassen /Gnatz 81/.

Es wird außerdem ein *Modulkonzept* benutzt, das weitgehend mit /Wirth 77/ übereinstimmt, welches geeignet ist,die Funktionsweise peripherer Geräte zu beschreiben und
welches durch das Schlüsselwort <u>device</u> gekennzeichnet sein soll: Das wesentliche
Charakteristikum sind die *modulinternen Zustandsvariablen*; der Aufruf von Prozeduren
des Moduls hängt nicht nur von den Prozedurparametern ab, sondern auch von diesen Zustandsvariablen und damit, anders als z.B. in /Laut 80/, u.U. implizit von der Hi-
storie der vorausgehenden Prozeduraufrufe. Die Zustandsvariablen sind ausschließlich
durch die Prozeduren, die in einem Treiberprogramm aufgerufen werden können, manipu-
lierbar (vgl. Anhang).

Den Zustandsvariablen kann neben der mathematisch-programmiersprachlichen Bedeutung
wieder eine zusätzliche technische Interpretation zugeordnet werden: Sie können als
Abstraktion von Ausgabemedien aufgefaßt werden, etwa des Bildschirms eines Sichtge-
räts, der Papierbahn eines Schnelldruckers, der Stellung eines Zeichenwerkzeuges am
Plotter oder der Position einer Werkzeughalterung eines Handhabungssystems.

Unterlegt man also naheliegenderweise die Terminologie der Automatisierungstechnik,
dann können diese Zustandsvariable bzw. die Operationen, welche die Zustände verän-
dern, als Abstraktionen von Effektoren, die nicht-deterministischen Konstruktionen
als Abstraktion von Sensoren eines Gerätes aufgefaßt werden.

Absicht dieses Aufsatzes ist es, eine übersichtliche Zusammenstellung einiger methodischer Aspekte für die Spezifikation interaktiver Systeme sowie der darauf aufbauenden
Entwicklung zu geben. Das spezielle Beispiel der syntaxgesteuerten Eingabe ist lediglich von untergeordnetem Interesse. Da das Beispiel eine *Programmentwicklung durch
schrittweise Umformung* vorführen soll, wird das darin enthaltene, grammatische Problem innerhalb des programmiersprachlichen Rahmens und angepaßt an einzelne Programm-
entwicklungsschritte behandelt. Wesentlich vom Standpunkt der Programmentwicklungs-
methodik ist lediglich, daß ein Theorem aus einer speziellen mathematischen Theorie -
hier aus der Theorie der formalen Sprachen - zur Umformung herangezogen wird. Häufig sind ja Programmumformungen von bloß schematischer Gestalt, d.h. von der mathematischen Theorie des speziellen Problems unabhängig.

Das Beispiel hätte übrigens auch wie in /Gnatz 81/ aus dem Bereich der Rechnergraphik
genommen werden können. Gerade bei einem System, wie es beispielsweise in /GKS/ definiert wird, ist die Konstruktion verschiedener Modulzerlegungen, entsprechend ver-
schiedenartiger DD/DI-Schnittstellen (<u>device</u>-<u>dependent</u> / <u>device</u>-<u>independent</u>), von
eminent praktischer Bedeutung. Die programmiersprachliche Notation folgt im wesentlichen dem /CIP-L-Sprachreport 81/.

2. Zeichenketten und zeichenweise Ein/Ausgabe

Die nachfolgenden Beispiele stützen sich auf einen eingeschränkten Zeichenvorrat <u>char</u>
mit

<u>mode</u> <u>char</u> ≡ <u>atomic</u> {a, b, c, <u>(</u> , <u>)</u>, <u>+</u>, <u>x</u>, leer, *}

sowie auf Zeichenketten über diesem Zeichenvorrat. Letztere seien durch folgenden Typ
festgelegt.

```
type STRING ≡ (sort char, char leer) string, mty, make, &, top, rest :
     sort string ,
     string mty ,
     funct (char) string make ,
     funct (string, string) string & ,
     funct (string s : s ≠ mty) char top ,
     funct (string s : s ≠ mty) string rest ,

  laws
     ∀ string r, string s, string t, char x :
     r & (s & t) = (r & s) & t ,
     r & mty = mty & r = r ,
     x = leer  ↔  make(x) = mty ,
     x ≠ leer  ⟶  top(r & make(x)) = x ,
     x ≠ leer  ⟶  rest(r & make(x)) = r

  endoftype
```

Die Funktionsweise einer reinen *Ausgabe-* oder *Anzeigeeinheit* für Zeichenketten der
Art <u>string</u> spezifizieren wir durch den Modul

```
(1)        device ANZEIGE ≡ (sort char, char leer) delete, put :
              type (string, mty, make, &, top, rest) ≡ STRING(char, leer) ;
              var string anzeige := mty ;
              proc delete ≡:
                   anzeige := mty ;
              proc put ≡ (char x) :
                   anzeige := anzeige & make(x)
           endofdevice
```

Technisch kann die Zustandsvariable anzeige als ein Band aufgefaßt werden, auf das
durch die Operation put das Zeichen x in der jeweils nächsten, freien Schreibposition aufgebracht und das anschließend in die nächste Schreibposition transportiert
wird. Das Zeichen leer hat jedoch entsprechend den Axiomen von STRING eine Son-
derstellung: put(leer) bewirkt keine Veränderung des Inhalts der Variablen anzeige.
Die Operation delete schließlich bewirkt das Löschen der bisherigen Ausgabe; dies
kann beispielsweise durch Auflegen eines neuen Bandes geschehen.

Als Beispiel einer reinen *Eingabeeinheit* kann eine Tastatur für die neun Zeichen aus dem Alphabet <u>char</u> durch folgenden Modul spezifiziert werden: [1]

$$\text{\underline{device} STST} \equiv (\text{\underline{sort} \underline{char}, \underline{char} a, b, c, \underline{(}, \underline{)}, \underline{+}, \underline{x}, leer, *) read :}$$

$$\underline{proc} read \equiv (\underline{var} \underline{char} x) :$$

$$x := (a \parallel b \parallel c \parallel \underline{(} \parallel \underline{)} \parallel \underline{+} \parallel \underline{x} \parallel leer \parallel *)$$

$$\underline{endofdevice}$$

Die Breite des endlichen Auswahlausdrucks in der Zuweisung an x ist dabei die Menge
{a, b, c, <u>(</u>, <u>)</u>, <u>+</u>, <u>x</u>, leer, *} . Der Ausdruck liefert in nicht-deterministischer Weise irgendein Element aus dieser Menge.

Die Benutzung des <u>some</u>-Operators[2] anstelle der endlichen Auswahl erfordert lediglich
das Alphabet <u>alpha</u> als Modul*parameter* (vgl. Anhang):

$$\underline{device} TST \equiv (\underline{sort} \underline{alpha}) read :$$

$$\underline{proc} read \equiv (\underline{var} \underline{alpha} x) :$$

$$x := \underline{some} \underline{alpha} q : \underline{true}$$

$$\underline{endofdevice}$$

Es ist dann TST(<u>char</u>) dieselbe Eingabeeinheit wie STST(<u>char</u>, a, b, c, <u>(</u>, <u>)</u>, <u>+</u>, <u>x</u>,
leer, *). <u>true</u> ist das Prädikat, durch welches sämtliche Zeichen aus <u>alpha</u> der
Breite des <u>some</u>-Ausdrucks zugeschlagen werden. Der Variablen x wird ein Zeichen aus
dieser Breite zugewiesen.

Eine etwas komfortablere Tastatur erlaubt auch das *Blockieren aller bzw. Lösen einzelner Tasten* durch das Treiberprogramm. Man hat damit einen Modul,der sowohl Eingabe-
als auch Ausgabeoperationen enthält. Er enthält eine Reihung t boolescher Variabler,
deren Komponenten mit den Zeichen aus <u>char</u> indiziert werden.

$$\underline{device} BTST \equiv (\underline{sort} \underline{char}, \underline{char} a, b, c, \underline{(}, \underline{)}, \underline{+}, \underline{x}, leer, *) block, free, read :$$

$$\underline{char} \underline{array} \underline{var} \underline{bool} t := (\underline{false}, ..., \underline{false}) ;$$

$$\underline{proc} block \equiv :$$

$$t := (\underline{false}, ..., \underline{false}) ;$$

$$\underline{proc} free \equiv (\underline{char} q) :$$

$$t[q] := \underline{true} ;$$

$$\underline{proc} read \equiv (\underline{var} \underline{char} x) :$$

$$x := \underline{some} \underline{char} q : t[q] \vee (q = *)$$

$$\underline{endofdevice}$$

In einer zusätzlichen technischen Interpretation könnte jedem Zeichen q ein Anzeige-

---

[1] Abkürzend wird hier <u>char</u> a, b, ..., * anstelle von <u>char</u> a, <u>char</u> b, ..., <u>char</u> *
geschrieben.

[2] "comprehensive choice" in /CIP-L-Sprachreport 81/.

lämpchen t[q] zugeordnet sein, welches genau dann aufleuchtet, wenn die jeweilige Taste entsperrt ist, eine Technik, die insbesondere für Funktionstasten beim graphischen Dialog oder in Prozeßleitwarten eingesetzt wird.

Man beachte übrigens, daß in BTST die *-Taste auch dann gedrückt werden kann, wenn sie nicht entsperrt ist und das zugehörige Lämpchen nicht aufleuchtet. Der Auswahlausdruck ist also stets definiert (vgl. /Broy, Gnatz, Wirsing 79/). Die *-Taste wird damit escape-Taste. Hätte man die Prozedur read in der Gestalt

$$\underline{\text{proc}} \ read \equiv (\underline{\text{var}} \ \underline{\text{char}} \ x) :$$
$$x := \underline{\text{some}} \ \underline{\text{char}} \ q : t[q]$$

spezifiziert, dann müßte ein Treiberprogramm sicherstellen, daß jedem Aufruf von read ein Aufruf von read oder von free, nicht jedoch ein Aufruf von block vorangeht. Wird diese Bedingung verletzt, kommt es im Modul BTST zu einem Fehler: Die Breite des Auswahlausdruckes ist dann die leere Menge und enthält somit kein Element, das ausgewählt werden könnte.

Ein solches Phänomen ist beim Entwurf eines Moduls zu vermeiden. Man hätte übrigens anstelle des escape-Zeichens * auch eine *Fehlermeldung* einführen können:

$$\underline{\text{proc}} \ read \equiv (\underline{\text{var}} \ \underline{\text{char}} \ x, \ \underline{\text{var}} \ \underline{\text{bool}} \ error) :$$
$$\lceil \ error := \quad \exists \ \underline{\text{char}} \ q : t[q] \ ;$$
$$x := \underline{\text{some}} \ \underline{\text{char}} \ q : t[q] \ \vee \ \neg \ error \ \rfloor \quad .$$

3. Syntaxgesteuerte Eingabe

Diskutiert werden nun die Spezifikation und Entwicklung einer *abstrakten Ein/Ausgabeeinheit, welche die zeichenweise Eingabe von Worten mit einer gegebenen Syntax überwacht:* Es wird sichergestellt, daß, wenn die Sequenz der bereits eingegebenen Zeichen Anfang eines solchen Wortes ist, durch das nächste eingegebene Zeichen zusammen mit dieser Sequenz wieder ein (um dieses Zeichen verlängerter) Anfang eines solchen Wortes entsteht.

Das Beispiel dient hier lediglich als "toy problem". Mit dem Problemkreis des syntaxgeführten Dialogs haben sich ausführlich auseinandergesetzt etwa /Gorny 75/ und /Hoffmann 74/.

Als leicht überschaubares Beispiel wählen wir die Grammatik

$$E ::= S \mid S \underline{+} E$$
$$S ::= F \mid F \underline{x} S$$
$$F ::= a \mid b \mid c \mid \underline{(} \ E \ \underline{)}$$

mit den sieben Terminalzeichen a, b, c, $\underline{(}$, $\underline{)}$, $\underline{+}$, $\underline{x}$ $\in$ $\underline{\text{char}}$ und mit E als Axiom. L(E) sei die zugehörige Sprache.

Die beiden übrigen Zeichen leer, $*$ $\in$ <u>char</u> dienen als Sonderzeichen: leer bedeutet
Abschluß der Eingabe eines Wortes; $*$ dient wieder als escape-Symbol.

Zunächst stellen wir die Grammatik als Typ dar (vgl. dazu Teil III in /CIP-L-Sprach-
report 81/): [1]

$$\begin{aligned}
&\underline{mode}\ E \equiv me(\underline{S}\ em)\ |\ plus(\underline{S}\ su,\ \underline{E}\ ex)\ ,\\
&\underline{mode}\ S \equiv ms(\underline{F}\ sm)\ |\ mal(\underline{F}\ fc,\ \underline{S}\ sf)\ ,\\
&\underline{mode}\ F \equiv \underline{atomic}\ \{as,\ bs,\ cs\}\ |\ kl(\underline{E}\ lk)
\end{aligned}$$

und gehen damit über zu einer abstrakten Syntax der zur Grammatik gehörenden Sprache.

Wir geben nun eine eindeutige, totale Abbildung es der Objekte aus $\underline{E}$ auf Zeichenketten der Art <u>string</u> über dem Alphabet <u>char</u> an: es soll genau die Worte in $L(E)$
liefern. Die Spezifikation der zeichenweisen Eingabe von Worten aus $L(E)$ wird sich
dann im wesentlichen auf diese Abbildung es abstützen. [2]

```
funct es ≡ (E e) string :
      if e is me then ss(em(e))
      orif e is plus then ss(su(e)) & make(+) & es(ex(e))
      fi

funct ss ≡ (S s) string :
      if s is ms then fs(sm(s))
      orif s is mal then fs(fc(s)) & make(x) & ss(sf(s))
      fi

funct fs ≡ (F f) string :
      if f = as then make(a)
      orif f = bs then make(b)
      orif f = cs then make(c)
      orif f is kl then make(() & es(lk(d)) & make())
      fi
```

Liest man beispielsweise die Objekte in $\underline{E}$ als "Syntaxbäume", dann ist die Funktion
es ein Übersetzer, der die Baumdarstellung in eine entsprechende Zeichenkette um-
setzt ("tree-to-string"-Umsetzung).

Mit Hilfe der Funktion es läßt sich das Prädikat "$r \in$ <u>string</u> ist Anfang eines Wortes aus $L(E)$" in der folgenden Form fassen:

$$\exists\ \underline{string}\ s,\ \underline{E}\ e\ :\ es(e) = r\ \&\ s\ .$$

Damit ist auch die leere Zeichenkette mty Anfang eines Wortes aus $L(E)$, obwohl

---

[1] In einer Kurzform der allgemeinen Typnotation für spezielle monomorphe Typen in
CIP-L. Sorten sind hier $\underline{E}$, $\underline{S}$, $\underline{F}$, Konstruktorfunktionen me, plus, ms, mal, kl,
Destruktorfunktionen em, su, ex, sm, fc, sf, lk und Konstante as, bs, cs.
[2] <u>orif</u> bedeutet nicht-deterministische, <u>elsf</u> sequentielle Fallunterscheidung.

mty selbst nicht in L(E) ist.

Als Kernstück der zeichenweisen, syntaxgesteuerten Eingabe spezifizieren wir nun in deskriptiver Form eine *mehrdeutige* Funktion next. Der Deutlichkeit halber wird dabei das Schlüsselwort ambfunct ("ambiguous function") benutzt. [1]

$$\text{ambfunct next} \equiv (\underline{\text{string}}\ r : \exists\ \underline{\text{string}}\ s, \underline{E}\ e : es(e) = r\ \&\ s)\ \underline{\text{char}} :$$
$$\underline{\text{some}}\ \underline{\text{char}}\ z : p(r, z)$$

wobei gilt

$$p(r, z) = (z = *)$$
$$\vee\ (\exists\ \underline{E}\ e : es(e) = r \wedge z = \text{leer})$$
$$\vee\ (\exists\ \underline{\text{string}}\ t, \underline{E}\ e : es(e) = r\ \&\ make(z)\ \&\ t \wedge z \neq \text{leer})\ .$$

Dabei haben die beiden Sonderzeichen leer und * die bereits erwähnte Bedeutung. Sie wird präzisiert durch die nachfolgende, zusammenfassende Spezifikation des abstrakten Ein/Ausgabegerätes:

```
device TIP1 = (sort char, char a, b, c, (, ), +, x, leer, *) clear, get :
    type (string, mty, make, &, top, rest) = STRING(char, leer) ;

    sort E   = ... ;
    sort S   = ... ;
    sort F   = ... ;

    funct es  = ... ;
    funct ss  = ... ;
    funct fs  = ... ;

    ambfunct next  = ... ;

    (var string anzeige, var char cl) := (mty, leer) ;

    proc clear =:
        (anzeige, cl) := (mty, leer) ;
    proc get = (var char vc) :
        ⌈ if cl = leer then anzeige := mty fi ;
          char h = next(anzeige) ;
          (anzeige, cl, vc) :=
               if h = * then (mty, leer, *)
                        else (anzeige & make(h), h, h) fi ⌋

    endofdevice
```

Der Variablen anzeige ordnen wir hier dieselbe technische Interpretation wie im Modul ANZEIGE zu. Ein Anwenderprogramm (Treiber), das über TIP1 als "Betriebsmittel" verfügt, manipuliert die internen Variablen von TIP1 über die beiden Prozedu-

---

[1] CIP-L macht syntaktisch keinen Unterschied zwischen Funktionen und "mehrdeutigen Funktionen". Die Existenzaussage in der Parameterliste beschreibt den exakten Definitionsbereich von next als Teilmenge von string.

ren clear und get. clear überführt den Modul in den "Grundzustand", der mit dem Initialisierungszustand übereinstimmt. Insbesondere die Anzeige wird dabei gelöscht. get spezifiziert die eigentliche Interaktion zwischen Anwenderprogramm und Dialogpartner. Durch einen Aufruf von get im Anwenderprogramm erhält der Dialogpartner die Möglichkeit, ein Zeichen entsprechend der mehrdeutigen Funktion next einzugeben. Dieses Zeichen wird über vc an das Anwenderprogramm weitergereicht. Das Sonderzeichen * fungiert als escape-Symbol, das auch dem Dialogpartner erlaubt, den Modul in den Grundzustand zu überführen. Durch das Sonderzeichen leer wird die Eingabe eines Wortes w aus $L(E)$ abgeschlossen; w bleibt jedoch in der Anzeige stehen. Erst mit der Eingabe eines weiteren Zeichens wird die Anzeige durch Löschung von w für ein neues Wort freigemacht. Diese Verzögerung der Löschoperation bewerkstelligt die Variable cl (vgl. auch Abschnitt 5).

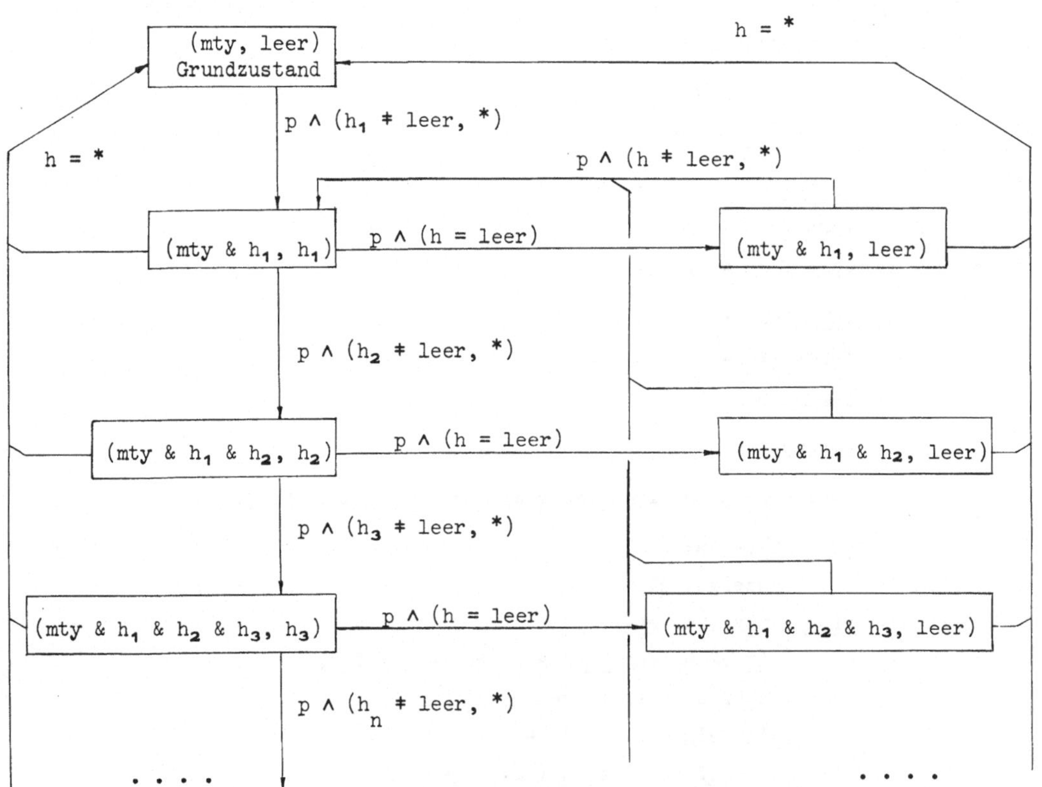

Abbildung: Zustandsübergangsdiagramm für die Aufrufe von get.
Jeder Aufruf von clear führt in den Grundzustand.

TIP1 spezifiziert als abstraktes Ein/Ausgabegerät die Nahtstelle zwischen Anwenderprogramm und Dialogpartner. Man spricht auch vom Kommunikationsmodul. Man beachte, daß diese Spezifikation auf einer Abstraktionsebene erfolgt, die nicht von prozeßorientierten Begriffen wie z.B. <u>warte auf Ereignis</u> Gebrauch macht.

4. Zerlegung in Teilsysteme

Die Spezifikation von TIP1 soll nun in mehreren Schritten so umgeformt werden, daß
ein funktionell äquivalenter Modul entsteht, der sich jedoch hierarchisch auf ANZEIGE
und BTST abstützt. Während in TIP1 im Grunde auf die spezielle Gestalt der Sprache L(E) nicht Bezug genommen wird, macht jedoch die weitere Entwicklung davon wesentlich Gebrauch: Offensichtlich gilt für die mehrdeutige Funktion next das folgende

<u>Lemma</u>:

1)   next(mty) hat dieselbe Breite wie der Ausdruck

$$\underline{\text{some}}\ \underline{\text{char}}\ z\ :\ (z = *)$$
$$\lor\ (\exists\ \underline{\text{string}}\ s,\ \underline{E}\ e\ :\ es(e) = make(z)\ \&\ s\ \land\ z \neq leer)$$

   also auch dieselbe Breite wie

$$(*\ [\!]\ a\ [\!]\ b\ [\!]\ c\ [\!]\ \underline{(}\ )\ .$$

2)   **Für alle** $r \in \underline{\text{string}}$, $x \in \underline{\text{char}}$, $x \neq leer$ mit der Eigenschaft

$$\exists\ \underline{\text{string}}\ s,\ \underline{E}\ e\ :\ es(e) = r\ \&\ make(x)\ \&\ s$$

   gilt: next(r & make(x))   hat dieselbe Breite wie der Ausdruck

$$\underline{\text{some}}\ \underline{\text{char}}\ z\ :$$
$$(z = *)$$
$$\lor\ (\exists\ \underline{E}\ e\ :\ es(e) = r\ \&\ make(x)\ \land\ z = leer)$$
$$\lor\ (\exists\ \underline{\text{string}}\ s,\ \underline{E}\ e\ :\ es(e) = r\ \&\ make(x)\ \&\ make(z)\ \&\ s\ \land\ z \neq leer)$$

   oder wie

```
(* [] if x ∈ {a, b, c, ),} then
       (± [] x [] if zähl(r & make(x)) = 0 then leer else ) fi)
     orif x ∈ {(, +, x} then
       (( [] a [] b [] c)
     fi)
```

   wobei zähl die Differenz der Anzahl von öffnenden und schließenden Klammern
   liefert:

```
funct zähl ≡ (string r) int :
    if r = mty then 0 else
        if top(r) = ) then zähl(rest(r)) - 1
        orif top(r) = ( then zähl(rest(r)) + 1
        orif top(r) ∉ {(, )} then zähl(rest(r))  fi
    fi .
```

<u>Ende des Lemmas</u>.

Aus diesem Lemma ergibt sich, daß next auch in die Form

$$\underline{\text{ambfunct}}\ \text{next} = (\underline{\text{string}}\ r : \exists\ \underline{\text{string}}\ s,\ \underline{E}\ e : es(e) = r\ \&\ s)\ \underline{\text{char}} :$$
$$(*\ [\!]\ \underline{\text{if}}\ r = \text{mty}\ \underline{\text{then}}\ (a\ [\!]\ b\ [\!]\ c\ [\!]\ \underline{(}\ )\ \underline{\text{else}}$$
$$\underline{\text{if}}\ \text{top}(r) \in \{a,\ b,\ c,\ \underline{)}\}\ \underline{\text{then}}$$
$$(\underline{+}\ [\!]\ x\ [\!]\ \underline{\text{if}}\ \text{zähl}(r) = 0\ \underline{\text{then}}\ \text{leer}\ \underline{\text{else}}\ \underline{)}\ \underline{\text{fi}})$$
$$\underline{\text{orif}}\ \text{top}(r) \in \{\underline{(},\ \underline{+},\ \underline{x}\}\ \underline{\text{then}}$$
$$(a\ [\!]\ b\ [\!]\ c\ [\!]\ \underline{(}\ )$$
$$\underline{\text{fi}}$$
$$\underline{\text{fi}})$$

gebracht werden kann. Das Zählen der Klammern in der Zeichenkette r kann jedoch vermieden werden, wenn man zu einer Funktion nx mit einem zweiten Parameter übergeht und spezifiziert:

$$\underline{\text{ambfunct}}\ \text{nx} = (\underline{\text{string}}\ r,\ \underline{\text{int}}\ k :$$
$$\text{zähl}(r) = k$$
$$\wedge\ \exists\ \underline{\text{string}},\ s,\ \underline{E}\ e : es(e) = r\ \&\ s)(\underline{\text{char}},\ \underline{\text{int}}) :$$
$$\lceil\ \underline{\text{char}}\ h = \text{next}(r)\ ;\ (h,\ \text{zähl}(r\ \&\ \text{make}(h)))\ \rfloor$$

Eliminiert man hier die Funktion next und zähl mit Hilfe ihrer Definitionen und der Beziehung zähl(r) = k, so ergibt sich nach einer entsprechenden Vereinfachung

$$\underline{\text{ambfunct}}\ \text{nx} = (\underline{\text{string}}\ r,\ \underline{\text{int}}\ k :$$
$$\text{zähl}(r) = k$$
$$\wedge\ \exists\ \underline{\text{string}}\ s,\ \underline{E}\ e : es(e) = r\ \&\ s)(\underline{\text{char}},\ \underline{\text{int}}) :$$
$$((*,\ 0)\ [\!]\ \underline{\text{if}}\ r = \text{mty}\ \underline{\text{then}}$$
$$\underline{\text{char}}\ h = (a\ [\!]\ b\ [\!]\ c\ [\!]\ \underline{(}\ )\ ;$$
$$(h,\ \underline{\text{if}}\ h = \underline{(}\ \underline{\text{then}}\ 1\ \underline{\text{else}}\ 0\ \underline{\text{fi}})$$
$$\underline{\text{else}}$$
$$\underline{\text{if}}\ \text{top}(r) \in \{a,\ b,\ c,\ \underline{)}\}\ \underline{\text{then}}$$
$$\underline{\text{char}}\ h = (\underline{+}\ [\!]\ x\ [\!]\ \underline{\text{if}}\ k = 0\ \underline{\text{then}}\ \text{leer}\ \underline{\text{else}}\ \underline{)}\ \underline{\text{fi}})\ ;$$
$$(h,\ \underline{\text{if}}\ h = \underline{)}\ \underline{\text{then}}\ k\text{-}1\ \underline{\text{else}}\ k\ \underline{\text{fi}})$$
$$\underline{\text{orif}}\ \text{top}(r) \in \{\underline{(},\ \underline{+},\ \underline{x}\}\ \underline{\text{then}}$$
$$\underline{\text{char}}\ h = (a\ [\!]\ b\ [\!]\ c\ [\!]\ \underline{(}\ )\ ;$$
$$(h,\ \underline{\text{if}}\ h = \underline{(}\ \underline{\text{then}}\ k\text{+}1\ \underline{\text{else}}\ k\ \underline{\text{fi}})$$
$$\underline{\text{fi}}$$
$$\underline{\text{fi}})$$

Damit ergibt sich eine modifizierte Version TIP2 des abstrakten Ein/Ausgabegerätes mit einer weiteren Zustandsvariablen kl, welche den Klammerdefekt (d.i. Anzahl der öffnenden minus Anzahl der schließenden Klammern) für den jeweiligen Anfang eines Wortes aus L(E) enthält:

```
device TIP2 ≡ (sort char, char a, b, c, (, ), +, x, leer, *) clear, get :
    ⋮
    ambfunct nx ≡ ... ;
    (var string anzeige, var char cl, var int kl) := (mty, leer, 0) ;
    proc clear ≡:
        (anzeige, cl, kl) := (mty, leer, 0) ;
    proc get ≡ (var char vc) :
     ⌈ ⌈(char h, int d) ≡ nx(cl, kl) ‖ if cl = leer then anzeige := mty fi ⌋ ;
        if h = *
            then (anzeige, cl, kl, vc) := (mty, leer, 0, *)
            else (anzeige, cl, kl, vc) := (anzeige & make(h), h, d, h) fi      ⌋
endofdevice
```

Inspiziert man nx, so zeigt sich, daß neben dem Klammerdefizit, das hier mit k bezeichnet ist, lediglich $top(r)$ benötigt wird, um die Breite der mehrdeutigen Funktion nx zu spezifizieren. An der Aufrufstelle von nt in get gilt für anzeige   mty immer $top(\text{anzeige}) = cl$. Dies erlaubt den Übergang zu folgender Funktion nt:

```
        ambfunct nt ≡ (char z, int k :
                        z = leer ∧ k = 0
                    ∨ z ≠ leer ∧ ∃ string s, string t, E e :
                            es(e) = s & make(z) & t
                        ∧ k = zähl(s & make(z))) (char, int) :
            ((*, 0) ‖ if z = leer then
                        char h ≡ (a ‖ b ‖ c ‖ ( ) ;
                        (h, if h = ( then 1 else 0 fi)
                      else
                        if z ∈ {a, b, c, )} then
                            char h ≡ (+ ‖ x ‖ if k = 0 then leer else ) fi) ;
                            (h, if h = ) then k-1 else k fi)
                        orif z ∈ {(, +, x }then
                            char h ≡ (a ‖ b ‖ c ‖ ( ) ;
                            (h, if h = ( then k+1 else k fi)
                        fi
                    fi)
```

Damit erhält man eine Version TIP3 des abstrakten Ein/Ausgabegerätes: Es genügt, die Zustandsvariablen cl und kl zur Bestimmung der möglichen nächsten Eingabezeichen heranzuziehen: Die Variable anzeige und deren Manipulation ist damit separierbar geworden. Im Anschluß an TIP3 wird diese Separierbarkeit benutzt, um die hierarchische Abstützung auf ANZEIGE durchzuführen.

```
device TIP3 ≡ (sort char, char a, b, c, (, ), +, x, leer, *) clear, get :
    ⋮
    ambfunct nt ≡ ... ;
    (var string anzeige, var char cl, var int kl) := (mty, leer, 0) ;
    proc clear ≡:
        (anzeige, cl, kl) := (mty, leer, 0) ;
    proc get ≡ (var char vc) :
        ⌈ ⟦(char h, int d) ≡ nt(cl, kl) ‖ if cl = leer then anzeige := mty fi ⟧ ;
          if h = *
                then (anzeige, cl, kl, vc) := (mty, leer, 0, *)
                else (anzeige, cl, kl, vc) := (anzeige & make(h), h, d, h) fi          ⌋
endofdevice
```

Berücksichtigt man nun (vgl. /Broy 80/), daß die kollektive Zuweisung

$$(x_1, \ldots, x_i, \ldots, x_n) := (E_1, \ldots, E_i, \ldots, E_n)$$

äquivalent ist zu den parallel auszuführenden Zuweisungen

$$\llbracket\; x_1 := E_1 \;\|\; \ldots \;\|\; x_i := E_i \;\|\; \ldots \;\|\; x_n := E_n \rrbracket$$

falls für $i = 1, \ldots, n$ in E_i von den Variablen $x_1, \ldots, x_n$ höchstens die Variable x_i vorkommt, dann läßt sich etwa clear in naheliegender Weise umschreiben in

```
        proc clear ≡:
            ⟦ anzeige := mty ‖ (cl, kl) := (leer, 0) ⟧
```

oder unter Abstützung aus ANZEIGE in

```
        proc clear ≡:
            ⟦ call delete ‖ (cl, kl) := (leer, 0) ⟧
```

Entsprechend erhält man für get

```
        proc get ≡ (var char vc) :
            ⌈ ⟦(char h, int d) ≡ nt(cl, kl) ‖ if cl = leer then call delete fi ⟧ ;
              if h = *
                    then ⟦ call delete ‖ (cl, kl, vc) := (leer, d, h) ⟧
                    else ⟦ call put(h) ‖ (cl, kl, vc) := (h, d, h) ⟧ fi ⌋
```

oder wenn man die Konstantenbezeichnungen h und d eliminiert

```
        proc get ≡ (var char vc) :
            ⌈ ⟦(vc, kl) := nt(cl, kl) ‖ if cl = leer then call delete fi ⟧ ;
              if vc = *
                    then ⟦ call delete ‖ cl := leer ⟧
                    else ⟦ call put(vc) ‖ cl := vc ⟧ fi ⌋
```

Eliminiert man schließlich den Aufruf von nt in der Prozedur get, dann erhält man
nun zusammenfassend eine Version TIP4:

```
    device TIP4 ≡ (sort char, char a, b, c, (, ), +, x, leer, *) clear, get :
          ⋮
        device (delete, put) ≡ ANZEIGE (char, leer) ;
        (var char cl, var int kl) := (leer, 0) ;
        proc clear ≡:
            ⟦ call delete ∥ (cl, kl) := (leer, 0) ⟧
        proc get ≡ (var char vc) :
            ⌈ ⟦ if cl = leer then
                    vc := (a ⫿ b ⫿ c ⫿ ( ⫿ *) ;
                    kl := if vc = ( then 1 else 0 fi
                else
                  if cl ∈ {a, b, c, )} then
                      vc := (+ ⫿ x ⫿ if kl = 0 then leer else ) fi ⫿ *) ;
                      if vc = ) then kl := kl-1 fi
                    orif cl ∈ {(, +, x} then
                      vc := (a ⫿ b ⫿ c ⫿ ( ⫿ *) ;
                      if vc = ( then kl := kl+1 fi
                  fi ; if vc = * then kl := 0 fi
                fi ∥ if cl = leer then call delete fi ⟧ ;
              if vc = *
                then ⟦ call delete ∥ cl := leer ⟧
                else ⟦ call put(vc) ∥ cl := vc ⟧ fi ⌋
    endofdevice
```

Damit ist die Abstützung auf ANZEIGE vollzogen (vgl. Anhang).

Die Abstützung auf BTST wird durch Umformung der endlichen Auswahlausdrücke erreicht.
Man benutzt wie in BTST eine Reihung t von booleschen Variablen, welche den Zeichen
in char, also den "Tasten" einer abstrakten Tastatur zugeordnet sind.

Unter der Zusicherung

$$(t[a], \ldots, t[*]) = (\underline{false}, \ldots, \underline{false})$$

läßt sich z.B. die Zuweisung

$$vc := (a \, ⫿ \, b \, ⫿ \, c \, ⫿ \, (\, ⫿ \, *)$$

ersetzen durch die Sequenz der folgenden drei Zuweisungen:

$$(t[a], t[b], t[c], t[(], t[*]) := (\underline{true}, \ldots, \underline{true}) ;$$
$$vc := \underline{some} \; \underline{char} \; q : t[q] \lor (q = *) ;$$
$$(t[\underline{a}], \ldots, t[*]) := (\underline{false}, \ldots, \underline{false}) \quad .$$

Nach der Ausführung dieser Sequenz ist die obige Zusicherung wieder gültig. Damit
ergibt die Abstützung auf BTST die Sequenz

⟦ call free(a) ‖ call free(b) ‖ call free(c) ‖ call free(( ) ‖ call free(*) ⟧ ;
   call read(vc) ;
   call block   .

Damit kann nun auch die Abstützung auf BTST ausgeführt werden. Die in TIP1 für Spe-
zifikationszwecke erforderlichen Definitionen von E, S, F usw. sind überflüssig, da
sie in den Prozeduren clear und get nicht mehr benutzt werden. Man hat damit

   device TIP5 ≡ (sort char, char a, b, c, (,), +, x, leer, *) clear, get :
      device(delete, put) ≡ ANZEIGE(char, leer) ;
      device(block, free, read) ≡ BTST(char, a, b, c, (,), +, x, leer, *) ;
      (var char cl, var int kl) := (leer, 0) ;
      proc clear ≡:
        ⟦ call delete ‖ (cl, kl) := (leer, 0) ⟧ ;
      proc get ≡ (var char vc) :
      ⌈ ⟦ if cl = leer then
           ⟦ call free(a) ‖ call free(b) ‖ call free(c) ‖
          call free(() ‖ call free( ) ⟧ ;
          call read(vc) ;
          ⟦ call block ‖ kl := if vc = (then 1 else 0 fi ⟧
        else
            if cl ∈ {a, b, c,)} then
              ⟦ call free(+) ‖ call free(x) ‖
              call free (if kl = 0 then leer else) fi) ‖ call free(*) ⟧ ;
              call read(vc) ;
              ⟦ call block ‖ if vc =) then kl := kl-1 fi ⟧
            orif cl ∈ {(, +, x,} then
              ⟦ call free(a) ‖ call free(b) ‖ call free(c) ‖
              call free(() ‖ call free(*) ⟧ ;
              call read(c) ;
              ⟦ call block ‖ if vc = (then kl := kl+1 fi ⟧
            fi ; if vc = * then kl := 0 fi
          fi ‖ if cl = leer then call delete fi ⟧ ;
        if vc = *
          then ⟦ call delete ‖ cl := leer ⟧
          else ⟦ call put(vc) ‖ cl := vc ⟧ fi ⌉

    endofdevice

TIP5 kann als abstraktes Gerät verstanden werden, welches die beiden Module ANZEIGE
und BTST als "Bauteile" enthält.

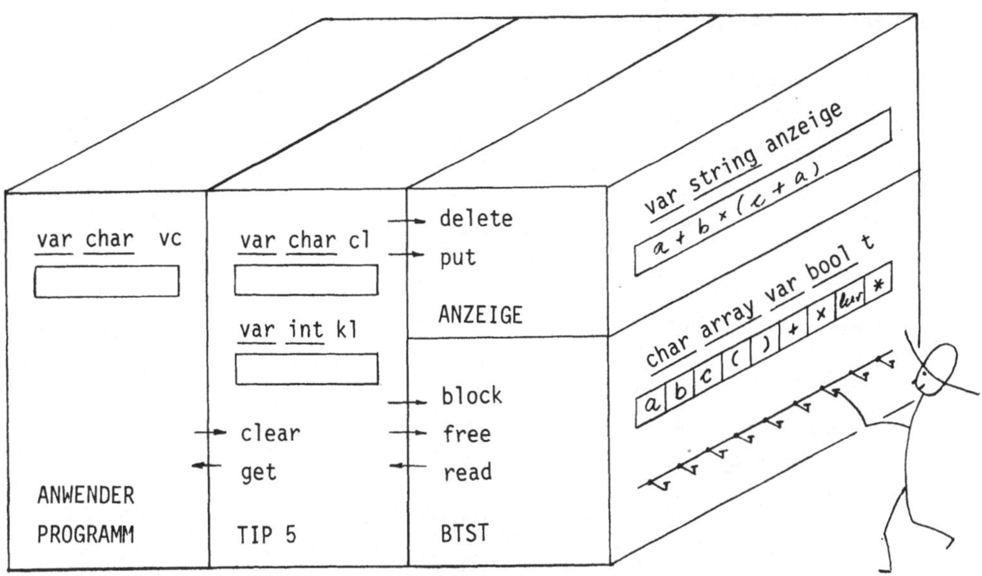

5. Zur Konstruktionssystematik interaktiver Systeme

Die in den Abschnitten 3. und 4. am speziellen Beipiel vorgeführte Programment-
wicklungstechnik ist allgemein einsetzbar. Dieser Aspekt eröffnet einen Ausblick auf
eine *Systematik interaktiver Systeme* : In /Kupka, Wilsing 80/ wird ein abstraktes
Dialogsystem als 6-Tupel $(I, O, S, \delta, \lambda, s_0)$ mit

- Mengen I, O, S
- (totalen) Abbildungen $\delta : I \times S \to S$ und $\lambda : I \times S \to O$
- $s_0 \in S$

definiert. Dabei sind die Elemente von I, O und S die abstrakten Eingaben, die abstrakten Ausgaben bzw. die abstrakten Zustände. Die Semantik des Dialogsystems kann
durch Axiome festgelegt werden. Mit den Mitteln von /CIP-L-Sprachreport 81/ läßt sich
ein solches abstraktes Dialogsystem als abstrakter Datentyp schreiben, wobei das 6-Tupel
in die Signatur des Typs übergeht:

```
type ADS ≡ I, O, S, δ, λ, s0 :
     sort I, sort O, sort S ,
     funct (I, S) S δ ,
     funct (I, S) O λ ,
     S s0
laws
     ...
endoftype
```

Über einem solchen Typ ADS lassen sich nun Programme, Funktionen, Prozeduren, Moduln usw. formulieren. Einige typische Fälle seien nachfolgend kurz aufgelistet:

A)   ein abgeschlossenes Dialogsystem

```
⌈ type (input, output, state, d, l, s₀) ≡ ADS ;
  var state z := s₀ ;
  var output a ;
  do  input i ≡ some input j : true ;
      (z, a) := (d(i, z), l(i, z))
  od                                              ⌋
```

B)   ein schrittgesteuerter Eingabedialog

```
type (input, output, state, d, l, s₀) ≡ ADS ,
device SE ≡ clear, step :
    var state z := s₀ ;
    var output a ;
    proc clear ≡:
        z := s₀ ;
    proc step ≡ (var input vi)
        ⌈ vi := some input i : true ;
          (z, a) := (d(vi, z), l(vi, z))  ⌋
endofdevice
```

C)   ein Kommunikationsmodul

```
type (input, output, state, d, l, s₀) ≡ ADS ,
device KM ≡ put, out, step, inform :
    var state z := s₀ ;
    var output a ;
    proc put ≡ (state s) :
        z := s ;
    proc out ≡ (output p) :
        a := p ;
    proc step ≡ (var input vi) :
        ⌈ vi := some input i : true ;
          (z, a) := (d(vi, z), l(vi, z)) ⌋ ;
    proc inform ≡ (var state vc) :
        vc := z
endofdevice
```

Diese Liste könnte fortgesetzt werden; sie macht jedoch bereits deutlich, daß für die
Zwecke der Spezifikation die Beschränkung auf Automaten ADS zu starr ist. Im Prinzip
kann man beliebige abstrakte Datentypen zulassen (vgl. z.B. /Wirsing et al. 80/). Der
innere Aufbau der Mengen input, output, state kann dadurch bequemer behandelt werden

Auch wünscht man sich bei den Funktionen d, l, s_0 eine reichhaltigere Palette. Die
Architektur eines interaktiven Systems wird ohnehin wesentlich durch die Kontrollstruk-
turen mitbestimmt. So will man etwa Terminierungsbedingungen explizit formulieren können oder aber man macht die Eingabe abhängig vom aktuellen Zustand oder von der letzten
Ausgabe. Letzteres ist typisch für das Arbeiten mit dem Lichtgriffel bei graphischen Ge-
räten. Man kommt somit zu Erweiterungen von ADS etwa in folgender Richtung

```
        type EADS ≡ I, O, S, δ, λ, τ, ν, s₀ :
            sort I, sort O, sort S ,
            funct (I j, S z : ν(j, z)) S δ ,
            funct (I j, S z : ν(j, z)) O λ ,
            funct (S) bool τ ,
            funct (I, S) bool ν ,
            S s₀
        laws
            ...
        endoftype
```

Damit läßt sich beispielsweise ein Eingabemodul mit folgender Architektur spezifizieren:

```
D)        type (input, output, state, d, l, t, n, s₀) ≡ EADS ;
          device DKM ≡ clear, get :
              var state z := s₀ ;
              var output a ;
              proc clear ≡ (output p) :
                  (z, a) := (s₀ , p) ;
              proc get ≡ (var state vs) :
               ⌈ while ¬ t(z) do
                      input i ≡ some input j : n(j, z) ;
                      (z, a) := (d(i, z), l(i, z))
                  od ;

                  vs := z                                    ⌋
          endofdevice
```

Die Beispiele A) - D) sind als Programmspezifikationen aufzufassen, die als Ausgangspunkt von Programmentwicklungen dienen können. Es steht heute ein reichhaltiges In-
strumentarium zur Verfügung, das eine Weiterentwicklung der Konstruktionssystematik interaktiver Systeme in einem einheitlichen, programmiertechnischen Rahmen ermöglicht.

Die Anwendungsmöglichkeiten sind weitreichend: So bekommt man etwa den einfachsten Fall
einer Methodenbankspezifikation als ein abgeschlossenes Dialogsystem. Zustandsvariable
ist eine Datenbank bk, wobei man die Deklaration var datenbank bk auf einen geeig-

neten Datentyp DATENBANK abgestützt. Als Zustandsübergangsfunktion benutzt man eine Reihung mk von Funktionen, welche die Menge $\underline{datenbank}$ in sich abbilden. Diese Funktionen nennt man auch "Methoden": Die Reihung werde mit den Elementen einer Art $\underline{index}$ indiziert, so daß also

$$\underline{index}\ \underline{array}\ (\underline{ambfunct}\ (\underline{datenbank})\ \underline{datenbank})\ mk$$

gilt. Man erhält für den Dialog die folgende stark vereinfachte Grundform:

```
do
    index dx ≡ some index j : m(j, bk) ;
    bk := mk[dx](bk)
od  .
```

Dabei ist m ein Prädikat: $m(dx, bk)$ ist eine hinreichende Bedingung für die Ausführbarkeit des Funktionsaufrufes $mk[dx](bk)$. Die Methoden $mk[dx]$ können selbst wieder Dialogsysteme sein:

```
mk[dx] = (datenbank bk : m(dx, bk)) datenbank :
    ⌈  (var state z, var output a) := (f(bk), g(bk)) ;
       while ¬ t(z)
           do input i ≡ some input j : n(j, z) ;
              (z, a) := (d(i, z), l(i, z))
           od ;
       h(z, bk)
```

wo f, g und h geeignet zu wählende Funktionen sind.

6. Schlußbemerkung

Für die Erstellung eines Anwenderprogramms genügt die kompakte, deskriptive Spezifikation TIP1, die - verglichen mit TIP5 - besser überschaubar ist: Das Anwenderprogramm braucht sich weder um die algorithmischen Details von TIP5 noch um die Art der Modularisierung zu kümmern.

Ein wesentlicher Aspekt der aufgezeigten Entwicklung ist die Auslagerung von Variablen in hierarchisch untergeordnete Module: Formale Programmentwicklungsmethoden dürften sich auch für die schrittweise Entwicklung der "Systemarchitektur" mit Vorteil einsetzen lassen. Dabei ergibt sich gegebenenfalls die parallele Benutzung von Konstituenten eines Moduls automatisch bei seiner Kreation.

Wichtig ist aber auch die Feststellung, daß die nichtdeterministischen Konstruktionen in einen untergeordneten Modul verlagert werden. Die Funktion get in TIP5 ist ein deterministisches Programm: Die Unbestimmtheit der Eingabe liegt nunmehr lediglich in der Breite der möglichen Inhalte der Variablen vc ("Parameter-Nichtdeterminismus").

Die gelegentlich unterstellte, technische Interpretation der Module als Apparaturen ist
hier lediglich informell zu verstehen: Die Bindung der programmiersprachlichen Entitä-
ten an physikalische Komponenten erfordert eigentlich noch eine Weiterentwicklung.
Die parallele Anweisung ⟦ call free(a) ‖ call free(b) ‖ ... ⟧ kann nicht unmittelbar physikalisch interpretiert werden. Dies würde eine geeignete Vervielfachung von
Konstituenten von BTST erfordern oder aber eine Sequentialisierung der parallelen
Anweisungen.

<u>Anhang: Elimination und Kreation von Moduln</u>

Die Abstützung eines Moduls auf einen anderen kann durch Textersetzung erklärt werden:
Eine Applikationsdeklaration, z.B.

(2)   <u>device</u> (del, pt) ≡ ANZEIGE (<u>ch</u>, er) ,

des Moduls ANZEIGE aus Abschnitt 2 kann in folgender Weise eliminiert werden:

1)   Die Liste der Deklarationen im Inneren von (1) wird kopiert. Diese Kopie heiße

2)   Kommen aktuelle Bezeichnungen von (2) in den linken Seiten der Deklarationen von
     A auch als nicht-formale Bezeichnungen vor, so sind letztere in der Kopie konsis-
     tent umzubenennen. Bei dieser Umbenennung ist gleichzeitig sicherzustellen, daß
     alle nicht-formalen Bezeichnungen von A von allen Bezeichnungen verschieden sind,
     die an der Applikationsstelle (2) sichtbar sind. Durch diese Umbenennung ent-
     stehe aus A ein Textstück B.

3)   In B werden die formalen Bezeichnungen der Parameter und Konstituenten aus (1)
     <u>char</u>, leer bzw. delete, put durch die entsprechenden aktuellen aus (2) er-
     setzt. Es entsteht ein Textstück C:
             <u>type</u> (<u>string</u>, mty, make, &, top, rest) ≡ STRING (<u>ch</u>, er) ;
             <u>var</u> <u>string</u> anzeige := mty ;
             <u>proc</u> del ≡: anzeige := mty ;
             <u>proc</u> pt ≡ (<u>ch</u> x) : anzeige & make(x)

4)   Die Applikationsdeklaration (2) wird durch C ersetzt.

Umgekehrt kann eine Sequenz von Deklarationen durch eine Applikationsdeklaration eines
Moduls ersetzt werden, falls der obige Eliminationsprozeß die ursprüngliche Sequenz
wieder herstellt und diese Sequenz in folgendem Sinn in sich abgeschlossen ist (Sepa-
rierbarkeitsbedingung):

     a) Die Umgebung der Applikationsdeklaration stützt sich nicht auf das Textstück
         B ab.

b) Umgekehrt stützt sich B höchstens mit Typ- oder Modulbezeichnungen auf die Umgebung der Applikationsdeklaration ab.

D.h. ein Modul kommuniziert mit seiner Umgebung nur über seine Parameter und Konstituenten. Variable dürfen weder als Parameter noch als Konstituenten von Moduln vorkommen.

Dank

Meinen Kollegen M. Broy, A. Laut, T.A. Matzner, H.-O. Riethmayer und H. Wössner verdanke ich eine Reihe wertvoller Anregungen im Zusammenhang mit der hier behandelten Thematik. Für hilfreiche Hinweise habe ich auch den Gutachtern zu danken.

Referenzen

/Broy 80/
M. Broy: Transformation parallel ablaufender Programme. Dissertation, TU München, Fakultät für Mathematik, 1980

/Broy, Gnatz, Wirsing 79/
Broy, R. Gnatz, M. Wirsing: Semantics of nondeterministic and noncontinuous constructs. In: F.L. Bauer, M. Broy (eds.): Program Construction. Lecture Notes in Computer Science, 69, Berlin-Heidelberg-New York: Springer (1979), 553-592

/CIP-L-Sprachreport 81/
F.L.Bauer, M.Broy, W. Dosch, R. Gnatz, F. Geiselbrechtinger, W. Hesse, B. Krieg-Brückner, A. Laut, T.A. Matzner, B. Möller, H. Partsch, P. Pepper, K. Samelson (†), M. Wirsing, H. Wössner: Report on a wide spectrum language for program specification and development (tentative version). TU München, Institut für Informatik, TUM-I8104, May 1981

/GKS/
Graphical Kernel System (GKS), Functional Description. Draft International Standard, ISO TC97/SC5/WG2; 1981-May-25, Version: 6.6

/Gnatz 81/
R. Gnatz: Referenzmodell für Graphische Systeme, Versuch einer Axiomatik. In:
J. Encarnacao, W. Straßer (Hrsg.): Graphics und Portabilität - das graphische Kernsystem GKS. München: Oldenbourg (1981), 357-389

/Kupka, Wilsing 74/
I. Kupka, M. Wilsing: Functions describing interactive programming. In:
A. Günther et al. (eds.): International Computing Symposium 1973, Davos. Amsterdam: North-Holland (1974), 41-45

/Kupka, Wilsing 80/
I. Kupka, M. Wilsing: Conversational languages. Chichester-New York-Brisbane-Toronto: Wiley (1980)

/Gorny 75/
P. Gorny: Program generation in a syntax guided dialogue. 2. Auflage.
Ruhr-Universität Bochum, Institut für konstruktiven Ingenieurbau - Angewandte
Informatik, Bericht 1/75, März 1975

/Hoffmann 74/
H.-J. Hoffmann: Programming by selection. In: A. Günther et al. (eds.): International computing symposium 1973, Davos. Amsterdam: North-Holland (1974), 59-65

/Laut 80/
A. Laut: Safe Procedural Implementations of Algebraic Types. Information Processing Letters 11, 4/5, 147-151, 1980

/McCarthy 63/
J. McCarthy: Towards a mathematical science of computation. Proc. IFIP Congress 62.
Amsterdam: North-Holland (1963), 21-28

/Riethmayer 81/
H.-O. Riethmayer: Die Entwicklung der Bedienungskomponente des CIP-Systems.
9. Treffen zum Interaktiven Programmieren, 25. Februar 1981, Oldenburg i.O., Notizen
zum Interaktiven Programmieren, Organ der Fachgruppe Interaktives Programmieren im
Fachausschuß 2 der Gesellschaft für Informatik, Heft 6, März 1981, 47-76

/Seillac II/
R.A. Guedj, P.J.W. Ten Hagen, F.R.A. Hopgood, H.A. Tucker, D.A. Duce (eds.):
Methodology of Interaction. IFIP Workshop, Seillac, France, May 1979.
Amsterdam: North-Holland (1980)

/Wirsing et al. 80/
M. Wirsing, P. Pepper, H. Partsch, W. Dosch, M. Broy: On hierarchies of abstract
data types. TU München, Institut für Informatik, TUM-I8007, 1980

/Wirth 77/
N. Wirth: Modula: A language for modular multiprogramming. Software - Practice
and Experience, 7, 3-35, Jan. 1977

<u>Programmieren mit graphischen Mitteln:</u>

<u>Die Sprache GRADE</u>

<u>und ihre Implementation*</u>

Hans-Eckart Sengler

URW-Unternehmensberatung

Hamburg

Abstract

An overview is given on the programming language GRADE and its implementation in a pilot version of a GRADE-system.

The language is an attempt to utilize graphical means of describing systems, well known in engineering disciplines or in program documentation, directly for programming. The aim is to make existent programs easier to comprehend by the experienced user. In a GRADE program therefore, the semantically most important structures are being represented graphically: the component structure, the potential flow of control and the potential flow of data. The notation was developed from that of Petri Nets, the semantics are based on PASCAL.

In the GRADE-system a language-specific editor allows the editing of graphics and text. It stores a program with its component structure directly accessible, reducing the necessary syntactical analysis by the compiler. A supervisor controls the execution of a compiled program, showing the source program on a graphical display and within it the actual flow of data and control.

---

*   Die diesem Bericht zugrunde liegenden Arbeiten wurden mit Mitteln des Bundesministers für Forschung und Technologie (Förderungskennzeichen 083 0214) gefördert. Die Verantwortung für den Inhalt liegt allein beim Autor.

1. Idee und Zielsetzung

GRADE ist ein Versuch, dem Programmierer moderne Programmier-Konzepte
und graphische Darstellungsmethoden nicht nur als Hilfsmittel der Entwicklung oder Dokumentation zur Verfügung zu stellen, sondern sie
direkt zur Programmierung einzusetzen.

GRADE bezeichnet zum einen eine Programmiersprache, in der der Datenfluß, der Kontrollfluß und die Komponentenstruktur von Programmen
graphisch durch Netze dargestellt werden, ähnlich den Petri-Netzen [1].
Als Abstraktionsmittel stehen der "Prozessor" - vergleichbar der Prozedur üblicher Sprachen - und der "Speicher" zur Verfügung - eine Realisierung abstrakter Datenstrukturen. Als Kontrollstruktur werden die
Sequenzbildung und E.W. Dijkstra's "Guarded Commands" eingesetzt [1].
Die Sprache ist (bisher) auf die Beschreibung sequentieller Prozesse
beschränkt.

GRADE bezeichnet zum anderen ein Programmiersystem, das die Programmiersprache GRADE realisiert. Ein spezieller graphischer Editor erlaubt das
interaktive Gestalten von Programmen und prüft bereits deren syntaktische
Korrektheit. Er legt die graphischen Darstellungen in einer Form ab,
die eine anschließende Übersetzung möglichst einfach macht. Ein Compiler
erzeugt daraus ausführbaren Code, ein Supervisor überwacht die Ausführung und stellt sie auf Wunsch am Bildschirm graphisch dar.

Die Sprache GRADE entstand im Rahmen eines Forschungsvorhabens des
Autors an der Universität Hamburg. Dessen Ziel bestand darin, Eigenschaften von Programmiersprachen zu finden, die insbesondere große und
komplexe Programmsysteme für den ausgebildeten Programmierer möglichst
verständlich machen. Diese Arbeit zeigt unter anderem die Notwendigkeit
auf, die für das Verstehen eines Programms wichtigsten semantischen
Strukturen - den potentiellen Kontrollfluß, den potentiellen Datenfluß
und die Komponentenstruktur (Gliederung in Blöcke, Moduln o.ä.) - möglichst schnell und eindeutig erkennbar darzustellen. Eine hohe Verständlichkeit der Programme hätte nicht nur zur Folge, daß Programmierer
schneller und damit kostengünstiger Änderungen und Verbesserungen

---

[1] Im folgenden werden Petri-Netze und insbesondere ihre Interpretation
     als Netze aus Instanzen und Kanälen als bekannt angenommen. Ein
     Überblick findet sich in [7].

durchführen können, sondern auch, daß schon bei der Programmerstellung weniger Fehler auftreten und daß auf eine zusätzliche Beschreibung der Programmkonstruktion (Flußdiagramme, Nasse-Schneiderman-Diagramme) verzichtet werden kann.

Ein GRADE-System entsteht derzeit in einer Pilotversion bei der Firma URW Unternehmensberatung in Hamburg. Seine Entwicklung wird vom BMFT (GMD) gefördert.

2. Die GRADE-Sprache (Überblick)

GRADE kann als eine spezielle Interpretation und Erweiterung der Netze aus Instanzen und Kanälen nach C.A.Petri erklärt werden. Ein solches Netz wird durch Rechtecke (Instanzen), Kreise (Kanäle) und sie verbindende, gerichtete Kanten dargestellt. Kanten dürfen dabei nur Kanäle mit Instanzen verbinden.

Beispiel:

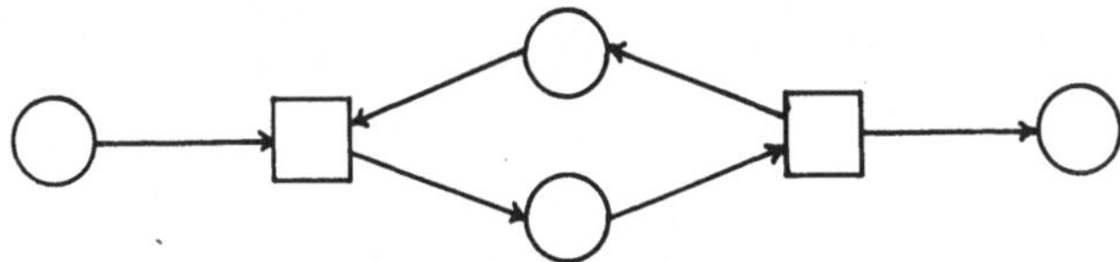

Diese Darstellung wird für GRADE übernommen und wie folgt interpretiert:

Eine Kante ist eine <u>Datenleitung</u>. Über eine Datenleitung können Daten eines Datentyps in der Richtung der Leitung transportiert werden. Die in GRADE möglichen Datentypen entsprechen denen von PASCAL [4]. Der Name des Datentyps einer Datenleitung wird als Name der Datenleitung aufgefaßt und muß an die Kante geschrieben werden.

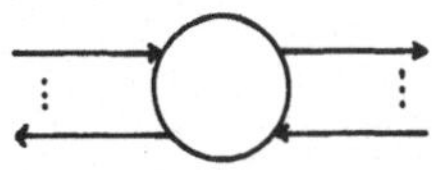

Datenleitung

Ein Kreis ist ein <u>Speicher</u> (Kanal). Über Datenleitungen können zu einem Speicher Daten geschickt oder von ihm geholt werden. Das Konzept Speicher in GRADE umfaßt die Variablen üblicher Programmiersprachen, aber auch die Konstanten und die Ein-/Ausgabegeräte, vordefiniert in

Speicher, allgemein

GRADE sind ferner Speicher mit den
Funktionen "stack" und "queue"; der
Programmierer hat auch die Möglichkeit, selbst Speicher zu definieren
(s.u.).

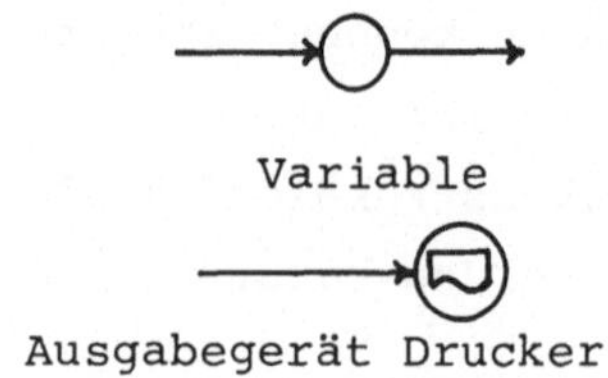

Ein Rechteck symbolisiert einen _Prozessor_ (Instanz). Ein Prozessor
kann aus Speichern, mit denen er über Datenleitungen verbunden ist,
Daten holen oder Daten zu ihnen
schicken. Das Konzept Prozessor
in GRADE umfaßt die Operationen
üblicher Programmiersprachen.
Der Zuweisung äquivalent ist
die Transportoperation. Der
Programmierer hat zudem die
Möglichkeit, selbst Prozessoren
zu definieren.

Die Einführung expliziter Datenleitungen mit Datentyp ergibt für
die Sprache folgende Besonderheiten:

o Der Speicher besitzt nicht die Eigenschaft, einem Datentyp anzuge-
   hören (im Gegensatz zu den Variablen üblicher Programmiersprachen).
   Dadurch erst läßt sich das Konzept Speicher auf Datenquellen und
   Datensenken allgemeiner ausdehnen, also auch auf E/A-Geräte.

o Die konkrete Funktion eines vordefinierten Speichers wird kontext-
   abhängig (z.B. _real_- oder _integer_-Variable), ähnlich wie dies bei
   Operationen in vielen Sprachen üblich ist.

o Die verschiedenen Zugriffsformen auf Daten (Konstanten, lokale/
   globale Variable, Parameter verschiedener Typen, Geräte) werden
   einheitlich durch die Verbindung mit einer Datenleitung dargestellt.

Zu klären bleibt, unter welchen Bedingungen ein Prozessor _aktiv_ wird.
Während durch Petri-Netze _parallele_ Aktivierungen beschrieben werden
sollen, wurde für GRADE (zunächst) ein rein _sequentielles_ Konzept entworfen.

In jedem GRADE-Programm existiert genau ein <u>Aktivierungsimpuls</u>, der dem
Programm bei seinem Start (vom Betriebssystem) übergeben wird und den es
bei seiner Beendigung zurückgibt. Erreicht der Impuls einen Prozessor,
so wird dieser aktiv. Erst wenn der Prozessor seine Aktivität beendet
hat, gibt er den Impuls zurück.

Der Aktivierungsimpuls durchläuft im Programm eine <u>Aktivierungsleitung</u>.
Sie ist eine explizite Darstellung der Kontrollstruktur des Programms.
Die Aktivierungsleitung hat die
Form eines Kamms, dessen Zinken
jeweils noch eine Verzweigung
enthalten können. An den Zinken sind Prozessoren ange-
schlossen. Der Aktivierungsimpuls durchläuft den Kamm
von links nach rechts und läuft
dabei nacheinander je einmal
in jede Zinke (Sequenzbildung).

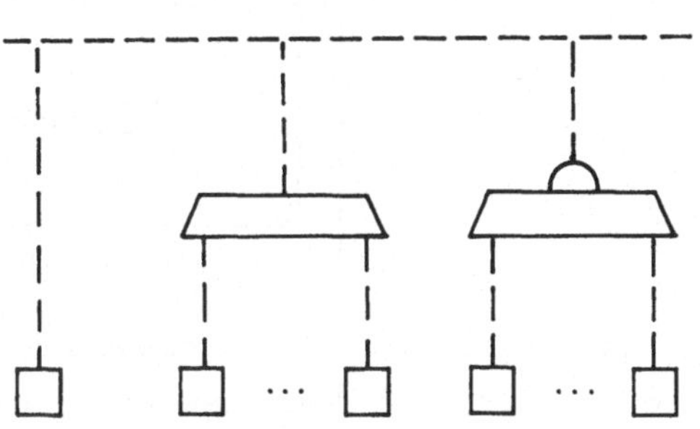

Aktivierungsleitung (mit angeschlossenen Prozessoren)

Es gibt zwei Arten von Verzweigungen, die eine Zinke enthalten kann:
die <u>Alternative</u> und die <u>Wiederholung</u>. Ihre Bedeutung entspricht der von
E.W.Dijkstra's "Guarded Commands"
IF und DO. Die Entscheidung,
welcher der unteren Ausgänge
für den Aktivierungsimpuls
gewählt wird, erfolgt aufgrund von logischen Aus-
drücken, die in das Trapez-
symbol geschrieben werden.

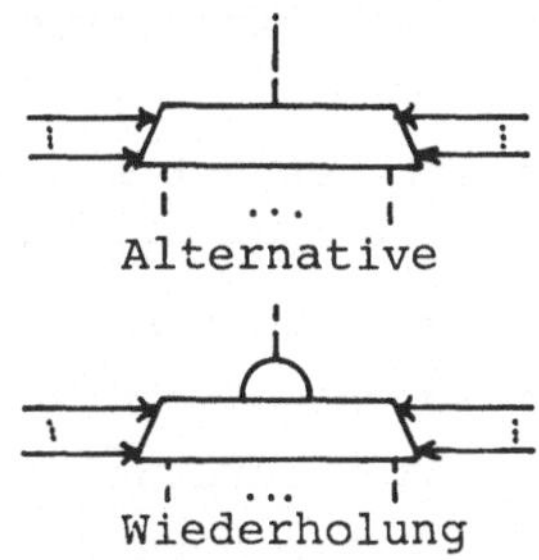

Alternative

Wiederholung

Operanden in den Ausdrücken können Konstanten und Namen von Datenleitungen sein. Zur Auswertung der Ausdrücke einer Verzweigung wird
von jeder angeschlossenen Datenleitung ein Datum geholt.

Beispiel:

(Berechnung des größten gemeinsamen Teilers von A und B)

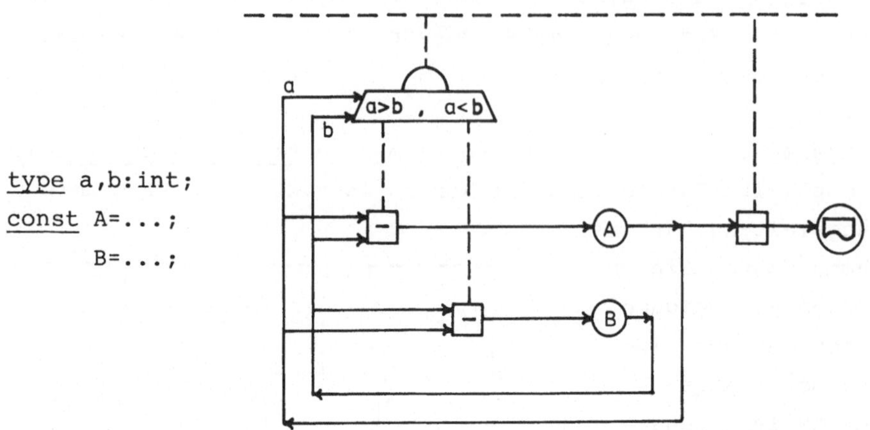

```
type a,b:int;
const A=...;
      B=...;
```

Durch das Eintragen der Konstanten A und B in die Kreissymbole erhalten diese Speicher Anfangswerte. Solange ein Speicherinhalt größer als der andere ist, wird die entsprechende Subtraktionsoperation aktiviert. Sind beide Speicherinhalte gleich, so bricht die Wiederholung ab, und der Inhalt des oberen Speichers wird auf den Drucker ausgegeben.

Mit den Hilfsmitteln Datenleitung, Speicher, Prozessor und Aktivierungsleitung kann der Programmierer eigene Prozessoren und Speicher nach folgenden Regeln konstruieren:

Ein Prozessor besteht aus einer Aktivierungsleitung mit beliebig vielen angeschlossenen Prozessoren. Die Prozessoren und die Verzweigungen der Aktivierungsleitung können über Datenleitungen an lokale, oder, aus dem Prozessor heraus auf globale Speicher zugreifen.

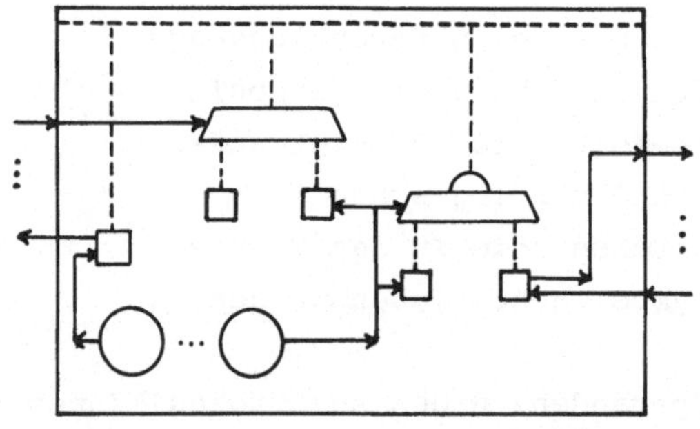

Prinzipbild konstruierter Prozessor

Um mehreren Prozessoren und Verzweigungen den Zugriff auf einen Speicher zu erlauben, dürfen Datenleitungen in Form eines Baums verzweigt sein, wobei die Wurzel des Baums den Anschluß an den Speicher bilden muß.

Die Konstruktion eines Prozessors entspricht der Definition einer Prozedur in üblichen Sprachen. Ein konstruierter Prozessor kann benannt werden und dann wie jeder andere Prozessor an anderen Stellen des Programms (auch mehrfach) verwendet werden. Die Typen der Datenleitungen müssen kompatibel sein. Das Einsetzen darf nicht (indirekt oder direkt) rekursiv erfolgen.

Ein Speicher enthält für jede außen anschließbare Datenleitung genau einen Prozessor. Dieser der Datenleitung "zugeordnete" Prozessor ist mit ihr und mit beliebig vielen lokalen Speichern verbunden. Auch hier dürfen Datenleitungen von lokalen Speichern baumartig verzweigt sein.

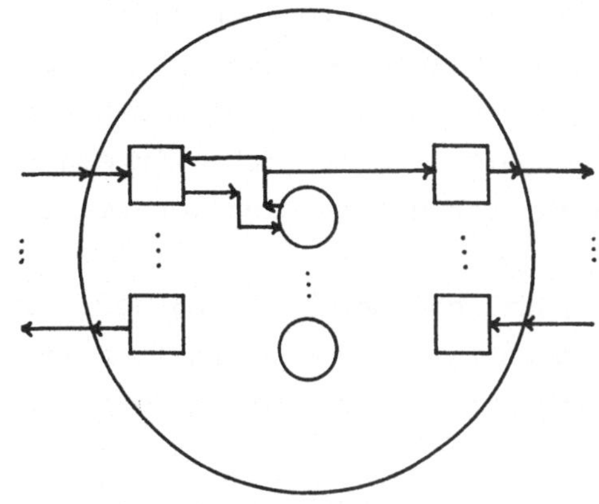

Prinzipbild konstruierter Speicher

Der konstruierte Speicher erlaubt die Modellierung abstrakter Datenstrukturen. Auf eine Datenmenge (innere Speicher) kann nur durch Zugriffsprozeduren (Prozessoren) zugegriffen werden. Die Aktivierung der Prozessoren erfolgt hier nicht explizit über eine Aktivierungsleitung, sondern implizit dadurch, daß ein äußerer Prozessor ein Datum schicken oder holen will. Der innere Prozessor muß so konstruiert sein, daß er genau einmal diesen Transportwunsch erfüllt. Das transportierte Datum kann während der Aktivität des Prozessors als in einem nicht gezeichneten Leitungsspeicher befindlich gedacht werden:

Damit sind auch die formalen Anforderungen an die Verfeinerung eines Speichers erfüllt, die an ihren Grenzen nur Speicher besitzen darf.

impliziter Leitungsspeicher

Wie bei den Prozessoren können auch konstruierte Speicher benannt und dann mehrfach in einem Programm eingesetzt werden, wiederum jedoch nicht rekursiv. Wird ein Prozessor oder Speicher nur durch Angabe seines Namens an einer Stelle eines Programms eingesetzt, so hat das die gleiche Bedeutung, als sei er erneut definiert worden. Das Einsetzen

entspricht also nicht einem "Aufrufen", vielmehr der Makro-Ersetzung.
Die Implementation kann jedoch über Unterprogramme erfolgen.

Durch die Konstruktionsregeln für Prozessoren und Speicher ergibt sich
als Komponentenstruktur eine Hierarchie. Ein GRADE-Programm ist ein
Prozessor, der keine Datenleitungen zu globalen Speichern besitzt und
dessen sämtliche innere Komponenten im Programm, in einer Bibliothek
oder in der Sprache definiert sind. Zusätzlich müssen alle Datentypen
und Konstanten definiert sein, und zwar entweder lokal zu einem Prozessor bzw. Speicher oder global in einer speziellen Programmsektion.
Ihre Definition erfolgt ähnlich wie in PASCAL im normalen Text.

Eine ausführliche Beschreibung der Sprache GRADE findet sich in [8].
Auf die wichtigsten Besonderheiten im Vergleich zu üblichen höheren
Programmiersprachen sei abschließend hingewiesen:

o Die für das Verständnis wesentlichen Strukturen eines Programms
   werden graphisch dargestellt.

o Es gibt nur einen Parametermechanismus (nicht: globale Variable und
   Parameter verschiedener Arten).

o Der Zugriff ist unabhängig vom Datentyp dargestellt. Damit sind konstruierte Speicher leicht austauschbar, ohne daß sie benutzende
   Prozessoren geändert werden müssen [2].

o Über eine Datenleitung kann nicht nur ein Datum (wie bei const- oder
   ref-Parametern) zu einem Prozessor gelangen, sondern eine Folge von
   Daten.

o Es gibt nur zwei Abstraktionskonzepte (üblich: Block, Schleife(n),
   Prozedur, Funktion).

o Ein- und Ausgabe sind nicht als Operationen (Read, Write o.ä.),
   sondern als Erweiterung des Variablenkonzepts definiert.

3. Das GRADE-System (Überblick)

Ein Programmiersystem für die Sprache GRADE muß die üblichen Aufgaben
eines Programmiersystems erfüllen, d.h. es muß erlauben, Programme zu
editieren und zu verwalten sowie zu übersetzen und den erzeugten Code
auszuführen. Folgende Besonderheiten ergeben sich für die GRADE-Sprache:

o Es kann kein üblicher Texteditor verwendet werden, da neben dem Text
   (Definitionen, Kommentare) auch Graphik (Prozessoren und Speicher)
   editiert werden muß.

o Der konzeptionelle Abstand zwischen dem graphischen Quellprogramm
   und dem ausführbaren Code ist größer als bei Textsprachen. Der
   Programmierer benötigt daher (zumindest nach Meinung des Autors)
   eine quellsprachbezogene Überwachungsmöglichkeit für die Ausführung
   von Programmen.

Das Pilot-GRADE-System [1] wurde mit dem Ziel entwickelt, mit einem
Text-Programmiersystem konkurrieren zu können.
Das bedeutet:

o Die Bedienung, speziell das Editieren von Programmen, muß für den
   Programmierer ähnlich einfach sein wie bei einem Textprogramm.

o Der Speicheraufwand und die Ausführungszeit sowohl der System-
   programme als auch der Benutzerprogramme sollten üblichen Systemen
   vergleichbar sein.

Diese Anforderungen ließen sich nur verwirklichen bei Einsatz eines
eigenen, speziell für die GRADE-Sprache entwickelten Editors. Das
Editieren von Text entspricht bei diesem Editor dem üblicher Text-
editoren. Das Editieren von Graphik ist auf das Erzeugen, Löschen,
Verschieben, Benennen und eventuell Kommentieren von GRADE-Symbolen
beschränkt. Der Befehlssatz konnte dadurch auf elf einbuchstabige
Kommandos begrenzt werden.

---

[1] Implementiert auf einer DEC LSI-11/23 unter RSX. Als Terminal wird
     ein DEC VT 100 mit Graphik-Zusatz VT 640 eingesetzt, als Hardcopy
     ein Aristomat-Zeichentisch. Das System ist in PASCAL geschrieben,
     der Entwurf erfolgte jedoch in GRADE, um ein späteres Umschreiben
     zu erleichtern.

Ein Positionieren innerhalb einer Graphik ist sowohl in kleinen Raster-
schritten als auch durch Springen zwischen schon vorhandenen Symbolen
möglich. Das Positionieren erfolgt durch acht Richtungstasten. Der Einsatz eines Lichtgriffels (bzw. Tablett, Rollkugel) wurde erwogen, aber
wegen aufwendigerer Bedienung und Programmierung abgelehnt.

Das Positionieren innerhalb eines Programms ist bezüglich der Komponentenstruktur möglich. Die Kommandos "up" und "down" (realisiert durch
Kontrollzeichen) lassen den Editor zu dem in der Hierarchie darüber
bzw. darunter gelegenen Prozessor oder Speicher übergehen. Bei "down"
muß dazu in der Graphik auf das entsprechende Symbol positioniert sein.
Auch durch Angabe seines Namens ist der Übergang zu einem anderen Prozessor oder Speicher möglich.

Bevor eine Graphik oder die Definitionen von Datentypen und Konstanten
vom Editor abgespeichert werden, wird ihre Korrektheit bezüglich der
GRADE-Syntax geprüft. Bei einer Graphik verhindert der Editor schon
beim Entstehen das Verletzen der Syntax (z.B. das Verbinden zweier
Prozessoren durch eine Datenleitung); vor dem Abspeichern prüft er
noch die Vollständigkeit der Benennungen von Symbolen. Der Benutzer
wird auf Syntaxfehler hingewiesen. Soll das Abspeichern dennoch erfolgen, so wird das Programmteil in seiner rechnerinternen Darstellung
als fehlerhaft markiert.

Dieses Vorgehen hat zur Folge, daß der Programmierer sehr frühzeitig
auf syntaktische Fehler hingewiesen wird und daß der Compiler weitgehend auf Syntaxprüfungen verzichten kann. Ist ein Teil eines Programms
als fehlerhaft markiert, so wird dessen Übersetzung abgelehnt. Der
Compiler muß jedoch die Kompatibilität getrennt editierter Programmteile prüfen.

Der Editor legt die Komponenten und die durch Aktivierungsleitungen
und Datenleitungen gebildete Struktur einer Graphik in einer Direkt-
zugriffsdatei ab. Das bedeutet für den Compiler, daß ein wesentlicher
Teil der Analysephase (parsing) entfällt, lediglich die Ausdrücke in
Verzweigungen sind auf die übliche Weise zu behandeln.

Der Compiler erzeugt in einer ersten Ausbaustufe interpretierbaren
Zwischencode, langfristig ist die Erzeugung bindbaren Objektcodes vorgesehen. Der Compiler unterscheidet bei der Codeerzeugung zwischen ein-

fach und mehrfach im Programm eingesetzten Prozessoren, die als "inline-code" bzw. als "subroutine" erzeugt werden. Der Objektcode soll vom normalen Binder (TKB im RSX-System) verarbeitet werden.

Eine Besonderheit bildet der Supervisor, der die quellsprachbezogene Überwachung der Ausführung eines GRADE-Programms erlaubt. Eine Darstellung der Ausführung ist für den Programmierer dann am einfachsten verständlich, wenn sie sich möglichst nah an das vom Programmierer selbst geschriebene Programm anlehnt. Der Supervisor benutzt daher neben dem ausführbaren Code die vom Editor abgelegte rechnerinterne Darstellung eines Programms und stellt dem Programmierer darin den tatsächlichen Kontroll- und Datenfluß dar.

Dazu hat der Compiler im Objektcode die Namen der jeweiligen Prozessoren und Speicher abgelegt, ferner in der rechnerinternen Programmdarstellung (also im Quellprogramm!) die relativen Code-Adressen der einzelnen Symbole. Über die Namen kann der Supervisor auf die entsprechende graphische Darstellung zugreifen und sie ausgeben, an Hand der Adressen kann er in der graphischen Darstellung den Kontrollfluß durch einen wandernden Punkt, den Datenfluß durch ein Aufleuchten der jeweiligen Datenleitung und ein Ausgeben des gerade transportierten Wertes zeigen.

Die Methode, den Compiler im Quellprogramm Informationen ablegen zu lassen, hat den Zweck, den Objektcode kurz zu halten und trotzdem eine vollständige Darstellung der Ausführung zu bieten. Sie hat den Nachteil, daß eine Überwachung der Ausführung viele Zugriffe zur rechnerinternen Programmdarstellung erfordert und damit langsam ist. Eine ausführliche Beschreibung des GRADE-Systems und seiner Bedienung findet sich in [3].

4. Einschätzung und Ausblick

Die Aussichten einer graphischen Sprache wie GRADE sind schwer einzuschätzen. Zum einen lassen sich Vorteile erkennen, wie: Verringerung des Dokumentationsaufwandes, schnelleres Einarbeiten in vorhandene Programme, weniger Programmfehler. Sie müssen jedoch erst durch einen praktischen Einsatz der Sprache geprüft und bewertet werden. Auf der anderen Seite steht die Notwendigkeit, graphiktüchtige Geräte zur Programmentwicklung einzusetzen, was für den Betreiber eine finanzielle Mehrbelastung bedeutet. Nicht zu unterschätzen sind auch die Akzeptanzprobleme bei Programmierern, die bisher eine Textsprache benutzen.

Ein wesentlicher Vorteil einer graphischen Sprache hat sich jedoch schon bei den wenigen Beispielen herausgestellt, die in GRADE programmiert wurden: Die graphische Darstellung macht die Komplexität von Strukturen augenfällig. Der Programmierer sieht schon beim Programmentwurf diese Komplexität und bemüht sich viel stärker als bei Textdarstellungen darum, sie zu verringern.

Das GRADE-System, so wie es als Pilotversion existiert, erfüllt eine Reihe von Ansprüchen, die für Text-Programmiersysteme gefordert wurden, aber dort nur schwer erreichbar sind [5]. Die Forderung nach einfacher Bedienbarkeit wird nach Meinung des Autors erfüllt. Ob das System aber auch von anderen Programmierern akzeptiert wird und ob seine technischen Daten denen üblicher Systeme vergleichbar sind, kann sich erst nach einer intensiven praktischen Nutzung zeigen.

Sprache und System werden dabei sicherlich in vielen Punkten verbessert werden müssen. Bei der Sprache wurde bisher bewußt versucht, mit möglichst wenigen Konzepten auszukommen. Probleme lassen sich bei der Anpassung an spezielle Systemumgebungen und bei der Behandlung von Ausnahmebedingungen erkennen. Auch die graphische Darstellung kann sicherlich verbessert und dem menschlichen Erkennungsvermögen angepaßt werden (andere Formen, Einsatz von Farben o.ä.) [6].

Literaturhinweise

1. Dijkstra, E.W.: Guarded Commands, Nondeterminacy and Formal Derivation of Programs; CACM Vol 18 (1975) 8, S. 453-457

2. Geschke, C.M., Mitchell, J.G.: On the Problem of Uniform References to Data Structures; IEEE-SE Vol 1 (1975) 2, S. 207-219

3. Huneke, H., Sengler, H.E.: GRADE-Bedienungsanleitung; URW Unternehmensberatung; interne Mitteilung, Mai 1981

4. Jensen, K., Wirth, N.: PASCAL, User Manual and Report; Lecture Notes in Computer Science Vol 18, Springer, Berlin 1974

5. Oberquelle, H.: Objektorientierte Informationsverarbeitung und benutzergerechtes Editieren, Teil 1: Grundlagen; Universität Hamburg, FB Informatik, Bericht IFI-HH-B-62/79

6. Oberquelle, H.: Communication by Graphic Net Representations; Universität Hamburg, FB Informatik, Bericht IFI-HH-B-75/81

7. Petri, C.A.: Introduction to General Net Theory; und andere Artikel in: W. Brauer (Hrsg.): Net Theory and Applications; Springer, Berlin 1980, S. 1-19

8. Sengler, H.E.: GRADE-Sprachbeschreibung; URW Unternehmensberatung, interne Mitteilung, Mai 1981

Ein System zur rechnerunterstützten Spezifikation

Lutz Hirschmann

mbp   Mathematischer Beratungs-
und Programmierungsdienst GmbH
4600 Dortmund, Semerteichstr. 47

Zusammenfassung

Das Ergebnis der Phase Systementwurf, nämlich die Beschreibung der entstandenen Moduln und ihrer Interaktion, bezeichnen wir als Spezifikation.

Es wird ein Formalismus vorgestellt, mit dem die Spezifikation in einfacher Weise beschrieben werden kann. Besonderer Wert wird dabei auf die Behandlung abstrakter Datentypen gelegt.

Durch ein Werkzeug wird die Konsistenz der Spezifikation geprüft. Darüber hinaus können Programmrahmen in verschiedenen Programmiersprachen generiert werden, wodurch ein rechnergestützter Übergang von der Entwurfs- zur Programmierungsphase ermöglicht wird.

Es wird über Erfahrungen berichtet, die mit diesem Spezifikationssystem in einem industriellen Projekt gemacht worden sind.

1. Anforderungen an ein Spezifikationssystem aus industrieller Sicht

Am Anfang eines Berichts über ein Spezifikationsverfahren empfiehlt es sich noch immer, eine Begriffsklärung voranzustellen. Ein mögliches und sehr grobes Phasenmodell für den Softwareentwicklungszyklus läßt sich untergliedern in die folgenden

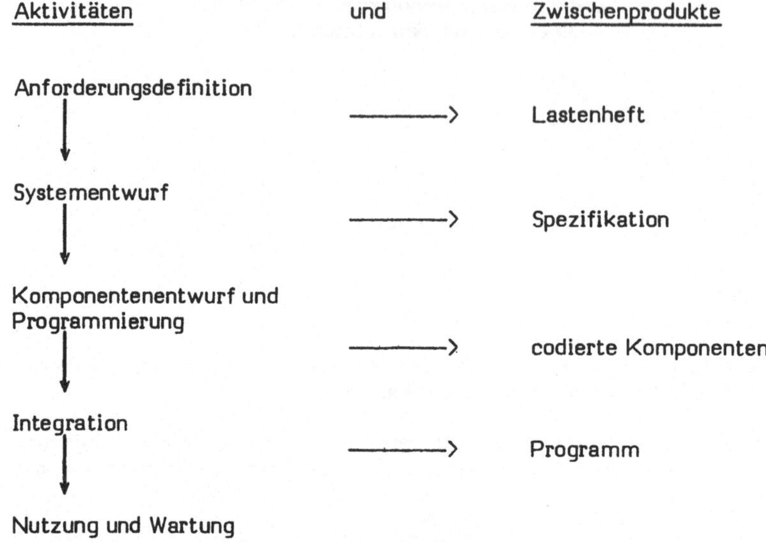

Spezifikation in diesem Sinn bezeichnet das Ergebnis des Systementwurfs, d.h. die Zerlegung des Gesamtsystems in überschaubare, von einem Programmierer in angemessener Zeit implementierbare Komponenten und die Definition der Interaktion zwischen ihnen. Die Spezifikation ist Ausgangspunkt für die Programmierung und Grundlage für die Integration.

Eine Spezifikationssprache ist ein Formalismus zur Beschreibung der Spezifikation.

Nachdem im Bereich der Programmiersprachen eine gewisse Konsolidierung eingetreten ist, zielt die derzeitige Entwicklung auf Sprachen zur Beschreibung der im Entwicklungszyklus davorliegenden Zwischenprodukte.

Spezifikationssprachen sind aktueller Forschungsgegenstand, doch erwartet man von ihrem Einsatz schon jetzt eine Verbesserung der Softwarequalität.

Neben der Unterstützung der allgemeinen Spezifikationsgrundsätze, wie

- Wahrung des Geheimnisprinzips (information hiding)

- Wohldefiniertheit der Schnittstellen zwischen den Komponenten

- Implementierungsunabhängigkeit

muß eine Spezifikationssprache folgenden Kriterien genügen, wenn sie industriell einsetzbar sein soll:

- Verständlichkeit. Die Spezifikationssprache muß von Softwareingenieuren in angemessener Zeit erlernbar sein. Der Aufwand zur Erstellung der Spezifikation muß in einem vertretbaren Verhältnis zu Einsparungen in späteren Entwicklungsphasen stehen. Da die Spezifikation auch die Grundlage für die vom gesamten Projektteam vorgenommene Entwurfsrückschau (design-review) bildet, ist eine gute Lesbarkeit von großer Bedeutung.

- Praktikabilität. Die Spezifikationssprache muß eine wirkungsvolle Hilfe für die real vorkommenden Problemstellungen und die heute übliche Komplexität von Software bieten. Die elegante Spezifikation eines Kellers sagt noch nichts aus über die Brauchbarkeit des Verfahrens in einem Projekt, in dem ein 50.000 bis 100.000 Zeilen umfassendes Programm-System zu erstellen ist. Der Formalisierungsgrad einer industriell einsetzbaren Spezifikationssprache muß in besonderem Maße ausgewogen sein und darf die Spezifikation komplexer Software nicht behindern. Formale Verifizierbarkeit ist heute noch ein nachgeordnetes Kriterium.

Diese aus der praktischen Arbeit entstandenen Kriterien verbieten noch die Anwendung von neueren Forschungsergebnissen, wie z.B. der algebraischen Spezifikation /Gut 77/, obwohl wir diesen große Bedeutung beimessen.

Für die industrielle Softwareentwicklung läßt sich daraus die Aufgabe ableiten, die neueren Ergebnisse auf dem Gebiet der Spezifikation in weniger formaler, aber dafür mehr praktikabler Weise einsetzbar zu machen.

Dazu haben wir vorhandene Spezifikationssprachen geprüft. Die Konzepte in SPECIAL /Ro 76/ finden wir interessant, aber in der Praxis kaum anwendbar. SPEZI /Ko 79/ und eine Notation zur Software-Modularisierung /Den 79/ gaben uns wesentliche Anregungen für die Entwicklung des Spezifikationssystems easy. Wie die meisten neueren Spezifikationsverfahren basiert easy auf den Ideen von abstrakten Maschinen und abstrakten Datentypen.

2.   Konzepte der Spezifikationssprache easy

Eine Spezifikation in easy ist in Pakete gegliedert. Ein <u>Paket</u> dient zur Formulierung der beim Systementwurf entstandenen Komponenten und faßt logisch zusammengehörende Programmteile zusammen.

Die Kommunikation zwischen Paketen wird durch ihre Schnittstellenbeschreibung definiert. Objekte der Schnittstellenbeschreibung sind Prozeduren, Typen und Konstanten. Die in der <u>Exportschnittstelle</u> angegebenen Objekte sind Ressourcen, die in diesem Paket implementiert und anderen Paketen zur Verfügung gestellt werden. Aus anderen Paketen benutzte Ressourcen werden in der <u>Importschnittstelle</u> angegeben.

<u>Prozeduren</u> bestehen aus dem Prozedurnamen und der Parameterangabe, wobei für jeden Parameter Name, Typ und Übergabeart (in, out, in-out) angegeben werden. Der Zugriff auf die Daten eines Pakets kann von außen nur über Prozeduren erfolgen, so daß die Implementierungsunabhängigkeit der Datenstrukturen und damit das Prinzip des information hiding gewahrt bleibt, wie es für abstrakte Datentypen heute üblich ist. Der Informationsfluß zwischen den Paketen ist ausschließlich durch Prozedurparameter festgelegt.

Während die Syntax der Prozeduren präzise formalisiert ist, wird für die Angabe ihres Effekts kein bestimmter Formalismus erzwungen, denn das Bestehen auf einer formalen operationellen oder gar algebraischen Semantikbeschreibung scheint uns mit der angestrebten Praktikabilität nicht vereinbar, auch wenn wir dadurch auf die Möglichkeit einer formalen Verifikation des Programms gegen die Spezifikation verzichten müssen. Die Beschreibung des Effekts einer Prozedur erfolgt daher in "sorgfältiger Umgangssprache" evtl. mit der Angabe eines Implementierungsbeispiels.

<u>Konstanten</u> werden in der Schnittstellenbeschreibung durch ihren Namen und ihren Typ angegeben.

easy unterstützt das Konzept der abstrakten Datentypen. Daher sind auch <u>Typen</u> Bestandteile der Schnittstellenbeschreibung und müssen von dem Paket exportiert werden, in dem die betreffende Datenstruktur implementiert werden soll. Typen werden durch ihre Namen spezifiziert und informell erläutert. Die Typen von Parametern importierter Prozeduren und von importierten Konstanten müssen in dem importierenden Paket bekannt sein, so daß aus der Spezifikation ersichtlich ist, welche Datentypen in welchen Paketen benutzt werden.

Das Bekanntsein eines Typs in einem Paket erlaubt darin die Deklaration und den Gebrauch von Daten dieses Typs. Zwei Typen sind - ebenso wie Prozeduren und Konstanten - genau dann gleich, wenn ihre Namen gleich sind.

Nachdem in den Export- und Import-Abschnitten die Schnittstellenobjekte festgelegt sind, werden im Sequence-Abschnitt in informeller Weise Reihenfolgebedingungen in der Benutzung exportierter Prozeduren beschrieben.

Danach folgt der Error-Abschnitt mit Hinweisen auf Restriktionen, Grenzen und Fehlerreaktion, die bei der Verwendung der exportierten Objekte zu beachten sind.

Das folgende Beispiel soll einen Eindruck von der Spezifikationssprache easy geben. Es ist Teil der Spezifikation für ein easy unterstützendes Werkzeug, auf das im nächsten Abschnitt noch ausführlicher eingegangen wird.

PACKAGE lexical-analysis

     VERSION 1 FROM 10.08.1981 BY Hirschmann

DESCRIPTION

     Dieses Paket führt die lexikalische Analyse einer easy-Spezifikation durch. Die lexikalischen Einheiten werden klassifiziert, und easy-Identifier werden in die Namensliste eingetragen.

EXPORT

     PROC next-lex (OUT lexclass: type, OUT repr: name, OUT int: line-number)

     DESCRIPTION Von der aktuellen Position ausgehend, analysiert next-lex die Quelldatei und gibt Typ, Name und Zeilennummer der als nächste lexikalische Einheit erkannten Zeichenkette über die Parameter aus.

     TYPE lexclass
     DESCRIPTION Der Typ lexclass umfaßt die Elemente "Name", "Schlüsselwort" und "Dateiende".

     PROC initialize-lexical-analysis (IN file: source-file, OUT errmsg: return-code)
     DESCRIPTION Initialisierungsroutine für die Lexikalanalyse. Die Quelldatei wird zum Lesen eröffnet, die aktuelle Leseposition zeigt auf Dateianfang.

PROC finalize-lexical-analysis

DESCRIPTION Abschlußroutine für Lexikalanalyse, schließen der Quelldatei.

CONST repr: by-sy, const-sy, description-sy,

    ** ... und weitere easy-Schlüsselworte ...

    type-sy, version-sy

DESCRIPTION Diese Konstanten sind reservierte Namen und werden in easy als Schlüsselworte benutzt.

IMPORT

FROM basic-io: PROC open-file (IN file: d),

                         PROC close-file,

                         PROC get-char (OUT char: c),

                         TYPE file.

FROM namelist: PROC enter-identifier (IN string: name, OUT repr: key),

                         TYPE repr.

FROM error-messages: PROC report-error (IN int: line-nr, IN errmsg: err-nr),

                         TYPE errmsg,

                         CONST errmsg: open-err, illegal-char, illegal-seq, ok.

SEQUENCE

Die exportierten Prozeduren müssen in folgender Reihenfolge benutzt werden:

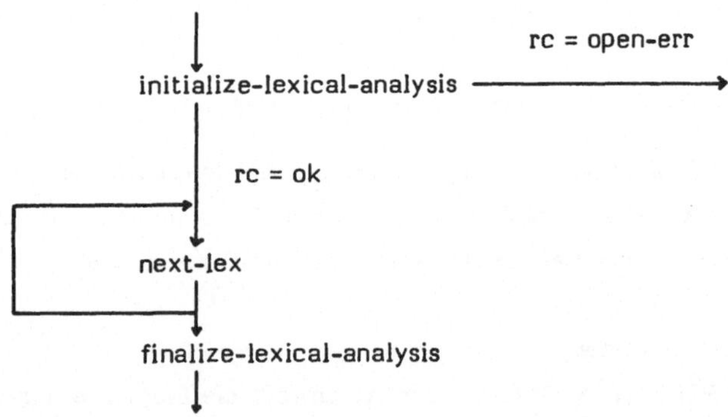

ERROR Falls die Quelldatei nicht vorhanden ist oder sich nicht öffnen läßt, liefert der Aufruf von initialize-lexical-analysis den return-code "open-err" zurück. Bei erfolgreicher Initialisierung hat der return-code den Wert "ok". Ein möglicher Überlauf der Namensliste wird vom Paket namelist behandelt.

ENDPACK   lexical-analysis

Für die Spezifikation der Kommunikation zwischen Paketen ist die Export-/Importrelation das geeignete Ausdrucksmittel, dies gilt aber nur eingeschränkt für den Informationsfluß am "Rand" des Systems, z.B. bei Dialoganwendungen. Der "Importeur", hier ein menschlicher Benutzer, liegt außerhalb der Pakete.

Zur Spezifikation dieses Sachverhalts gibt es besonders gekennzeichnete E/A-Prozeduren, deren Parameter den Informationsfluß zwischen dem spezifizierten System und der Umgebung angeben. Diese E/A-Prozeduren werden in einem besonderen, mit "External" bezeichneten Abschnitt des Pakets untergebracht.

easy enthält zum jetzigen Zeitpunkt keine Sprachmittel zur Formulierung nebenläufiger Prozesse. Wir gehen davon aus, daß auch Echtzeitanwendungen in erster Linie nach dem Kriterium der Zusammenfassung der wichtigsten Datenstrukturen zu spezifizieren sind, wie es das Paketkonzept nahelegt. Zu einer solchen Spezifikation gibt es i.a. mehrere Prozeßaufteilungen, so daß die Beschränkung auf eine dieser Möglichkeiten leicht zu einer Überspezifikation führt. In easy gibt es daher global zu allen Paketen einen Abschnitt "Configuration", in dem mögliche Prozeßaufteilungen oder Überlagerungsstrukturen beschrieben werden können.

Es gibt in easy keine Unterscheidung von verschiedenen Pakettypen (z.B. Funktionspaket oder Datenpaket) und auch keine vorgeschriebene Anordnung der Pakete (z.B. als strenge Hierarchie). Zwar sollte der Entwurf möglichst zu einer Hierarchisierung in Abstraktionsebenen führen, doch scheint uns eine Begrenzung der Paket-Interaktion auf hierarchische Beziehungen die allgemeine Anwendbarkeit der Spezifikationssprache zu stark einzuschränken.

3.   Werkzeug für easy

Zur Unterstützung der Arbeit mit der Spezifikationssprache wird ein Werkzeug entwickelt, dessen Funktionen im folgenden beschrieben werden.

<u>Erleichterung bei der Erstellung der Spezifikation</u>

Zur Reduzierung der Schreibarbeit können die Typen von Parametern importierter Prozeduren und die Typen importierter Konstanten automatisch importiert werden. Für den Import von Prozeduren reicht die Angabe des Prozedurnamens.

Um die Vorteile des Spezifikationssystems schon während des Systementwurfs nutzbar zu machen, in einer Phase also, in der die Spezifikation noch nicht vollständig ist, darf diese an genau definierten Stellen noch offen gelassen werden.

Für importierte Objekte kann die Angabe des exportierenden Pakets entfallen, das Werkzeug sucht ggf. danach. Umgekehrt kann auf die vollständige Angabe von importierten Objekten aus bestimmten Paketen verzichtet werden. In diesem Fall versucht das Werkzeug einen automatischen Import. Weil darunter die Präzision der Schnittstellenbeschreibung stark leidet, wird der Benutzer mahnend auf deren Vervollständigung hingewiesen.

Konsistenzprüfungen

Die Spezifikation wird u.a. daraufhin geprüft, ob die Namen der exportierten Objekte eindeutig sind, jedes importierte Objekt auch exportiert worden ist und ob die Schnittstellenstruktur "klar" ist, d.h. keine Re-Exporte stattfinden.

Dokumentationshilfe

Es werden Querverweislisten für jedes Paket und für die gesamte Spezifikation generiert. Die Verwendungsnachweise gestatten Aussagen darüber, welche Pakete von der Änderung bestimmter Objekte betroffen sind.

In einer späteren Ausbaustufe soll auch eine grafische Übersicht über die Pakete und ihre Interaktion erstellt werden.

Sicherung der Integrität

Die vollständige und korrekte Spezifikation ist noch keine Garantie für ein korrektes Programm. Der "klassische" - wenn auch in größerem Umfang wegen der immensen Schwierigkeiten kaum praktizierte - Weg ist die formale Verifikation des Programms gegen die Spezifikation.

Aufgrund der informellen Semantikbeschreibung ist dieses Verfahren bei der Verwendung von easy nicht möglich, doch versuchen auch wir die korrekte Implementierung der Spezifikation zu erleichtern. Dazu soll aus der Spezifikation ein Programmrahmen in der jeweiligen Programmiersprache generiert werden, um sicherzustellen, daß die spezifizierten Schnittstellen bei der Programmierung eingehalten werden. Dieses Verfahren ist vorteilhafter gegenüber dem Ansatz, die Spezifikation direkt mit Sprachmitteln der Programmiersprache zu erstellen, insbesondere aus folgenden Gründen:

- Programmiersprachen führen durch ihre Ablauforientierung leicht zur Überspezifikation, während eine Spezifikationssprache ausgewogene Sprachmittel zur Formulierung des "was" (anstelle des "wie") hat und somit die Implementierungsunabhängigkeit eher gewährleisten kann.

- Die Paketstruktur, insbesondere aber die Angabe von Datentypen ist für die Spezifikation auch dann wertvoll, wenn die vorgesehene Programmiersprache nicht über solche Konzepte verfügt.

- Für die Spezifikation steht ein einheitlicher, projektübergreifender und programmiersprachunabhängiger Formalismus zur Verfügung.

Die Abbildung der Spezifikation auf einen Programmrahmen ist verhältnismäßig einfach für neuere Programmiersprachen wie Ada. Für jedes easy-Paket kann ein Ada-package-head generiert werden, weitere Angaben, z.B. der Importe, erfolgen als Kommentar.

Schwieriger ist diese Abbildung etwa bei Fortran oder Assembler, wo es keine Datentypen und (von manchen Assemblern abgesehen) keine Konstrukte zur globalen Strukturierung gibt. Aber gerade bei der - noch häufigen - Verwendung dieser Sprachen ist eine Spezifikation unter Verwendung dieser aktuellen Konzepte besonders hilfreich.

Im Fall von Fortran können easy-Pakete auf Fortran-Unterprogramme und easy-Prozeduren auf entries in Fortran-Unterprogrammen abgebildet werden. Die Parameterübergabe zwischen den entries kann über entry-Parameter oder über common-Bereiche abgewickelt werden. Dem bei Verwendung der zweiten Möglichkeit auftretenden Verlust an Sicherheit der Schnittstellen, hervorgerufen durch die Möglichkeit von im Sinne der Spezifikation unzulässigen Zugriffen auf den common-Bereich, muß durch entsprechende Programmierrichtlinien entgegengewirkt werden.

Vollständige Datenabstraktion läßt sich in Fortran praktisch kaum durchhalten. In den meisten Fällen wird vor Beginn der Implementierung für jeden exportierten Datentyp dessen Repräsentation festgelegt, das Werkzeug überträgt diese in die importierenden Pakete. Der generierte Programmrahmen enthält dann alle notwendigen Informationen, die ein Programmierer braucht, um die Implementierung eines dem easy-Paket entsprechenden Fortran-Unterprogramms verhältnismäßig unabhängig vornehmen zu können.

Entwicklung des Werkzeugs

Die Spezifikation des Werkzeugs selbst wurde in easy vorgenommen, als Implementierungssprache wurde Pascal verwendet. Aus Kapazitätsgründen war es bis jetzt nicht möglich, alle spezifizierten Pakete zu implementieren.

Für die praktische Anwendung am dringendsten benötigt wurde die Dokumentationsunterstützung, um beim Spezifizieren nicht die Übersicht über die große Menge der Schnittstellenobjekte zu verlieren. Die Programmierung dieser Funktion wurde daher zuerst in Angriff genommen, syntaktische und semantische Analyse folgten danach. Daß die sukzessive Implementierung des Werkzeugs in dieser Folge ohne größere Schwierigkeiten möglich war, konnte schon als erster Erfolg der easy-Spezifikation gewertet werden.

4. Praktische Erfahrung mit easy

Die Spezifikationssprache easy wurde außer bei der Erstellung des Werkzeugs auch in einem Projekt zur Entwicklung eines Verkehrsleitsystems erprobt. Für die Entwicklung dieses Produktes waren mehrere Mannjahre angesetzt, Rahmenbedingungen des Auftraggebers waren u. a. die Verwendung von Fortran und die leichte Erweiterbarkeit der VerkehrswegeStruktur. Insbesondere die letzte Anforderung war nur mit einer sauberen Spezifikation der Software zu erfüllen, für die 20% der Entwicklungskosten aufgewendet wurden.

Positive Erfahrungen

Die Akzeptanz von easy im Projektteam war gut. Wesentliche Gründe dafür waren neben der Aufgeschlossenheit der Mitarbeiter für neue Techniken wohl die Einführung der Spezifikationstechnik an Hand eines Problems aus der Aufgabenstellung sowie die Bereitschaft, die ersten praktischen Erfahrungen sofort in einer Neufassung der Spezifikationssprache zu berücksichtigen.

Positiv beurteilt wurde vor allem die durch easy geschaffene Transparenz der Spezifikation; jedes Mitglied im Projektteam hatte einen guten Überblick über den Stand des Entwurfs, denn dieser war durch die Spezifikation zu jeder Zeit dokumentiert. Die von easy ausgehende Notwendigkeit der präzisen Schnittstellenbeschreibung führte frühzeitig zur Aufdeckung logischer Inkonsistenzen. Das Vorgehen, erst vollständig zu beschreiben, <u>was</u> gemacht wird, bevor die Implementierung in Angriff genommen wird, wurde als qualitätssteigernd bewertet.

Als außerordentlich nützlich wurde weiterhin angesehen, daß der Entwurf in einer definierten Form vorlag, die die Kommunikation im Projektteam während der Entwicklungsphase erleichterte und als Grundlage für eine kritische Entwurfsrückschau dienen konnte. Dadurch entfiel der gefährliche, monatelange "Blindflug" zwischen Aufgabenstellung und Programmierung, und Entwurfsfehler konnten noch mit verhältnismäßig geringem Aufwand korrigiert werden. Die durch die formale Festlegung der Spezifikationssprache erzielte Normierung der Spezifikation erleichterte den Teammitgliedern die Einarbeitung in die von ihren Kollegen erstellten Spezifikationen.

Die Präzision der umgangssprachlich angegebenen Semantik von Paketen, Prozeduren und Typen konnte nach Anlegen eines Glossars, in dem alle für das Projekt wichtigen Begriffe verbindlich definiert sind, wesentlich gesteigert werden. Ein in jedem Paket optional vorkommender Abschnitt "Terminology" macht das Glossar zum Bestandteil der Spezifikation.

Eine Aussage zu den Veränderungen der Entwicklungskosten durch den Einsatz von easy ist schwierig zu machen, weil wir natürlich nicht das gleiche Produkt unter gleichen Voraussetzungen parallel in konventioneller Weise entwickeln konnten. Nach unseren Beobachtungen verursachte die Spezifikation bei der Entwicklung des Verkehrsleitsystems einen etwas größeren Aufwand als bei konventioneller Vorgehensweise eingeplant worden wäre, der jedoch bei der Programmierung wieder eingespart wurde.

Die entscheidenden Einsparungen durch die in easy erstellte Spezifikation erwarten wir bei den Wartungskosten. Aufgrund der klaren und gut dokumentierten Struktur der Programme scheint die Halbierung dieser Kosten eine realistische Erwartung zu sein. Bei den heute üblichen Aufwendungen für Fehlerbeseitigung und funktionale Erweiterung nach Auslieferung des Produkts wären nach 2 Jahren die gesamten Kosten für die Spezifikation aufgewogen.

<u>Probleme</u>

Zunächst erwies sich das Arbeiten mit der Spezifikationssprache als gewöhnungsbedürftig. Das Auseinanderhalten von Export-/Importrelation einerseits und Datenfluß andererseits, sowie die Trennung des logischen Konzepts Paket von dem physikalischen Konzept des Lademoduls erforderte einige Diskussionen.

Die durch das Niederschreiben der vollständigen Spezifikation entstandene Arbeit wurde bisweilen als lästig empfunden, insbesondere, wenn es sich um Schnittstellen handelte, die "eigentlich klar" waren.

Der Weg von der fertigen Spezifikation zum Programm schien in manchen Fällen noch immer etwas steinig, insbesondere dann, wenn Spezifikation und Programmierung von verschiedenen Personen vorgenommen wurden.

Schlußbemerkungen

Eine Spezifikationssprache ist keine Systementwurfsmethode. Sie kann nur die heuristischen Empfehlungen, etwa von Parnas /Par 72/ oder Myers /My 75/, unterstützen, jedoch nicht die Kreativität des Entwerfers ersetzen. Deshalb konnten wir auch nicht klären, wo die optimale Paketgröße liegt, und ob es empfehlenswert ist, in die Spezifikationssprache ein Konstrukt aufzunehmen, mit dem Verfeinerungen von Paketen darstellbar sind (z. Zt. ist dies in easy nicht vorgesehen). Zu große Pakete führen leicht dazu, daß beim Systementwurf Probleme übersehen werden, zu kleine Pakete treiben den Aufwand für die Spezifikation beinahe "trivialer" Schnittstellen in die Höhe und vergrößern die Komplexität des Gesamtsystems.

Noch nicht befriedigend gelöst ist die Spezifikation nebenläufiger Prozesse, und auch die Semantikbeschreibung von Prozeduren und Typen muß nicht für alle Zeit rein informell bleiben. Doch für beide Aspekte haben wir bis jetzt noch keine Notationen gefunden, die ebenso präzise wie praktikabel wären.

Nachdem easy in der jetzigen Form schon den Übergang von der Spezifikation zum Programm unterstützt, wäre der nächste mögliche Schritt, eine Unterstützung auch für den Übergang vom Lastenheft zur Spezifikation zu versuchen. Ohne sich in den Problemen einer Entwurfsmethode zu verstricken, könnte vielleicht geprüft werden, ob die in geeigneter Weise zu formulierenden Anforderungen an das Softwaresystem durch die Spezifikation abgedeckt sind.

Bei allen Bemühungen, die Softwareentwicklung zu rationalisieren, sollten aber die Rückwirkungen auf die Arbeitsbedingungen der am Softwareerstellungsprozeß beteiligten Menschen bedacht werden. In der derzeitigen Software-Engineering-Environment-Euphorie (SE^3) scheint uns dieser Aspekt manchmal etwas zu kurz zu kommen.

<u>Anmerkungen</u>

Die Entwicklung des Spezifikationssystems easy erfolgte im Rahmen eines vom BMFT unter Nr. 083 0206 und mit Mitteln des mbp geförderten Projekts.

Für ihre Anregungen und Unterstützung danke ich meinen Kollegen N. Christensen und R. Desjardins.

<u>Literatur</u>

Den 79:   Denert, E.:
Software-Modularisierung
Informatik-Spektrum 2/4, S. 204-218, 1979.

Gut 77:   Guttag, J.V.:
Abstract Data Types and the Development of Data Structures
CACM 20/6, S. 396-404, 1977.

Ko 79:   Koch, W.:
SPEZI - eine Sprache zur Formulierung von Spezifikationen
TU Berlin, FB Informatik, Bericht Nr. 79-22, 1979.

My 75:   Myers, G.J.:
Reliable Software through Composite Design
Petrocelli/Charter, New York 1975.

Par 72:   Parnas, D.L.:
On the Criteria to be used in Decomposing Systems
into Modules, CACM 15/12, S. 1053-1058, 1972.

Ro 76:   Robinson, L.; Roubine, O.:
SPECIAL - A Specification and Assertion Language
Stanford Research Institute, Menlo Park, Ca., USA,
1976.

Projektorganisation nach dem Komponentenkonzept

Heiner Müller-Merbach

Institut für Betriebswirtschaftslehre
Technische Hochschule Darmstadt

Abstract

Phase concepts are prevailing in the literature on software design. In this paper,
a concept of parallel components will be introduced which is in contrast to the
concepts of succeeding phases.

1. Projektorganisation als Schlüssel für erfolgreiche Software-Entwicklung

In der Literatur zur Software-Entwicklung treten neuerdings Fragen der Projektorganisation immer stärker in den Vordergrund. Bei vielen Autoren scheint Einigkeit
darüber zu bestehen, daß die Projektorganisation den Schlüssel für Erfolg bei der
Software-Entwicklung darstellt.

In der Diskussion zur Projektorganisation spielen die Phasenkonzepte, wie sie in
recht großer Anzahl entwickelt und empfohlen wurden, eine zentrale Rolle. Den Phasenkonzepten soll in diesem Beitrag ein Komponentenkonzept entgegengestellt werden.
Es besteht im wesentlichen aus dem Vorschlag, die unterschiedlichen Aktivitäten der
Software-Entwicklung als parallel ablaufende und sich zeitlich stark überlappende
Komponenten zu organisieren, nicht aber als zeitlich hintereinander geschaltete,
sich nicht überlappende Phasen.

Das Zerlegen konstruktiver Tätigkeiten in - zeitlich aufeinanderfolgende - Phasen
ist in der Literatur zur Software-Entwicklung ebenso üblich wie in der Literatur
zur Planung, zum Operations Research, zur technischen Konstruktionslehre, zur Orga-
nisationsgestaltung etc. Gleichwohl gibt es Forschungsergebnisse, die den Nutzen von
Phasenkonzepten in Frage stellen.

Im folgenden seien zunächst die Phasenkonzepte der Software-Entwicklung erörtert und
hinsichtlich ihrer Auswirkungen kritisch erörtert (Abschnitt 2). Anschließend wird
als Kontrast dazu das Komponentenkonzept vorgestellt (Abschnitt 3). Zum Abschluß
werden im Zusammenhang mit dem Komponentenkonzept einige Aspekte der Projektleitung
angesprochen (Abschnitt 4).

2. Phasenkonzepte und ihre Auswirkungen

Phasenkonzepte findet man in der Informatik-Literatur in großer Fülle, teilweise in den Einführungslehrbüchern zur Informatik wie etwa bei Schmitz und Seibt [13] , S. 4 ff., dann sehr zahlreich in den speziellen Büchern zur Software-Entwicklung wie etwa bei Katzan [10], S. 29 ff., und Sneed [14] , S. 30 ff., und Heinrich [7] , S. 17 ff., und in zahlreichen Aufsätzen zur Software-Entwicklung wie etwa bei Balzert [2], bei Denert und Hesse [5], bei Endres [6], bei Hesse [8, 9] und vielen anderen.

Phasenkonzepte der Software-Entwicklung scheinen in der EDV-Praxis auch weit verbreitet zu sein. So berichten Abel et al. [1], S. 71, über den Befund einer empirischen Erhebung: "Von den 26 befragten Unternehmen gaben nur fünf an, kein Phasenmodell zu verwenden." Sie schränken allerdings ein, daß nur acht der 26 Firmen ein "genau ausgearbeitetes" Phasenkonzept zum Einsatz bringen. Ferner berichten sie, daß die in größeren EDV-Abteilungen für große Projekte eingesetzten Konzepte aus fünf bis sechs Phasen bestünden, in kleineren EDV-Abteilungen jedoch Konzepte mit nur drei bis vier Phasen verwendet würden. Sie selbst schlagen (auf S. 69) ein Konzept vor, das nach der Initialisierung aus acht Phasen besteht, nämlich:

    1 - Studie (Voruntersuchung)
    2 - Definition (Grobkonzept)
    3 - Systementwurf (Sachlogisches Teilkonzept)
    4 - Komponentenentwurf (Technisches Detailkonzept)
    5 - Programmierung
    6 - Validation
    7 - Übergabe
    8 - Nutzung

Abel et al. führen (auf S. 68) fünf Gründe für die Verwendung von Phasenkonzepten an und betonen (auf S. 72 f.), daß sich die Phasenkonzepte bei den befragten Unternehmen, die mit ihnen arbeiten, offensichtlich bewährt haben. Es ist allerdings nicht zu erkennen, ob sich die Bewährung auf die Phasenkonzepte bezieht oder auf die Tatsache, daß das Arbeiten mit einem Phasenkonzept nur kennzeichnet, daß der organisatorischen Strukturierung der Software-Entwicklung eine besondere Aufmerksamkeit und Sorgfalt gewidmet wurde.

Phasenkonzepte gibt es nicht nur im Bereich der Software-Entwicklung. So betont Endres [6], S. 157: "Das Prinzip (nämlich das Phasenkonzept) findet seine Anwendung bei jedem zielgerichteten größeren Unterfangen und erhält für die DV-Systementwicklung nur eine ganz spezifische inhaltliche Ausprägung." Interessant ist in diesem Zusammenhang ein mehrfach publizierter empirischer Befund von Witte [17,18] , der einen bestimmten Planungs- und Entscheidungsprozeß in deutschen Wirtschaftsunternehmen analysiert hat, nämlich den Prozeß der Entscheidung über die Installation von EDV-Anlagen. Er hat in keinem Fall das Vorliegen eines Phasenablaufs feststellen können. Ähnlich hat auch Conway [4] Planungsprozesse (im Sinne des Operations Research) beobachtet und ebenfalls keine realisierten Phasenabläufe feststellen können.

Nun ist die Feststellung der Nichtexistenz von Phasenabläufen in der Praxis kein
ausreichendes Argument gegen den potentiellen Nutzen von Phasenkonzepten; denn man
könnte sich durch diese Konzepte eine verbesserte Projektdisziplin erhoffen. Wenn
Phasenabläufe in der Praxis nicht festgestellt werden, kann es immerhin daran liegen,
daß Phasenkonzepte gar nicht bekannt waren.

Eigene - zugestandenermaßen punktuelle und daher nicht notwendigerweise repräsentative
 - Erfahrungen mit Phasenkonzepten haben fundamentale Schwierigkeiten und Nachteile
dieser Konzepte erkennbar werden lassen. Sie seien im folgenden skizziert:

● Eine gleichzeitige, überlappende Arbeit an verschiedenen Aktivitäten ist ausge-
  schlossen, soweit die Aktivitäten unterschiedlichen Phasen angehören. Das kann
  zu einer unnötigen Verlängerung der Projektdauer führen.

● Es kann sein, daß sich verschiedene Phasen gegenseitig voraussetzen, was zu einer
  Blockierung der Arbeit führt. Beispielsweise kann der Systementwurf davon abhängig
  sein, welche Hardware und welche System-Software verfügbar sein wird, während
  andererseits die Beschaffungsentscheidungen für die Hardware und die System-
  Software von dem fertiggestellten Systementwurf abhängig gemacht werden.

● Wenn ein Phasenwechsel identisch mit dem Übergang der Verantwortung von einer
  Abteilung zu einer anderen Abteilung ist, dann ist an dieser Stelle mit einer
  Ping-Pong-Wirkung zu rechnen. Wegen (tatsächlicher oder vermeintlicher) Unzu-
  länglichkeiten wird die zweite Abteilung immer wieder versuchen, die Annahme des
  entsprechenden Arbeitspapiers zu verweigern, und eine Überarbeitung (also einen
  Rücksprung in die vorhergehende Phase) verlangen.

● Die meisten Phasenschemata sind "EDV-nah" konzipiert und enthalten die Aspekte
  der organisatorischen Umstellung und der Wirtschaftlichkeitsanalyse nur unzuläng-
  lich.

Besonders große Schwierigkeiten scheinen durch die notwendige, aber häufig belastete
Zusammenarbeit zwischen der Fachabteilung (dem künftigen Benutzer der zu entwickelnden Software) und der EDV-Abteilung zu entstehen. Sie sprechen unterschiedliche
Sprachen, haben ein unterschiedliches Problemverständnis und einen voneinander stark
abweichenden Erfahrungshorizont. Häufig ist es die Aufgabe der Fachabteilung, die
Software-Aufgabe (aus der logischen Sicht des Benutzers) eindeutig und vollständig
zu beschreiben, so daß die EDV-Abteilung auf dieser Basis ein Software-System erstellen kann. Diese eindeutige und vollständige Beschreibung der Aufgabe läßt sich
vergleichen mit dem Auftrag an einen Architekten, ein Gebäude zu konzipieren bis hin
zur Festlegung der einzelnen Steckdosen, bevor mit dem Bauherrn eine Abstimmung des
Grundrisses stattgefunden hat. Der Verfasser hat es in der Praxis gelegentlich er-
lebt, daß gerade an dieser Stelle das Ping-Pong-Spiel begonnen wurde und Sollkonzepte
wegen "fehlender Steckdosen" von EDV-Abteilungen an Fachabteilungen zurückgewiesen
wurden, ohne daß globale Fassungen des Sollkonzeptes in der EDV-Abteilung zur
Diskussion angenommen wurden.

Nun wird allerdings in der Literatur immer wieder betont, daß die Phasenkonzepte
Rücksprünge auf vorhergehende Phasen durchaus nicht ausschlössen, sondern daß solche
Rücksprünge durchaus zu erwarten seien. Dennoch wird in der Entwicklungspraxis von

den betroffenen Mitarbeitern jeder Rücksprung als Kritik an der geleisteten Arbeit verstanden, und zwar nicht zu Unrecht. Das _Ideal_ des Phasenkonzepts besteht ja darin, daß alle Phasen nur _einmal_ bearbeitet werden und Rücksprünge nicht auftreten. Das ist aber unrealistisch. Es fragt sich daher, ob ein realistisches Ideal nicht von vornherein das zeitliche _Nebeneinander_ der einzelnen Aktivitäten zulassen sollte. Das ist der Grundgedanke des Komponentenkonzepts.

3. Das Komponentenkonzept

Die Entwicklung von Software stellt im allgemeinen eine komplexe Aufgabe dar, die durch die folgenden Merkmale gekennzeichnet ist:

● Es sind unterschiedliche Aktivitäten erforderlich, von denen nur einige andere voraussetzen.

● Es arbeiten verschiedene Mitarbeiter unterschiedlicher Abteilungen (Fachabteilung als künftiger Anwender, EDV-Abteilung, evtl. auch Organisationsabteilung, häufig auch weitere Fachabteilungen als künftige Mitbenutzer des Systems) an der gemeinsamen Aufgabe, und zwar im allgemeinen in starker zeitlicher Überlappung.

● Mit dem Arbeitsfortschritt entwickelt sich auch ein Kenntnis- und Erfahrungsfortschritt bei allen am Projekt Beteiligten. Dabei ist zu erwarten, daß laufend neue Ideen über das Projekt entstehen.

● Insbesondere ist zu erwarten, daß sich diejenigen am Projekt Beteiligten besonders stark gegenseitig in ihren Ideen befruchten, die mit unterschiedlichen Wissensgebieten, Denkgewohnheiten und Arbeitserfahrungen aufeinanderstoßen. Das werden insbesondere die Repräsentanten der unterschiedlichen Abteilungen sein.

Es erscheint daher sinnvoll, die verschiedenen Aktivitäten _gewollt parallel_ durchzuführen, die Mitarbeiter der verschiedenen Abteilungen _gewollt gleichzeitig_ einzusetzen, die Produktion neuer Ideen _während_ des Prozeßablaufs zu fördern und insbesondere die _gegenseitige_ geistige Befruchtung zu unterstützen. Das wird durch die Phasenkonzepte nicht gewährleistet. Vielmehr scheint diesbezüglich das Komponentenkonzept überlegen zu sein. Es wird im folgenden skizziert.

Das Komponentenkonzept unterscheidet sich von den Phasenkonzepten hinsichtlich des Umfanges oder der Zahl der Aktivitäten nicht grundsätzlich. Was den Umfang angeht, besteht allerdings insofern eine größere Flexibilität als bei den Phasenkonzepten, als jeder Projekt-Manager weitgehend frei in der Wahl und expliziten Kennzeichnung der einzelnen Aktivitäten ist.

Der Unterschied zwischen dem Komponentenkonzept und den Phasenkonzepten liegt in der _zeitlichen Anordnung_ der Aktivitäten. Beim Komponentenkonzept ist eine völlige Parallelität aller Aktivitäten zulässig. Das bedeutet allerdings nicht, daß sämtliche Aktivitäten gleichzeitig begonnen oder gleichzeitig abgeschlossen werden müßten. Zeitliche Verschiebungen zwischen unterschiedlichen Aktivitäten sind vielmehr normal.

Für jede Aktivität gibt es jedoch ein Reihenfolgeprinzip, welches den gesamten Entwicklungsprozeß prägen sollte, nämlich das Top-Down-Prinzip. Es ist in der Informatik bekannt und braucht hier bezüglich der einzelnen Aktivitäten nicht weiter spezifiziert zu werden. Wichtig erscheint jedoch, daß dieses Prinzip auch die <u>Verbindungen</u> zwischen den verschiedenen Aktivitäten prägt. Wenn man bezüglich einer Aktivität zu einem groben Lösungsvorschlag gekommen ist, dann kann auf dieser ersten Ebene die Verbindung mit anderen Aktivitäten hergestellt werden, so daß diese einerseits begonnen werden können, andererseits aber auch Rückmeldungen veranlaßt werden. Das wird später an Beispielen noch deutlich gemacht werden.

Auf der folgenden Seite sind in einer Skizze 14 verschiedene Komponenten genannt und in ihrer zeitlichen Verknüpfung bzw. Überlappung zusammengestellt. Die einzelnen Komponenten sind beispielhaft zu verstehen und können je nach Aufgabenstellung variiert, ergänzt oder reduziert werden. Im folgenden werden die Komponenten kurz erläutert.

<u>Komponente 1 - Problembeschreibung mit Zielsetzung und Anforderungen</u>

Zu jeder Software-Entwicklung ist die Problemstellung möglichst genau festzulegen und laufend zu aktualisieren. Diese Problemstellung soll die Zielsetzung des Systems als auch die Anforderungen umfassen. Änderungen der Problemstellung (insbesondere Erweiterungen) können sich bei der Hinzuziehung anderer Fachabteilungen ergeben. Sie können aber auch das Ergebnis von Rückmeldungen aus den 13 folgenden Komponenten sein. Im Sinne der Top-Down-Zerlegung wird anfangs nur eine globale Beschreibung der Problemstellung angefertigt werden, die mit dem Arbeitsfortschritt laufend stärker spezifiziert wird.

<u>Komponente 2 - Kostenschätzung und Wirtschaftlichkeitsrechnung</u>

Da EDV-Anwendungen auch dem Postulat der Wirtschaftlichkeit unterliegen (unterliegen müssen), ist eine Wirtschaftlichkeitsrechnung in Verbindung mit einer Kostenschätzung als laufende Aktivität während des gesamten Entwicklungprozesses zu sehen. Allerdings nimmt die Bedeutung dieser Komponente zum Ende des Prozesses ab, da hier weder Abbruchentscheidungen noch Beschleunigungsentscheidungen zu erwarten sein dürften. Ferner ist am Ende des Prozesses kaum zu erwarten, daß sich bei den Faktoren, die die Wirtschaftlichkeit beeinflussen, wesentliche Änderungen ergeben. Wichtig ist, daß die Wirtschaftlichkeitsrechnung früh beginnt und das Projekt über seine wesentliche Entwicklungszeit begleitet, wobei neue Erkenntnisse, die die Wirtschaftlichkeit betreffen, sofort in die Rechnung einbezogen werden müssen. Auch bei der Wirtschaftlichkeitsrechnung ist im Sinne der Top-Down-Zerlegung mit Grobrechnungen zu beginnen, die dann durch Detailrechnungen abgelöst werden.

<u>Komponente 3 - Analyse der Ist-Aufbauorganisation und Entwicklung der Soll-Aufbauorganisation</u>

EDV-Anwendungssysteme können einerseits von der bestehenden Aufbauorganisation beeinflußt sein und andererseits Einfluß auf eine sinnvolle neue Aufbauorganisation ausüben. Aus diesem Grunde ist es bei vielen EDV-Projekten nützlich, zunächst die Ist-Aufbauorganisation zu erheben, die in Verbindung mit dem EDV-Anwendungssystem steht. Soweit es erwägenswert erscheint, die Aufbauorganisation zu ändern, sollten die entsprechenden Vorbereitungen getroffen werden, wobei ebenfalls der Prozeß im Top-Down-Sinne zu gliedern wäre. Es ist jedoch zu betonen, daß es viele EDV-Anwendungssysteme gibt, durch die die Aufbauorganisation kaum oder gar nicht beeinflußt wird. In diesen Fällen kann es oft genügen, denjenigen Teil der Ist-Aufbauorganisation zu beschreiben, der den Rahmen für das EDV-Anwendungssystem bildet.

<u>Komponente 4 - Analyse der Ist-Ablauforganisation und Entwicklung der Soll-Ablauforganisation</u>

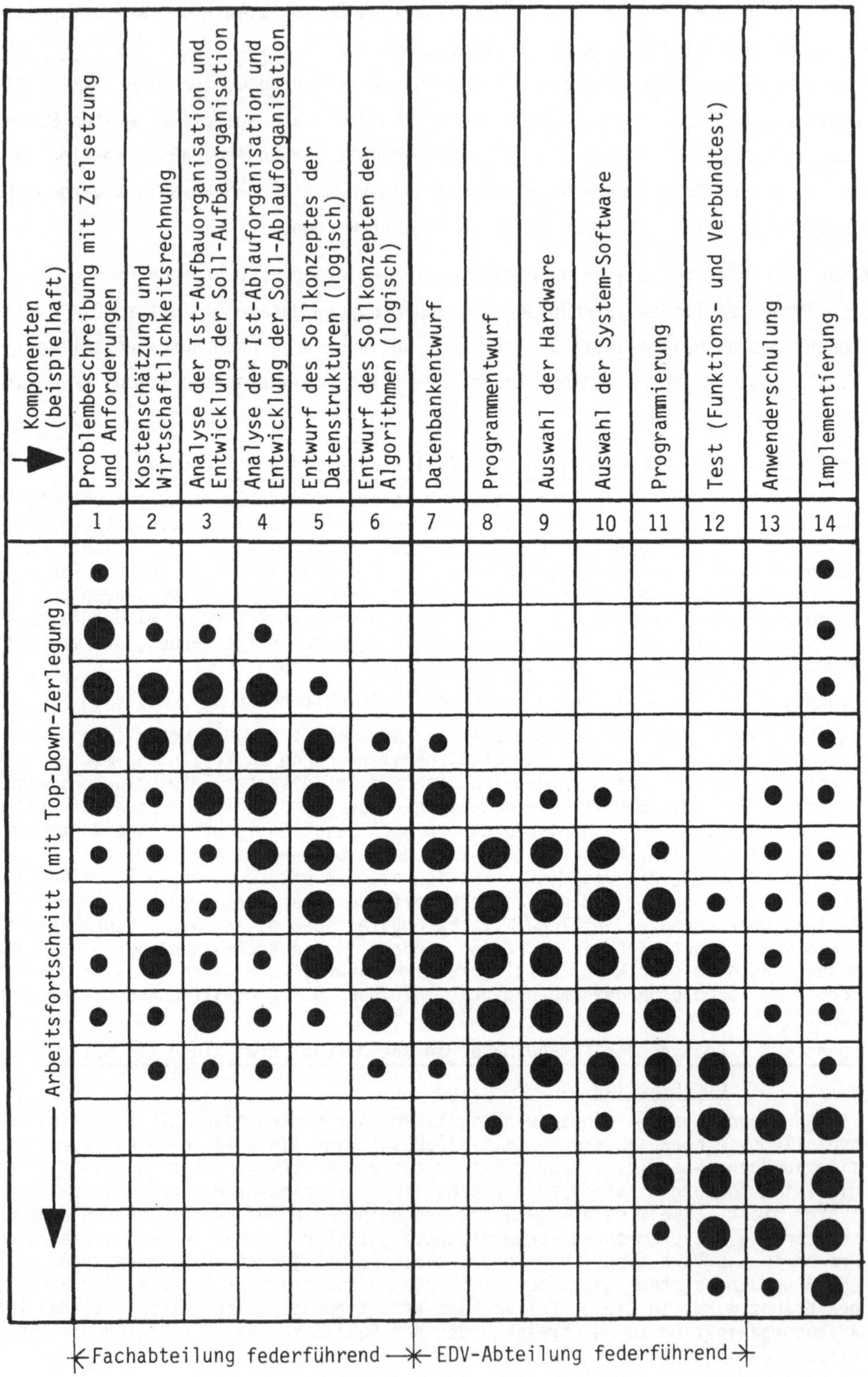

Komponenten (beispielhaft)

Arbeitsfortschritt (mit Top-Down-Zerlegung)

Nr.	Komponente
1	Problembeschreibung mit Zielsetzung und Anforderungen
2	Kostenschätzung und Wirtschaftlichkeitsrechnung
3	Analyse der Ist-Aufbauorganisation und Entwicklung der Soll-Aufbauorganisation
4	Analyse der Ist-Ablauforganisation und Entwicklung der Soll-Ablauforganisation
5	Entwurf des Sollkonzeptes der Datenstrukturen (logisch)
6	Entwurf des Sollkonzepten der Algorithmen (logisch)
7	Datenbankentwurf
8	Programmentwurf
9	Auswahl der Hardware
10	Auswahl der System-Software
11	Programmierung
12	Test (Funktions- und Verbundtest)
13	Anwenderschulung
14	Implementierung

←Fachabteilung federführend→←EDV-Abteilung federführend→

Beispielskizze zum Komponentenkonzept

Wenn auch nicht durch jedes EDV-Anwendungssystem die <u>Aufbau</u>organisation beeinflußt wird, so werden jedoch fast immer Änderungen der <u>Ablauf</u>organisation erforderlich sein. Andererseits wird die vorhandene Ablauforganisation häufig eine starke Präge-wirkung auf das EDV-Anwendungssystem haben. Aus diesen beiden Gründen ist es erstens wichtig, die Ist-Ablauforganisation zu erheben und zu analysieren und andererseits eine Soll-Ablauforganisation unter Einbeziehung des zu entwickelnden EDV-Anwendungssystems zu entwerfen. Erfahrene Organisatoren sollten für diese wichtige Komponente herangezogen werden.

Komponente 5 - Entwurf des Sollkonzeptes der Datenstrukturen (aus der logischen Sicht des Benutzers)

Das Sollkonzept (hier in die Komponenten 5 und 6 aufgegliedert) bildet das zentrale Dokument, in dem das EDV-Anwendungssystem aus der logischen Sicht des Benutzers dargestellt ist und das der EDV-Abteilung als wichtigste Grundlage für die EDV-bezogenen Entwurfsarbeiten dient. Den Datenstrukturen sei dabei hier eine gewisse Vorherrschaft gegenüber den Algorithmen (Komponente 6) gegeben. Wichtig ist hier wiederum die Vorgehensweise nach dem Prinzip der Top-Down-Zerlegung. Wichtig ist, daß ein Sollkonzept eindeutig und vollständig sein sollte, wobei die Vollständigkeit im Zuge der zunehmenden Detaillierung (in der Top-Down-Richtung) zu realisieren ist.

Komponente 6 - Entwurf des Sollkonzeptes der Algorithmen (aus der logischen Sicht des Benutzers)

Der zweite Teil des Sollkonzeptes betrifft die Algorithmen (Rechenverfahren) des EDV-Anwendungssystems. Sie sind hier wie die Datenstrukturen nur aus der logischen Sicht des Benutzers zu beschreiben, ohne daß die EDV-Realisation hier schon be-rücksichtigt werden müßte. Auch hier ist wieder eine schrittweise Spezifizierung im Sinne der Top-Down-Zerlegung angebracht.

Komponente 7 - Datenbankentwurf

Eng mit der Komponente 5 ist der von der EDV-Abteilung durchzuführende Datenbank-entwurf zu sehen. Hier wird die logische Sicht des Benutzers übertragen in die Sicht der EDV-Realisation. Dabei spielen Grundsatzfragen des Datenbankkonzepts (relationale versus hierarchische Datenbanken etc.) eine wichtige Rolle wie auch die Verfügbarkeit von entsprechender Datenbank-Software (vgl. Komponente 10). Von dieser Komponente 7 sind ggfs. Rückmeldungen und Empfehlungen an die Komponente 5 zu erwarten, die dort im Verlauf der Top-Down-Zerlegung berücksichtigt werden könnten.

Komponente 8 - Programmentwurf

An den Datenbankentwurf (Komponente 7) und an das Sollkonzept der Algorithmen (Komponente 6) schließt sich (in starker Überlappung) der Programmentwurf an. Mit ihm werden die algorithmischen Abläufe aus der logischen Sicht des Benutzers übertragen in die Sicht der EDV-Realisation. Diese Komponente bildet den Über-gang zur Programmierung (Komponente 11).

Komponente 9 - Auswahl der Hardware

Für verschiedene EDV-Anwendungssysteme ist eine eigene Hardware erforderlich. Da-bei kann es sich um eigens zu beschaffende EDV-Anlagen handeln, um Erweiterungen von bestehenden EDV-Anlagen oder um Zusatz- und Peripherie-Geräte (z.B. Terminals). Da Hardware-Beschaffungen unmittelbar mit meßbarem Aufwand verbunden sind, wird diese Komponente in enger Beziehung mit der Wirtschaftlichkeitsrechnung (Kompo-nente 2) stehen. Ferner gibt es gewöhnlich enge Beziehungen zur Ablauforganisa-tion (Komponente 4), insbesondere im Zusammenhang mit Dialog-Verarbeitung über neu einzusetzende Terminals.

Komponente 10 - Auswahl der System-Software

Es gibt eine Fülle an System-Software, die die eigene Programmierung wesentlich unterstützt, andererseits aber mit entsprechenden Miet- bzw. Beschaffungskosten verbunden ist (teilweise aber auch für zusätzlich erforderliche Hardware). Hierzu gehören beispielsweise die Datenbank-Software, Compiler, Hilfsprogramme etc.

Komponente 11 - Programmierung

Die Programmierung bedeutet das Umsetzen des Programmentwurfs (Komponente 8) in ein lauffähiges Programm (in einer vorzugebenden Programmiersprache). Auch hier ist das Prinzip der Top-Down-Zerlegung empfehlenswert, wobei hier die Top-Down-Hierarchie etwa der der Komponenten 7 und 8 bzw. 5 und 6 folgt. Generell sollten hier moderne Prinzipien der Programmierung eingehalten werden, etwa das Prinzip der "strukturierten Programmierung". Eine funktionsorientierte Modulierung des Programmsystems sollte ebenfalls angestrebt werden.

Komponente 12 - Test (Funktions- und Verbundtest)

Parallel mit der Programmierung sollte das Testen ablaufen. Dabei sind zunächst (isoliert für einzelne Programm-Module) Funktionstests vorzunehmen. Erst nach dem Testen aller Programmteile kann ein Verbundtest folgen. Wichtig ist in diesem Zusammenhang, daß die Testbeispiele entweder von der Fachabteilung geliefert werden oder gemeinsam von der Fachabteilung und der EDV-Abteilung entwickelt werden. Es ist von der EDV-Abteilung darauf zu achten, daß möglichst sämtliche Programmteile in allen Verzweigungen im Test durchlaufen werden.

Komponente 13 - Anwenderschulung

Über weite Strecken überlappend mit der Entwicklung des EDV-Anwendungssystems kann die Anwenderschulung vorgenommen werden. Diese hängt u.a. stark mit der Ablauforganisation (Komponente 4) zusammen, ferner mit der Hardware-Ausstattung an einzelnen Arbeitsplätzen (Komponente 9). Zur Anwenderschulung sollten sowohl die Fachabteilung als auch die EDV-Abteilung beitragen. Insbesondere ist hierzu Lehrmaterial bereitzustellen, was gewöhnlich nur gemeinsam durch beide Abteilungen erarbeitet werden kann. Auch bei der Anwenderschulung kann sich das Prinzip der Top-Down-Zerlegung bewähren. Man könnte sich vorstellen, daß die Anwender zunächst nur einen Überblick vermittelt bekommen, sodann in größerer Detaillierung einige für sie relevante Unterbereiche und schließlich in exakter Spezifizierung die sie betreffenden Teilbereiche erlernen. Im einzelnen ist die Anwenderschulung projektorientiert zu planen, da jedes EDV-Anwendungssystem unterschiedliche Anforderungen an die Anwender stellt und auch unterschiedlich stark von Mitarbeitern bedient wird, die mit EDV-Anlagen keine Erfahrung haben.

Komponente 14 - Implementierung

Als letzte Komponente sei die Implementierung betrachtet. Sie wird häufig als letzte Phase der Entwicklung von EDV-Anwendungssystemen bezeichnet. Tatsächlich erscheint es jedoch sinnvoll, gerade die Implementierung als fortwährend relevante Aktivität zu verstehen. Churchman [3],S. 21, setzt sie sogar an die erste Stelle des Phasenschemas: "I am often inclined to put the implementation question first, i.e. 'Can anything be changed?'". Die Implementierung ist eine Komponente, die zumindest die Projektleitung laufend beschäftigen sollte, selbst wenn der eigentliche Einsatz des EDV-Anwendungssystems eher am Ende des gesamten Prozesses stehen wird.

Die Überlappung der verschiedenen Komponenten läßt sich im Zusammenhang mit der Top-Down-Zerlegung an vielen Beispielen deutlich machen. Dazu seien zunächst die Komponenten 5 und 7 beispielhaft herausgegriffen.

Bei der logischen Konzipierung der Datenstrukturen mag es in der ersten Runde genügen, nur die "Objekttypen" (vgl. Wedekind und Ortner [16] und Wedekind [15]) in ihrem Umfang abzuschätzen und in ihrem Zusammenspiel darzustellen. Mit dieser Information kann die EDV-Abteilung schon Fragen der Datenbankgestaltung erörtern und ihre Vorschläge für die Realisierung artikulieren. In der Fachabteilung können sodann die Attribute zu den einzelnen Objekttypen entwickelt werden (Fortsetzung der Komponente 5). Mit ihnen kann die EDV-Abteilung die Arbeit am Datenbankentwurf fortsetzen. In

einer dritten Runde können dann die <u>Formate</u> spezifiziert werden, zunächst aus der
logischen Sicht des Benutzers (Komponente 5), sodann aus der Sicht der EDV-Realisation (Komponente 7).

Entsprechendes gilt für die Überlappung zwischen den Komponenten 5 und 6. Solange
auf der Ebene der Datenbeschreibung nur Objekttypen und ihre Abhängigkeiten gekennzeichnet sind, läßt sich über die Algorithmen nur aussagen, welche Objekttypen welche
anderen Objekttypen beeinflussen. Sind in der nächsten Runde die Attribute der Objekttypen bezeichnet, lassen sich schon formelmäßige Abhängigkeiten formulieren. Und wenn
schließlich die Daten spezifiziert sind, lassen sich die Algorithmen detailliert auf-
zeichnen.

Man erkennt an diesen Beispielen, daß die verschiedenen an der Software-Entwicklung
Beteiligten durch die Überlappungen laufend veranlaßt sind, gemeinsam zusammenzu-
arbeiten und die Vorschläge gegenseitig zu verarbeiten. Dabei wird der "Redaktions-
schluß" für jede Komponente (und zwar in der letzten Spezifizierungsstufe) weit nach
hinten verlegt. Das bedeutet, daß während großer Teile des Entwicklungsprozesses auch
solche Komponenten noch bereichert werden könnten, die bei den Phasenkonzepten als
erstes abgeschlossen sein müßten.

Das Komponentenschema bringt eine starke Verklammerung der verschiedenen Aktivitäten
und der verschiedenen Mitarbeiter der verschiedenen Abteilungen, die an dem Projekt
beteiligt sind. Die häufig zu beobachtenden Gräben zwischen den Fachabteilungen und
den EDV-Abteilungen könnten dadurch zu einem guten Teil beseitigt werden.

4. Das Komponentenkonzept und die Projektleitung

Das Komponentenkonzept stellt gewisse Anforderungen an die Projektleitung.

Zunächst einmal muß die Projektleitung das Projekt strukturieren, also die Komponenten
festlegen und sie untergliedern. Dabei können durchaus unterschiedliche Zusammenstellur-
gen von Komponenten sinnvoll werden, je nach Aufgabe (vgl. Müller-Merbach [11, 12]).
Die Projektleitung müßte also sämtliche Punkte, die in der obigen Skizze beispielhaft
eingetragen sind, spezifizieren. Das ist mit Sicherheit aufwendig, andererseits aber
ein wesentlicher Beitrag zum Verständnis der gesamten Aufgabe, die für ein Projekt
zu bearbeiten ist.

Darüber hinaus müßte die Projektleitung den Arbeitsaufwand für alle Teile der Komponenten abschätzen und den Mitarbeiterbedarf festlegen.

Die Projektleitung müßte sodann unter Berücksichtigung der verfügbaren Mitarbeiter
einen Netzplan über alle Teile der Komponenten aufstellen und eine Terminrechnung
für das gesamte Projekt durchführen und dabei den einzelnen Teilen der Komponenten
Solltermine zuordnen.

Schließlich müßten die einzelnen Teile der Komponenten den jeweiligen Mitarbeitern
als Aufgaben zugeordnet werden. Hinzu kommt die Überwachung der Arbeitsqualität und

der Termine für die einzelnen Aufgaben.

Die Projektleitung, wie sie auch organisiert sein mag, hat damit einen umfangreichen Aufgabenkomplex zu bearbeiten. Man mag an dieser Stelle gegen das Komponentenkonzept einwenden, daß die Phasenkonzepte der Projektleitung doch in der Projektgliederung viel Arbeit abnehmen, denn sie enthalten ja schon eine zeitliche Reihenfolge der Aktivitäten, was beim Komponentenkonzept nicht der Fall ist. Dieser Vorteil existiert allerdings nur scheinbar, da die Phasenkonzepte wegen der zumeist häufigen Rücksprünge gar nicht einzuhalten sind. Ist es da nicht ehrlicher, wenn man von vornherein den Prozeß in Form von Komponenten strukturiert?

Literatur

[1] Abel, E., Harraß, E., Schoenen, H.J., Schwald, A.: Untersuchung über Maßnahmen zur Verbesserung der Software-Produktion, Teil 2: Einsatz von Methoden der Software-Produktion in der Bundesrepublik Deutschland. Bericht Nr. 131 der Gesellschaft für Mathematik und Datenverarbeitung. München, Wien: Oldenbourg 1980.

[2] Balzert, H.: Methoden, Sprachen und Werkzeuge zur Definition, Dokumentation und Analyse von Anforderungen an Software-Produkte, Teil 1 und 2. Informatik-Spektrum 4, 145 und 246 (1981).

[3] Churchman, C.W.: Paradise Regained: A Hope for the Future of Systems Design Education. Education in Systems Science (hrsg. von B.A. Bayraktar et al.), S. 17 - 22. London: Taylor & Francis 1979.

[4] Conway, D.A.: Three Years in the Life of an O.R. Section, Vortrag auf dem Third European Congress on Operations Research, Amsterdam, 9. bis 11. April 1979.

[5] Denert, E., Hesse, W.: Projektmodell und Projektbibliothek: Grundlagen zuverlässiger Software-Entwicklung und Dokumentation. Informatik-Spektrum 3, 215 (1980).

[6] Endres, A.: Methoden der Programm- und Systemkonstruktion. Informatik-Spektrum 3, 156 (1980).

[7] Heinrich, L.J.: Systemplanung, Band 1: Analyse und Grobprojektierung von Informationssystemen. Berlin, New York: De Gruyter 1976.

[8] Hesse, W.: Das Projektmodell - Eine Grundlage für die ingenieurmäßige Software-Entwicklung. Informatik-Fachberichte Bd. 33, S. 107 - 122. Berlin, Heidelberg, New York: Springer 1980.

[9] Hesse, W.: Methoden und Werkzeuge zur Software-Entwicklung - Ein Marsch durch die Technologie-Landschaft. Informatik-Spektrum 4, 229 (1981).

[10] Katzan, H.: Methodischer Systementwurf - Eine Einführung in die HIPO-Technik. (deutsche Übersetzung). Köln-Braunsfeld: Rudolf Müller 1980.

[11] Müller-Merbach, H.: The Modeling Process: Steps Versus Components. Design and Implementation of Computer-based Information Systems (hrsg. von N. Szyperski und E. Grochla), S. 47 - 59. Alphen aan den Rijn: Sijthoff & Noordhoff 1979.

[12] Müller-Merbach, H.: Management Science Process: Phases or Components. Interfaces, 12 (1982, erscheint im Februar).

[13] Schmitz, P., Seibt, D.: Einführung in die anwendungsorientierte Informatik. München: Vahlen 1975.

[14] Sneed, H.: Software-Entwicklungsmethodik. Köln-Braunsfeld: Rudolf Müller 1980.

[15] Wedekind, H.: Datenbanksysteme I - Eine konstruktive Einführung in die Datenverarbeitung in Wirtschaft und Verwaltung (2. Auflage). Mannheim, Wien, Zürich: Bibliographisches Institut 1981.

[16] Wedekind, H., Ortner, E.: Systematisches Konstruieren von Datenbankanwendungen - Zur Methodologie der Angewandten Informatik. München, Wien: Hanser 1980.

[17] Witte, E.: Phasen-Theorem und Organisation komplexer Entscheidungsverläufe. Zeitschrift für betriebswirtschaftliche Forschung 10, 625 (1968).

[18] Witte, E.: Mikroskopie einer unternehmerischen Entscheidung - Bericht aus der empirischen Forschung. IBM-Nachrichten 19, 490 (1969).

A Case Study in Developing Reliable Software: The Construction of a Buffer Management System Used in Network Communication

R. Gotzhein, S. Keramidis, M. Reitenspieß

Institut für Mathematische Maschinen und Datenverarbeitung
Universität Erlangen-Nürnberg

Abstract

An industrial application will show the usefulness of a newer method
for constructing reliable software. The method combines the phases of
design and implementation of software production. Formulation and description of a problem, independent of its implementation, are possible. Relative to given consistency attributes of a problem, the correctness of a specified solution can be shown independent of its implementation. The correctness of the implementation relative to the
specification can be shown by using a representationfunction which
describes the relation between implementation and specification. The
industrial application which will be presented later will point out
that the method contributes to a simple and therefore clear system
structure. The reflections necessary for the specification were leading
to an efficient implementation. Error statistics which were prepared
during problem solving indicate that the application of the method reduced errors to a high degree. Especially design errors were detected
in an early stage.

1. Introduction

It is well known that a big part of information processing expenditures
stems from software. More than one half of the errors in programs already delivered arise from the concept and the design. Moreover, the
expenses for error correction and modification of delivered programs
are two to four times as high as the expenses before delivering. Formal and nonprecedural specification-methods and -languages can contrib-
ute to the avoidance or reduction of conceptual errors, if they allow
a unique design and a check of consistency attributes, independent of
the implementation. Thereby design errors can be revealed and erased
in time, that is, before they are integrated into the implementation.

To exclude implementation errors, well structured, high level programming languages and verification methods are necessary. With their
help, one can prove the implementation to accomplish the specification

requirements. Therefore, a specification method is of practical interest only, if it is closely connected to the implementation- and verification-technique.

Our software construction method consists of a specification-, an implementation-, and a verification-part. The description and programming of concurrency problems are integrated into this method. Due to the concrete application shown in the sequel, not all attributes of the method can be described. One aspect not mentioned is the possibility to model complex problems by a hierarchy of modules thereby reducing complexity. The notion of a module will be explained later. Another aspect is the usefulness of the method for real-time applications. The general model allows the comfortable synchronization of asynchronous activities so that real-time requirements can be taken into account.

In the following, the application of the method to an industrial project and the experiences accumulated thereby will be presented.

2.   Example: A Buffer Management System

The problem at hand was to design and implement a program for the buffer management in the network communication system SINEC, which is a trademark of the Siemens corporation. Another research topic was to what extent an existing buffer system can be replaced by a new one, which is better suited for use and more efficient with respect to memory and time. Picture 1 shows the environment the system should be integrated into. Besides others, the buffer management system should make the following operations available:

- transfer data
- request buffer
- release buffer.

In the following, this example will be used to illustrate our method.

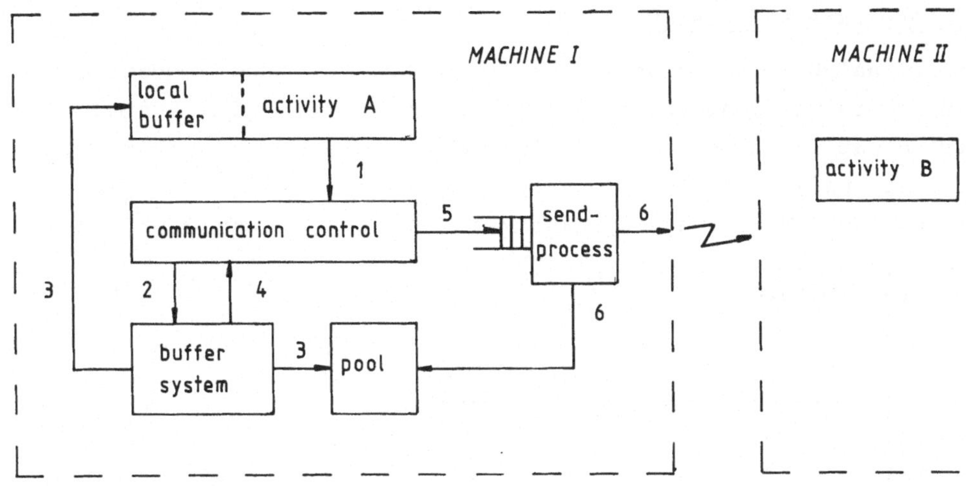

<u>Picture 1:</u> A data transfer sequence in the SINEC system

     1 Send-request: A wants to send a message to B
     2 Request to the buffer system: A message shall be
       transfered to a poolelement
     3 Selection of a buffer, transfer of the message
     4 Transfer of the buffer identification
     5 Placing the request to send in the waiting queue
       of the sending process
     6 Sending the message, waiting for receipt

3. A Software Construction Method

To construct the buffer management system, we proceeded in the following
well known way:

- After an exhaustive analysis of the problem and its given environment,
  a design was established. Some of the design decisions were influenced
  by simulation.

- The system-components given in the design were formally specified.

- Thereafter, the adherance of the specified objects to consistency
  attributes was proved.

- The specified components were implemented in PASCAL, and verified
  according to the classical verification method.

- Manually the PASCAL version was translated to the assembly language
  running on the target machine. After assemblation, it was tested,
  and integrated into the network communication system.

3.1 Analysis and Design

During analysis, an existing strategy "SNPS" for the allocation of
main memory was compared to a modified buddy-algorithm. A simulation
carried out for this reason yielded two effects. First, in the mean the
modified buddy-algorithm needs 15 % less main memory than "SNPS".
Second, the "SNPS" swapping rate was reduced for about 75 %.

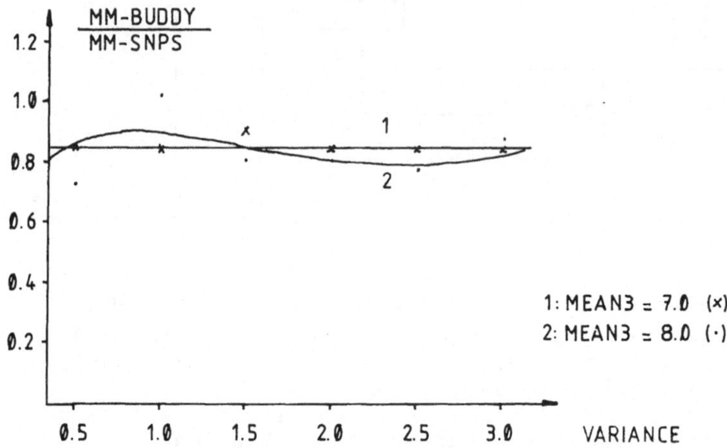

Picture 2: Relative main memory requirements for different
           profiles of requests to the buffer system

The results of the analysis led to the following rough design of the
buffer management system:

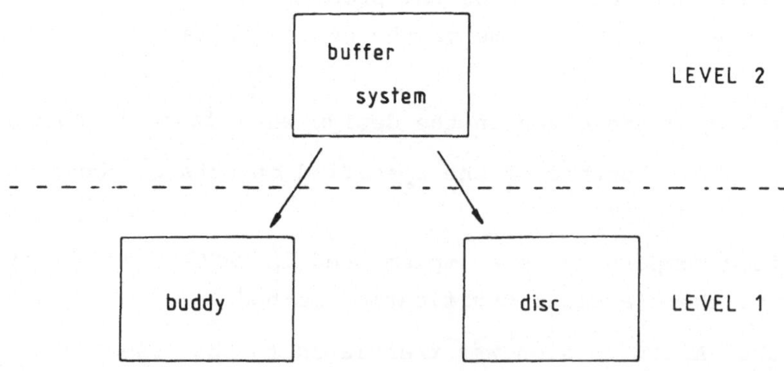

Picture 3: Call-hierarchy of the buffer management system

The buffer system of level 2 provides operations for buffer management.
The module "buddy" realizes the allocation strategy; the "disc"-module
supervises that part of the external memory which is dedicated to buffer
swapping. The following sections are restricted to the module "buddy".
The allocation strategy - a modified buddy-algorithm - can be character-
ized as follows:

- the main memory managed is of length $n*2^m$

- the length of memory blocks available is a power of two, therefore
  $2^k, 4 \leq k \leq m$

- each request M is adjusted to the least possible power of two,
  therefore $M \leq 2^k \land \forall k' < k : 2^{k'} < M$

- for each block-length $2^k, 4 \leq k \leq m$, there exists a separate list which
  contains all available blocks of equal length

- a request of length 2^k and an associated empty list causes an available block of length $2^n, k < n$ to be halved successively, until a block
  of length 2^k is formed

- the bisection of a block yields two so called buddy blocks; if both
  of them are available again, they are merged to a bigger block

- operations are "allocate" and "free".

3.2 Formal Specification of the Module "buddy"

An exhaustive presentation of our specification- and implementation-
method is given in [2]. This presentation is restricted to those parts
of the method which are necessary for the understanding of the statements. As we have mentioned above, the practical application of the
method and experiences made thereby are emphasized in this paper.

The abstraction mechanism of our method acts as a frame or schema for
specifying and implementing abstract data types. Picture 4 shows the
formal specification of the module "buddy". It consists of a specifi-
cation- and an implementation-part, and is initiated via a heading
line. With

MODULE buddy (factor: integer WHERE factor $\geq$ 1; logmax: (4..16));

the definition of an abstract data type named "buddy" is started.
"factor" and "logmax" are formal input parameters. The "WHERE"-con-

struct can restrict their range.

The specification part determines the module interface, that is, it determines the abstract view of all objects of this type. Predicate transformation is used for the sequential part of our specification language. But predicates may include structured objects, too. Some constructs of the module "buddy" specified on the previous page will be illustrated in the sequel.

The part "PARAMETERS", on one hand, defines the types of all values contained in the specification so the type can be left out in the remaining occurences. On the other hand, the abstract range of the objects of the type specified is fixed ("AR_AS"-construct). This means, the range of the abstract object "f" of type "buddy" is a set of blocks ("block"). In the part "MACROS", shorthands may be introduced.

The "OPERATIONS"-part characterizes the effects of each operation on the abstract objects ("EFFECTS"). The execution of the function "allocate" reserves a buffer of length 2^{loglen}. In case such a buffer exists, its address "addr" will be returned. Otherwise, the return value "addr" will become $\emptyset$. The "NBL"-construct is one of the constructs for the specification of asynchronous currents. The predicate proper is only dependant on the state of the given object.

In the "SYN"-part, noncompatibility-("NVTG") and priority-conditions ("PRIOR") are defined. Two operation calls (and therefore the calling processes, too) are named compatible, if they can be executed simultaneously. Otherwise, they are called noncompatible. According to the given specification of the module "buddy", all calls to the operations "allocate" and "free" are noncompatible two by two (mutual exclusion). The given priority-condition says that a call of "free" has higher priority than a call of "allocate". Compatibility- and priority-relations can be as complicated as necessary (see [2]). The "SYN"-part specifies common scheduling-restrictions upon operation-calls which work on single objects of a type. "NBL"-predicates, however, express synchronization restrictions which only depend on the state of an object. In general, an operation call can only be executed if the "SYN"- as well as the "NBL"-conditions are satisfied.

MODULE buddy (factor: integer WHERE factor $>$ 1; logmax: (4..16));

SPECIFICATION
    PARAMETERS
        TYPE address: $(\emptyset .. factor \cdot 2^{logmax})$;
        TYPE block: RECORD addr: address;
                            lng: (4.. logmax);
                            succ; pre d: $\uparrow$block;
                            st: (fr, us)
                END RECORD;
    $k_1, ..., k_{factor}, ..., k_{factor \cdot 2^{logmax-4}}$: block
        INIT $k_1 = (1, logmax, \uparrow k_{1+2^{logmax-4}}, nil, fr)$
        $\wedge\ k_{(factor-1) \cdot 2^{logmax-4}+1} = (((factor-1) \cdot 2^{logmax-4}+1) \cdot 16+1,\ logmax, nil,$
                                        $\uparrow k_{(factor-2) \cdot 2^{logmax-4}+1},\ fr)$
        $\wedge\ \forall j \in (1 \cdot 2^{logmax-4}+1, ..., (factor-2) \cdot 2^{logmax-4}+1) (\kappa_j = ((j-1) \cdot 16+1,\ logmax,$
                                        $\uparrow k_{j+2^{logmax-4}}, \uparrow k_{j-2^{logmax-4}}, fr))$;
    f: buddy AR_AS SET OF block
        INIT $f = \{k_i | i \in (\emptyset \cdot 2^{logmax-4}+1, ..., (factor-1) \cdot 2^{logmax-4}+1)\}$;
    root: ARRAY [4.. logmax] OF $\uparrow$ block
        INIT $root[logmax] = \uparrow k_1\ \wedge\ \forall n (4 \leqslant n < logmax \rightarrow root[n] = nil)$;
    length: $(1..2^{logmax})$;
    loglen: (4.. logmax);
    addr: address;
SYN
    NVTG: $(a_1, a_2) \in$ ALLOCATE $\cup$ FREE;
    PRIOR: $a_1 \in$ FREE $\wedge$ $a_2 \in$ ALLOCATE;
MACROS
    $f_m = \{k | k.st = fr\ \wedge\ k.lng = m\}$;
        /$*$ set of available blocks of length 2^m $*$/
    $\| f \| = \Sigma | f_m | \cdot 2^m$ WHERE $4 \leqslant m \leqslant$ logmax;
        /$*$ absolute size of main memory $*$/
OPERATIONS
    allocate (f, length, addr, loglen);
        NBL   true;
        EFFECTS   length = length' $\wedge$ $2^{loglen-1} <$ length $\leqslant 2^{loglen}$
                $\wedge$ $4 \leqslant$ loglen $\leqslant$ logmax
                $\wedge$ $[(\exists k) (k.st' = fr\ \wedge\ k.st = us\ \wedge\ k.lng' \geqslant 2^{loglen}\ \wedge\ k.addr = addr$
                        $\wedge\ \| f \| = \| f' \| - 2^{loglen})\quad \vee$
                    $(\neg \exists k) (\exists m) (loglen \leqslant m \leqslant logmax) (k.lng = m\ \wedge\ k.st = fr\ \wedge\ addr = \emptyset$
                                        $\wedge\ \| f \| = \| f' \|)\ ]$;
    free (f, loglen, addr);

IMPLEMENTATION

        /$*$ see   section   3.4 $*$/

MODULEEND.

<u>Picture 4:</u> Formal specification of the module "buddy"

3.3 Consistency Attributes

Before implementing a specified type, consistency attributes of objects
of this type are expected. Informally, these attributes of the module
"buddy" were given in section 3.1. They can be described formally by
the following invariants I_1 to I_4. The used variables refer to objects
declared in the part "PARAMETERS" of the specification.

$$I_1: \quad (\forall k \in f)(k.pred \neq nil \rightarrow k.pred\uparrow.succ = \uparrow k)$$

$$I_2: \quad (\forall k \in f)(k.succ \neq nil \rightarrow k.succ\uparrow.pred = \uparrow k)$$

$$I_3: \quad (\forall m)(4 \leq m \leq logmax)(|f_m| = n_m > \emptyset \rightarrow (\exists k_{i_1}, \ldots, k_{i_{n_m}} \in f_m)$$

$$((\forall j)(1 < j \leq n_m)(k_{i_j}.pred = \uparrow k_{i_{j-1}}) \wedge$$

$$(\forall j)(1 \leq j < n_m)(k_{i_j}.succ = \uparrow k_{i_{j+1}}) \wedge$$

$$k_{i_1}.pred = nil \wedge k_{i_{n_m}}.succ = nil \wedge$$

$$root[m] = \uparrow k_{i_1}))$$

$$I_4: \quad (\forall m)(4 \leq m < logmax)(\forall k_{i_1} \in f_m)(\neg \exists k_{i_2} \in f_m)(k_{i_2} = companion(k_{i_1}))$$

$$\text{where } k_{i_2} = companion(k_{i_1}) \Longleftrightarrow$$

$$(k_{i_1}.lng = k_{i_2}.lng \wedge$$

$$((k_{i_2}.addr = 1 \bmod 2^{(k_{i_2}.lng+1)} \wedge k_{i_1}.addr = k_{i_2}.addr + 2^{k_{i_2}.lng}) \vee$$

$$(k_{i_2}.addr \neq 1 \bmod 2^{(k_{i_2}.lng+1)} \wedge k_{i_1}.addr = k_{i_2}.addr - 2^{k_{i_2}.lng})))$$

From these invariants it can be derived that

- each object represents a set of chained lists; the array "root" contains the root of every list (I_3)

- the forward-/backward-chaining is required to be consistent (I_1, I_2)

- no two buddy-blocks are available at the same time (I_4).

These conditions are proved to be valid according to the following
schema:

a) The conditions are valid after initialization.

b) If the conditions are valid before execution of an operation, they
   are valid afterwards.

3.4   Implementation

As we have explained above, the abstract representation of a "buddy"
consists of a set of blocks ("block"). These blocks are chained in
lists associated with the given length of a block. An array "storage"
and a "tag"-vector implement an object of type "buddy". The representation function matching the ALPHARD-construct of the same name pre-
scribes how to construct abstract objects from concrete ones. For
a buddy-block "k_i" of type "block" the prescription looks like that:

- A concrete, available block with index "m" in the array "storage"
  has the abstract block "k_i" where i=(m-1)/16+1 as the value of the
  representation function.

- The element "tag [i]" of the "tag"-vector is associated with the
  component "k_i.st", and gives the state (free or used) of the block
  "k_i".

- The element "storage [m+1]" is associated with the component
  "k_i.succ".

- All other components of the block "k_i" are represented analogous.

The abstract operations are realized with PASCAL-procedures operating on
the given concrete objects. The correctness of these operations relative to concrete assertions has been proved according to the classical
verification method.

Based upon the representation function, the implementation has formally
been proved to satisfy the specification conditions.

The implementation of abstract synchronization conditions is restricted
to transform abstract predicates into concrete ones. The synchronization mechanism of the operating system must restrict the execution of
a called procedure to those cases where both the "SYN"- and the "NBL"-
conditions are fulfilled. For this reason, the concrete predicates are
made available to the operating system.[2] shows possible implementations of these ideas.

4. Experiences

The following shall explain two aspects when realizing the application described in part 3: On the one hand, a correspondance between specification and implementation has appeared. On the other hand, a positive influence from the method used can be deduced from error statistics prepared during the project.

4.1 The Method's Influence on Implementation

As it is widely known, the specification shall not restrict the implementation. In our work so far, we made the experience that the specification can have an influence on implementation algorithms. In the project described here, this can be shown by the following example:

Let $\| B^H \|$ equal the absolute allocated main memory, let $\| F^H \|$ equal the absolute available main memory. Then the following must hold:

$$\| F^H \| + \| B^H \| = factor \ * \ 2^{logmax} \qquad (*)$$

It is in question on which level (see picture 3) this statement must hold.

1st alternative: The statement is formulated on level 1 which contains the module "buddy". From this, it follows that the state information of a concrete object of type "buddy" must include variables defining $\| B^H \|$; it must include information about used blocks. These variables need memory and code for manipulating them.

2nd alternative: Statement (*) is formulated on level 2. This level already contains state information about used blocks defining $\| B^H \|$. Requirements to operations "allocate" and "free" of the module "buddy" can describe changes of $\| F \|$: At block allocation, $\| F \|$ is reduced by the block length, at block release, $\| F \|$ is increased accordingly.

The specification of both alternatives is possible, but the 2nd alternative leads to a more efficient implementation, because it needs less code as well as space.

The invariant I_4, already known, can be seen as another example for the influence of the specification on the implementation. This invariant prohibits a correct algorithm given in the literature ([4]) for the procedure "allocate". By doing so, thoughts leading to a more efficient algorithm were initiated.

4.2 The Methods's Influence on Efficiency

Several industrial projects conveyed by us showed that the expense for program delivery was according to expense estimates based upon experiences of the employers. The underestimation of real expenses in many cases is well known. For the industrial project this work is based on, the following values hold:

> To accomplish the project, 6 manmonths were necessary. 20 %
> allotted to the simulation-phase, 30 % allotted to the specifica-
> tion-phase, and 35 % allotted to implementation and verification.
> The leaving 15 % were necessary for translating the verified
> PASCAL-version into machine-language, for tests, and for integra-
> tion. During integration, three errors appeared all together. They
> could be traced back to special properties of the target machine
> or to missing experience in running this machine. They were found
> quickly. Usually, 45 % of all production costs are extimated only
> for integration.

As we have mentioned in the introduction, costs for error correction and modification of delivered programs are two to four times as high as the costs before delivering. When applicating our method to different projects, we made the experience that the expenses after the handing over of programs are less than before.

Literature

1. Boehm, B.W./Mc Clean, R.K./Urfrig, R.B.: Some experiences with
    automated aids to the design of large-scale reliable software.
    Int. Conf. on Reliable Software = ACM SIGPLAN Not. 10, 6,
    p. 105 - 113 (1975)

2. Keramidis, S./Reitenspieß, M./Weber, K.: Sprachkonstrukte und
    Betriebssystemunterstützung für asynchrone und verteilte Pro-
    zeßsysteme. In: Implementierungssprachen für nichtsequentielle
    Programmsysteme (J. Nehmer, ed.), German Chapter of the ACM,
    Report 7, p. 37 - 62. Stuttgart: Teubner 1981

3. Schneider, H.J.: Programmentwicklung als konstruktive Aufgabe.
    University Erlangen-Nürnberg, Technical Report, June 1981

4. Schnupp, P./Floyd, C.: Software - Programmentwicklung und Pro-
    jektorganisation. Berlin: W. de Gruyter 1976

From Requirements to their Formalization -

A Case Study on the Stepwise Development of Algebraic Specifications*

Helmut Partsch, Alfred Laut

Institut für Informatik
Technische Universität München

Abstract

The paper aims at demonstrating that the concept of algebraic abstract data types together with a suitable development methodology is suited for the specification of larger programs, too. Possible phases in a stepwise, goal-oriented development of such a formal, algebraic specification out of informal requirements are exhibited along with the sample specification of a program transformation system. This development is guided by a continuous communication between the specifier and his client where additional valuable hints are provided by the formal properties of algebraic types. It turns out that the formal techniques already developed within the CIP project at the Technical University Munich also apply to this front end of the transformational activities.

1. Introduction

In recent years different methodologies have been developed for bridging the gap between precise, understandable, yet inefficient and sometimes even non-algorithmic specifications on the one hand and efficient programs for specific machines on the other hand. Since most problems dealt with using these methodologies either were of a comparatively moderate size (e.g. problems from mathematics) or evolved directly from the everyday problems of a computer scientist, only little care has been taken of how to reach the starting point of a reasonable program development, viz. the formal specification.

Of course, there are already attempts to tackle the problem: In several AI approaches an automatic acquisition of specifications from the user's informal description is aimed at (cf. e.g. /Balzer et al. 76/, /Green, Barstow 78/). Although this seeme to be an attractive perspective, it is somewhat unrealistic in the present state of the art. The usual proceeding in industrial environments aims at a slightly formalized but more or less verbal specification, which is sometimes reached via several inter-

---

* This research was carried out within the Sonderforschungsbereich 49, Programmiertechnik, Munich.

mediate stages by means of ad hoc techniques similar to stepwise refinement (for an overview of different approaches see /Hesse 81/). Whereas these approaches show a considerable lack of preciseness such that the resulting specifications are not suited as a basis for formal development techniques such as verification or transformation, in most of the approaches using a formal specification language the problem of how to come up with a specification is not considered at all (cf. e.g. CLEAR /Burstall, Goguen 79/, AFFIRM /Gerhart et al. 80/, OBJ /Goguen, Tardo 79/, GIST /Goldman, Wile 80/). As an attempt to provide both, a formal specification language and suitable tools to develop a specification, ESPRESO (/Ludewig 80/) has to be mentioned.

Our approach is based on the assumption that the essential parts of nearly every system can be seen as black boxes relating input and output data according to the customer's wishes. Thus an algebraic specification which defines the relations between input data and output data by suitable axioms is advocated as the basis for the formulation of a specification (see e.g. /Bauer et al. 81/ - or for a more informal introduction /Bauer, Wössner 81/). We feel that these algebraic means provide a sufficiently comprehensive frame, which fulfils nearly all the requirements postulated for good specifications in the literature (cf. e.g. /Balzer, Goldman 79/, /Wassermann 80/):

- Algebraic data types (for short "ADT" or just "types") are a suitable tool for formulating precise, formally sound specifications.

- There are already methods for further developing such a specification (e.g. by transformations, cf. /Partsch, Broy 78/, /Laut 81/, /Laut, Partsch 81/).

- By stating only the properties of a solution and not its realization, an algebraic specification is as far as possible independent of any implementation, thus giving the freedom to find the most suitable one.

- Hierarchies of ADT (/Wirsing et al. 80/) provide the necessary modularity for structuring the design; moreover the modification of individual parts is facilitated.

- Algebraic specifications are easily comprehensible even for the non-expert by simply transcribing the formally stated properties into a verbal formulation.

- Adequacy can be made plausible by deriving suitable properties from the specification, which is considerably eased by the algebraic way of specification.

2. The stepwise development of algebraic specifications exemplified

Since ADT are nothing but a particular specification language, especially the problem of how to arrive at the specification from more or less vague ideas still has to be tackled. Similar to the development of programs we propose not to produce the whole specification in one sweep but rather to develop it in small steps, which are all accompanied by a specifier-customer dialogue. This continuous communication allows us to renounce the need for specific language constructs expressing informality (as e.g. in /Ludewig 80/) and to use the algebraic means right from the beginning instead. However, the formal approach requires that the partners of the dialogue do not presuppose anything implicitly, which might be a problem in particular for a customer from another discipline than computer science.

In the following we want to analyse and characterise some of the stages of this incremental process by treating the sample task of formally specifying the functional aspects of a program transformation system. (We did not care about the user-system interface and its systematic development, cf. /Riethmayer 80/.) As a representative section of the whole sample specification we will concentrate on the development of the part dealing with program(scheme)s.

2.1. Informal requirements

The specification development process usually starts with a set of informal requirements, which are communicated to a computer scientist (the specifier) by a customer. To give an impression of the intention and the complexity of the whole sample task and additionally to localize the part we actually use for our presentation, we will start with the entire collection of the (fictive) customer's wishes, which might be communicated to the specifier in the following way:

a) The system should allow for the inputting, retrieval, and printing of program parts written in an arbitrary context-free language. It should be able to store and retrieve them in different versions and allow for the building up of a program from several individual parts. Programs and program schemes should be treated alike by the system.

b) It should be possible to apply schematic transformation rules (i.e. pairs of related program schemes) from an extensible stock (that is to be kept by the system) at a distinguished location in a given program part - including the treatment of possible applicability conditions.

c) The system should provide a library of algebraic types together with applicative or procedural standard implementations. In particular the laws of these types should be available for transformation purposes. (This inclusion of algebraic types suggests that the otherwise unspecified language used has at least the characteristics of a scheme language; cf. /Bauer et al. 81/).

d) In addition to schematic transformations it should also be possible to apply
transformations given by suitable algorithms such as fold/unfold, suppression
of unchanged parameters in functions or procedures, transition from tail-re-
cursive functions to procedures, change of types, or transition from applicative
computation structures to procedural modules (cf. /Laut 80/).

e) The system should also support syntactically correct program manipulations in a
wider sense (e.g. insertion, deletion and replacement of program parts), for the
semantical correctness of which the user is responsible himself.

f) A program development using the facilities from b) to d) should be documented;
in particular , from the documentation it should be possible to redo a development with a modified program.

g) Apart from program manipulation also all means for the execution of programs (comprising testing of context-correctness or syntactic relations, or
translation into some existing programming language) should be provided.

2.2 A first collection of functionalities

Starting from such a bunch of half-baked user ideas, the specifier - together with
the customer - tries to extract the relevant information and to come up with an
initial (tentative) collection of possible object domains (sorts) and functions
relating them by their functionalities. The important aspect in this step is to
be seen in the fact that we advocate the functions to be the origin, which implicitly defines the necessary object domains, and not the other way round. The
reason for this is obvious: the only information we have so far is about *what to do* ,
we do not know *by which means*.

Requirement a) concerns the inputting of a program for which we introduce a function
parsep with a domain __string__ and a range __program__, which are characterised in more
detail only by the other functions. How to construct the domain is implicitly determined by the verbal formulation of the respective requirement. Thus the specifier
might formulate (we use the ALGOL-variant of CIP-L, cf. /Bauer et al. 81/; obvious
quantifications are frequently omitted):

> __funct__ (__string__) __program__ parsep , __co__ parse __program__ __oc__
> __funct__ (__program__) __string__ editp   __co__ at this level retrieval and printing are not
> distinguished __oc__ ,
> __funct__ (__pstore__, __pid__, __program__) __pstore__ storep __co__ program __store__, __program__ __identifier__ __oc__ ,
> __funct__ (__pstore__, __pid__) __program__ getp ,
> __funct__ (__program__, __program__) __program__ constructp

In an analogous way we get for some of the other functions that involve the sort
__program__ (__pos__ means "position"):

```
ad b)   funct (program p, pos s, rule r : applicable(p,s,r)) program applyrule ,
        funct (program, pos, rule) bool applicable ,

ad d)   funct (program p, pos s, talg t : isapplt(p,s,t)) program applytalg
                co transformation algorithm oc
        funct (program, pos, talg) bool isapplt ,

ad e)   funct (program, pos, program) (program, pos) insertp ,
        funct (program, pos) (program, pos) deletep ,
        funct (program, pos, program) (program, pos) replacep ,

ad g)   funct (program, data) value interpretep ,
        funct (program) bool synandcontcorr
          co syntactically correct and context correct oc ,
        funct (program) code translatep
```

Apart from correcting some trivial misunderstandings, the first reaction from the
customer's side concentrates on making things more precise. In particular this
comprises simple errors like missing parameters (necessary for more information), or
redundant functions the purpose of which is already covered by others. In this way,
constructp as intended above will be eliminated, since it is already covered by
the functions for requirement e). Thus the iterated conversation between customer
and specifier finally results in a collection of functionalities corresponding
roughly to the respective (initial) requirements.

2.3. Structuring the design

The next step in the development of a specification concentrates on structuring the
information collected so far and indicating primitives as a byproduct. We believe
(see also /Ludewig 80/) that postponing this decision, e.g. until having semantically specified the functions involved, would unnecessarily complicate the design
process. By the way, this first structuring of the logical design should not be
confused with the module structure of the later implementation, since it is still
open how the logical units correspond to implementation units: If e.g. it will turn
out that one of those units is too big for being implemented by a single module, a
local decomposition can be done; if on the other hand the logical decomposition is
already too fine, thus prohibiting an efficient implementation, a combination of
several units into a single one is appropriate. In either case the necessary changes
can be performed on the level of type definitions using techniques described elsewhere (cf. e.g. "type merging" in /Laut, Partsch 81/).

The basic idea for performing the structuring is to investigate the interdepen-
dencies of the functions; this naturally leads to filtering out the primitives (viz.

sorts without constructor functions) and finding subsets of sorts which are not connected via functions. For all subsets that are not singleton sets a further partitioning is appropriate where the criteria outlined in /Parnas 72/ may serve as a valuable guideline. In our experiment this first coarse as well as the later finer structuring was done in an informal (intuitive) way; finding more formal methods is still an area of future research. Applying these ideas to our specific example, we will come to the conclusion that some of the functions concerning the sort program logically belong to other types, e.g. applyrule, applicable (and similarly applytalg, isapplt) to RULE (resp. TALG), i.e. the component dealing with transformation rules (and algorithms, resp.), or storep, getp to PSTORE, i.e. the component for the administration of program parts. Thus for the component dealing with programs we provisionally get the following type fragment:

```
type  PROGRAM ≡ program, parsep, editp, insertp, deletep, replacep, interpretep.
                synandcontcorr, translatep :
      based on  string, pos, data, value, code,
               ...                                                    endoftype
```

2.4. Refining the system structure

The combined use of programs and markings (sort pos) suggests that the respect-ive components should be combined leading to the notion of a "marked program" (which, of course, implies some modifications of the functions involved).

Typically, marked programs can be seen as a pair consisting of the program and the marking. Hence we define:

```
type  MPROG ≡ mprog, markp, prog, loc, replacep, insertp, deletep, getmarkedp :
      based on  PROGRAM, pos ,
      mode mprog ≡ markp (program prog , pos loc) ,
      funct (mprog, program) mprog replacep ,
      funct (mprog, program) mprog insertp ,
      funct (mprog) mprog deletep ,
      funct (mprog) program getmarkedp                               endoftype
```

We assume that the remaining functions for objects of sort program are collected in a type PROGRAM that will be treated later on, since a detailed treatment of MPROG will imply some more properties for programs.

For this type fragment immediately the validity of the axioms

```
∀ mprog m , program p, pos l :
    P : prog(markp(p, l)) = p ,
```

```
L :  loc(markp(p, 1)) = 1,
M :  markp(prog(m), loc(m)) = m
```

is inferred from the semantics of mode definitions in CIP-L (modes are abbreviations for certain monomorphic types). In order to further fix its semantics, MPROG can be enriched by some obvious properties, which are expected by the customer:

- insertion and deletion are "inverse" operations,
- replacement can also be done by deletion and subsequent insertion.

Simple formalization of these properties leads to the incorporation of the axioms

```
∀ mprog m, program p :
  deletep(insertp(m, p)) = m ,
  insertp(deletep(m), getmarkedp(m)) = m ,
  replacep(m, p) = insertp(deletep(m), p).
```

A further refinement requires some design decisions about the markings of programs: We assume emptypos to mark the whole program and the operation & to add a selector localizing an immediately contained program part to a marking. For simplicity, the selectors will be represented as positive natural numbers (sort pnat) and hence the markings as sequences of numbers (cf. the "Dewey decimal notation" for trees, /Knuth 68/).

2.5. Detailed treatment of individual components

In this section we deal with the most crucial step in the whole design process, where the function domains have to be restricted as far as necessary and the semantics of the intended system has to be specified by defining suitable axioms. Since the envisaged system is already decomposed into logical units, each of them can be treated separately. Moreover our actual experiment showed that instead of working bottom-up it is preferable to elaborate the detailed specifications for the individual units top-down (with respect to the system structure): A "higher" unit often requires properties from the respective "lower" ones that are usually not considered when dealing with the "lower" unit first; by first dealing with the "higher" unit these requirements are simply inferred on the "lower" one and taken care of during its elaboration such that backtrack can be avoided.
While defining the semantics by formulating suitable axioms it is advisable to have already the formal criteria such as sufficient completeness in mind. This leads to first concentrating on the constructors and their properties and then defining the remaining functions relative to them (cf. /Guttag, Horning 78/, /Broy, Wirsing 81/). Frequently this leads to axioms which are different from those naively postulated; this in turn means that the previous axioms have to be verified as theorems based

on the new ones. Here the use of algebraic specification tools in connection with program transformations turns out to be advantageous too (cf. also /Gerhart et al. 80/): If a system for performing transformations is available (for an overview see /Partsch, Steinbrüggen 81/), the clerical work involved in proving or deriving theorems can be significantly supported by this system: either by simply doing the replacement steps in derivation chains (according to the axioms of the type), or - more advanced - by generating the verification conditions for data type induction proofs (cf. /Wirsing et al. 80/).

Sometimes it will also be advantageous to decompose the whole step into two more basic ones, the first of which yields a specification without any domain restrictions and the second modifies this result by superposing the respective restrictions (an example for this way of proceeding can be found in /Steinbrüggen 80/).

2.5.1. The component MPROG

For MPROG wea arrive at the following (sufficiently complete) specification. Note that replacep has no effect on the marking whereas for both insertp and deletep the environment of the marked position has to be taken care of.

```
type MPROG ≡ mprog, markp, prog, loc, replacep, insertp, deletep, getmarkedp:
     based on PROGRAM, pos, pnat ,
     mode mprog ≡ markp(program prog, pos loc : selectable(prog, loc)) ,
     funct (mprog m, program p : replaceable(prog(m), loc(m), p)) mprog replacep,
         law R : replaceable(p, s, p1) ⇒
                 replacep(markp(p, s), p₁) = markp(ins(del(p, s), s, p₁), s) ,
     funct(mprog m, pnat i, program p : insertable(prog(m), loc(m)& i, p)) mprog
                                        insertp ,
         law I : insertable(p, s & i, p₁) ⇒
                 insert(markp(p, s), i, p₁) = markp(ins(p, s & i, p₁), s) ,
     funct (mprog m, pnat i : deletable (prog(m), loc(m) & i)) mprog deletep ,
         law D :  deletable(p, s & i) ⇒
                 deletep(markp(p, s), i) = markp(del(p, s & i), s),
     funct (mprog) program getmarkedp ,
         law G : getmarkedp(markp(p, s)) = get(p, s)
                                                      endoftype
```

Note that in the above specification of MPROG the problems of the partiality with respect to selectability, insertability, replaceability, deletability as well as the preservation of syntactical correctness (including context-correctness) are transferred to the respective basic functions of PROGRAM .

Now we have to show that the previous properties of MPROG are derivable theorems. For this purpose a few assumptions are additionally made (which will be indicated

in the proof below) about the (in this context) primitive functions del, ins, and
get of PROGRAM .

$$insertable(prog(m), loc(m) \& i, p) \Rightarrow deletep(insertp(m, i, p), i) = m$$

Proof:

For the sake of simplicity we leave considerations on definedness (which are along
the same lines) to the reader.

Since markp is the only constructor for _mprog_ we have
(with (*) $m = markp(p_1, s)$)

$$
\begin{aligned}
&deletep(insertp(m, i, p), i) = &&((*))\\
&deletep(insertp(markp(p_1, s), i, p), i) = &&(I)\\
&deletep(markp(ins (p_1, s \& i, p), s), i) = &&(D)\\
&markp(del (ins (p_1, s \& i, p), s \& i), s) = &&((1) \text{ see below})\\
&markp(p_1, s) = m &&((*))
\end{aligned}
$$

where (1) is the property

$$del(ins(p, s, q), s) = p$$

which is to be provided by the component PROGRAM .   □

The other properties, viz.

$$insertp(deletep(markp(p, s), i), i, getmarkedp(markp(p, s \& i))) = markp(p, m),$$

$$replacep(markp(p, s \& i), p_1) = markp(prog(insertp(deletep(markp(p, s), i), i, p_1)), s \& i)$$

can be proved in an analogous way, again using properties similar to (1) above.

<u>2.5.2 The component PROGRAM</u>

As to the remaining functions intended for programs, another decomposition seems to
be advantageous. Remembering the customer's wish of language-independency, a partition
along this criterion is at hand. However, for further detailing the specification we
have to make at least some assumptions on objects of sort _program_ . Since independent
of the particular language used every program can be uniquely represented by its
syntax tree, we decide to define all objects of sort _program_ to be constructable
from the basic functions maketree and addchild provided by the basic type TREE
(cf. /Laut 81/). maketree(n) builds a singleton tree with node value n ;
addchild(t, t1) attaches t1 as rightmost child of t . Further we use the function
rank(t) yielding the number of children of the tree t and the function child(t,i)
which for $1 \le i \le rank(t)$ gives the i-th child of t .

Of course, not all the _tree_ objects are indeed suited to represent programs; the
admissible ones are further charaterized by the predicate synandcontcorr. This

function forms another type PR , which is based on TREE and which again leads
to a decomposition of PROGRAM into LDFPROG (language dependent functions for
programs) and the remaining functions that are collected in a type PROG. Note
that instead of working with primitive types we could also have used parametrized
types (cf./Wirsing, Broy 81/) with the syntax of the language as parameter.

Altogether we have the following hierarchical structure ("→" denotes the based on -
relation)

$$
\begin{array}{ccc}
 & \text{MPROG} & \\
 \swarrow & & \searrow \\
 \text{PROGRAM} & & \underline{\text{pos}} \\
 \swarrow \quad \searrow & & \\
 \text{LDFPROG} \quad \text{PROG} & & \\
 \searrow \quad \swarrow & & \\
 \text{PR} & & \\
 \downarrow & & \\
 \text{TREE} & &
\end{array}
$$

where

   <u>type</u> PR ≡ <u>program</u>, maketree, addchild, rank, child, synandcontcorr :
      <u>based</u> <u>on</u> TREE , <u>co</u> the sort <u>program</u> is supposed to be defined by TREE <u>oc</u>
      <u>funct</u> (<u>program</u>) <u>bool</u> synandcontcorr   <u>endoftype</u>

   <u>type</u> LDFPROG ≡ parsep, editp, interpretep, translatep :
      <u>based</u> <u>on</u> PR, <u>string</u>, <u>data</u>, <u>value</u>, <u>code</u> ,
      <u>funct</u> (<u>string</u>) <u>program</u> parsep ,
      <u>funct</u> (<u>program</u>) <u>string</u> editp ,
         <u>law</u> parsep(editp(p)) = p ,
      <u>funct</u> (<u>program</u>, <u>data</u>) <u>value</u> interpretep ,
      <u>funct</u> (<u>program</u>) <u>code</u> translatep   <u>endoftype</u>

   <u>type</u> PROG ≡ <u>program</u>, ins, get, del, replaceable, selectable, deletable, insertable :
      <u>based</u> <u>on</u> PR, <u>pnat</u>, <u>pos</u> ,
      <u>funct</u> (<u>program</u>, <u>pos</u>) <u>bool</u> selectable ,
         SELAO : selectable(p, emptypos) ,
         SELA1 : selectable(p,i & s) = <u>if</u> i ≤ rank(p) <u>then</u> selectable(child(p,i),s)
                                                    <u>else</u> <u>false</u>   <u>fi</u> ,
      <u>funct</u> (<u>program</u> p, <u>pos</u> s : selectable(p,s)) <u>program</u> get ,
         <u>laws</u> ∀ (<u>program</u> p, <u>pnat</u> i, <u>pos</u> s : selectable(p, i & s)) :
         GETO : get(p, emptypos) = p ,
         GET1 : get(p, i & s) = get(child(p, i), s) ,

      <u>funct</u> (<u>program</u>, <u>pos</u>, <u>program</u>) <u>bool</u> insable ,
         <u>laws</u> ∀ (<u>program</u> p, <u>pnat</u> i, <u>pos</u> s : ¬ isempty(s)) :
         INSAO : ¬ insable(p, emptypos) ,
         INSA1 : insable(p, i & emptypos) = (i ≤ rank(p) + 1) ,

INSA2 : insable(p, i & s) = <u>if</u> i ≤ rank(p) <u>then</u> insable(child(p,i), s)
<u>else</u> <u>false</u>   <u>fi</u>

<u>funct</u> (<u>program</u> p, <u>pos</u> s, <u>program</u> p_1 : insable(p, s, p_1)) <u>program</u> ins ,
    <u>laws</u> ∀ (<u>program</u> p, p_1, p', <u>pnat</u> i, <u>pos</u> s : insable(addchild(p, p'), i & s)) :
    INS1 : ins(p, (rank(p) + 1) & emptypos, p_1) = addchild(p, p_1),
    INS2 : i ≤ rank(p) + 1 ⟹ ins(addchild(p, p'), i & s, p_1) =
        <u>if</u> i = rank(p) + 1 ∧ ¬ isempty(s)
          <u>then</u> addchild(p, ins(p', s, p_1))
          <u>else</u> addchild(ins(p, i & s, p_1), p') <u>fi</u> ,

<u>funct</u> (<u>program</u> p, <u>pos</u> s : ¬ isempty(s) ∧ selectable(p, s)) <u>program</u> del ,
    <u>laws</u> ∀ (<u>program</u> p, p', <u>pnat</u> i, <u>pos</u> s : selectable(addchild(p, p'), i & s)) :
    DEL : del(addchild(p, p'), i & s) =
        <u>if</u> i = rank(p) + 1
          <u>then</u> <u>if</u> isempty(s) <u>then</u> p
                <u>else</u> addchild(p, del(p', s)) <u>fi</u>
          <u>else</u> addchild(del(p, i & s), p')   <u>fi</u> ,

<u>funct</u>(<u>program</u>, <u>pos</u>, <u>program</u>) <u>bool</u> replaceable,
<u>funct</u>(<u>program</u>, <u>pos</u>, <u>program</u>) <u>bool</u> insertable,
<u>funct</u>(<u>program</u>, <u>pos</u>) <u>bool</u> deletable,
    RA : replaceable(p, s, p_1) = <u>if</u> ¬ isempty(s) ∧ selectable(p, s)
          <u>then</u> synandcontcorr(ins(del(p, s), s, p_1)
          <u>else</u> <u>false</u>   <u>fi</u> ,

    IA : insertable(p, s, p_1) = <u>if</u> insable(p, s)
          <u>then</u> synandcontcorr(ins(p, s, p_1))
          <u>else</u> <u>false</u>   <u>fi</u> ,

    DA : deletable(p, s) = if ¬ isempty(s) ∧ selectable(p, s)
          <u>then</u> synandcontcorr(del(p, s))
          <u>else</u> <u>false</u>   <u>fi</u>   <u>endoftype</u>

and finally

  <u>type</u> PROGRAM ≡ <u>program</u>, ins, get, del, replaceable, selectable, deleteable,
            insertable, parsep, editp, interpretep, translatep :
    <u>based</u> <u>on</u> LDFPROG, PROG   <u>endoftype</u>

As in MPROG we have to show that the above specification allows the derivation of
the former properties such as
    insable(p_1, s) ⟹ del(ins(p_1, s, p_2), s) = p_1
or
    ¬ isempty(s) ∧ selectable(p, s) ⟹ ins(del(p,s), s, get(p, s)) = p
which again requires data type induction.

2.6. Formal examination of the specification

The specification obtained so far is now subjected to a formal process in order to
filter out information about (sufficient) completeness, consistency, monomorphicity
(or more general, existence of certain models) and leads to a formally sound, consoli-
dated specification, occasionally after some iterations where e.g. previously stated
properties have to be reformulated to meet the formalism.

We will not deal with all the details here since this would go beyound the scope
of the paper. A detailed treatment of these fundamental notions and how to formally
analyse hierarchical types can be found elsewhere (cf. e.g. /Guttag, Horning 78/,
/Wirsing, Broy 81/).

In /Laut 81/ the type TREE is shown to be consistent, sufficiently complete and
monomorphic. For PR , which is an operational enrichment (cf. /Broy et al. 80/)
of TREE , in its present form no definitive statement is possible since the
language-dependent function synandcontcorr is not yet specified at all. However,
from our restriction to context-free languages we know that this predicate is decidable
and that there exists a sufficiently complete and monomorphic specification.

The types LDFPROG, PROG, PROGRAM and, apart from the product mode, also MPROG
are operational enrichments, too. Here only some care has to be taken with respect
to hierarchy-consistency, e.g. when actually specifying parsep we have to make
sure that it is no further constructor for program objects. Monomorphicity
of all these types becomes plausible by the observation that all program (or mprog
resp.) objects are uniquely representable by the constructors provided by TREE ,
POS, and the product mode.

2.7. On Adequacy

It is well-known that it cannot be proved that a specification really reflects the
customer's wishes. But the confidence in the specification being a formalization
of what the customer actually wants can be significantly improved by formally
deriving additional properties of the specification, using the axioms, already proved
properties, and data type induction (see also /Parnas 72/, /Guttag, Horning 80/).
Obviously this "adequacy check" can be done in two directions: The customer may ask
questions (also about properties which are evident to himself) that have to be answered by the specification, or the specifier presents derived properties to the customer to be prompted (or also rejected, which would cause another iteration on the
specification). As already stated, mechanical support systems could help in reducing
the clerical work involved.

For our specific example the customer requires that (under suitable definedness restrictions) for the replace operation the property

$$\text{replaceable}(m, p_1) \wedge \text{replaceable}(m, p_2) \Rightarrow$$
$$\text{replace}(\text{replace}(m, p_1), p_2) = \text{replace}(m, p_2)$$

should hold. This can be prompted by the specification in the following way: w. l.o.g. we can assume $m = \text{markp}(p, s)$; then

$$\text{replace}(\text{replace}(m, p_1), p_2) =$$
$$\text{replace}(\text{replace}(\text{markp}(p, s), p_1), p_2) = \qquad \text{(R, twice)}$$
$$\text{markp}(\text{ins}(\text{del}(\text{ins}(\text{del}(p,s),s,p_1),s),s,p_2),s) = \text{(theorem}$$
$$\text{of } 2.5.2)$$
$$\text{markp}(\text{ins}(\text{del}(p,s),s,p_2),s) = \qquad \text{(R)}$$
$$\text{replace}(\text{markp}(p,s), p_2) = \text{replace}(m, p_2)$$

Another interesting question from the customer's side is whether the insert operation is commutative. When trying to prove

$$\text{insertable}(m, i, p_1) \wedge \text{insertable}(m, j, p_2) \wedge i \neq j \Rightarrow$$
$$\text{insertp}(\text{insertp}(m,i,p_1),j,p_2) = \text{insertp}(\text{insertp}(m,j,p_2), i,p_1)$$

it turns out that this property does not hold (which simply can be seen from the trivial case where $m = \text{markp}(\text{addchild}(p,p'), \text{emptypos})$, $i = \text{rank}(p), j = i + 1$).

But simultaneously the specifier got a hint for another closely related property, viz.

$$\text{insertable}(m,i,p_1) \wedge \text{insertable}(m,j,p_2) \wedge 0 < i \leq j \Rightarrow$$
$$\text{insertp}(\text{insertp}(m,i,p_1), j, p_2) = \text{insertp}(\text{insertp}(m,j-1,p_2), i,p_1)$$

which can be proved to hold (and which actually is the one the customer had in mind). Additionally similar properties can be proved to hold for the delete operation whereas for selecting marked programs some kind of "associativity" can be proved

$$\text{selectable}(p,s_1 \& s_2) \Rightarrow$$
$$\text{getmarkedp}(\text{markp}(\text{getmarkedp}(\text{markp}(p,s_1)), s_2)) = \text{getmarkedp}(\text{markp}(p,s_1 \& s_2))$$

Of course, similar to testing, this process of deriving additional properties cannot be exhaustive; more properties can be found e.g. in /Rosen 73/.

If in this final step no more backtracking is necessary for checking adequacy, the specification as elaborated till now can be taken as a "contract" for a further development, which both partners - the specifier and the customer - can agree upon.

3. Concluding remarks

The incremental way of developing an algebraic system specification by a continuous
specifier-customer dialogue as outlined in the previous section may be visualized
in the following diagram, which is to be considered as a guideline leaving enough
freedom for individual design decisions rather than an inflexible development scheme:

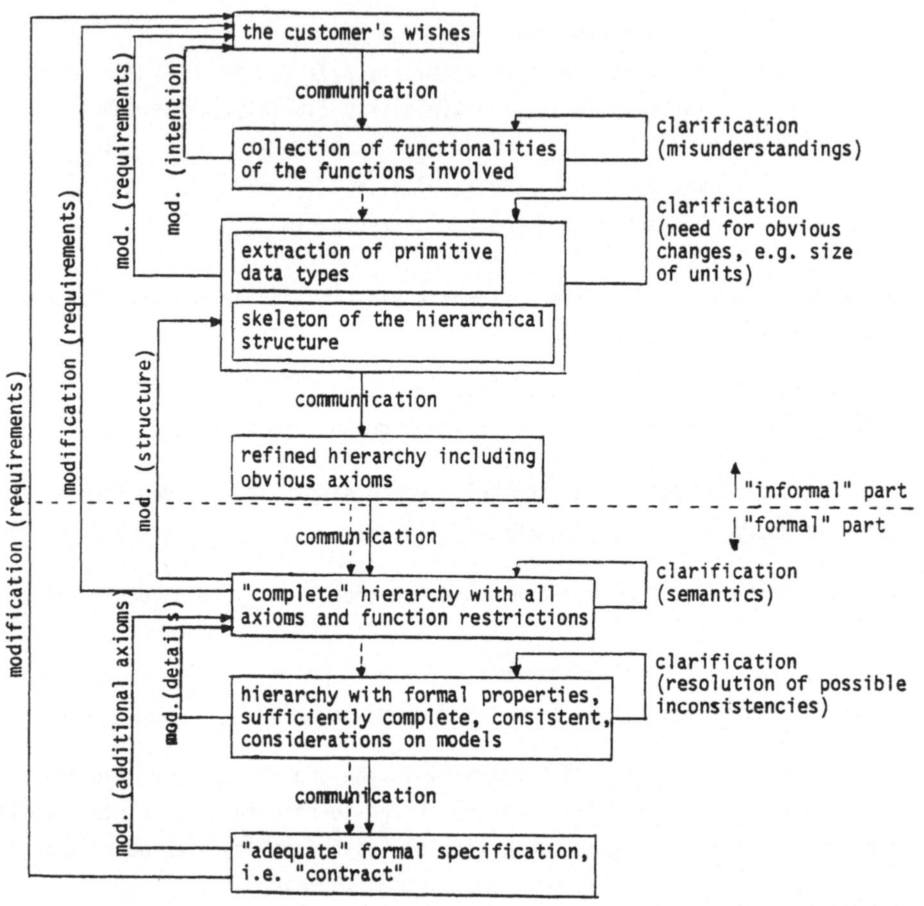

(--→ denotes activities from the specifier's side)

In this process (where maybe certain stages/actions can be combined whereas
others should be decomposed) usually several iterations will be necessary. Those
labelled by "clarification" comprise the explanation of a certain stage to the
customer and the processing of his reaction (if the design is influenced by it)
as well as information from the customer's side to make things more precise; those
labelled by "modification" indicate genuine backtrack steps (sometimes involved
by preceding clarification).

Summarizing, an incremental way of developing an algebraic specification as proposed and illustrated above has several advantages over always working with a complete specification as the only topic of communication:

A formal specification of a non-trivial system cannot be written all at once anyhow, and if the customer can intervene at every single step (where the design decisions involved are easily detected and localized and even can be marked as handles for possible future modifications), the amount of backtracking and duplication of work will drastically be reduced whereas the chance that the specification is adequate obviously increases. Moreover it will be easier for a non-expert customer to gradually understand small portions of a formal specification than to be confronted with all the formal stuff as a whole.

Another attractive aspect of the stepwise approach lies in the fact that some of the (anyhow necessary) activities can be done formally (and perhaps even mechanically) or at least guided by elaborate (formally based) methods, e. g. the extraction of primitives and the structuring of the functionalities into units, the addition of domain restrictions and their consequences for the axioms, the formal examination of ADTs for completeness and consistency, and the verification or derivation of additional properties of the specification.

<u>Acknowledgement:</u> We would like to thank P. Pepper, M. Wirsing, and H. Wössner for valuable comments and suggestions.

References

Balzer, R., Goldman, N. (1979): Principles of good software specification and their implications for specification languages. Proc. Int. Conf. on Specifications of Reliable Software, Cambridge, Ma., 1979

Balzer, R., Goldman, N., Wile, D. (1976): On the transformational implementation approach to programming. Proc. 2nd Int. Conf. on Software Engineering, San Francisco, Ca., 1976, 337-344

Bauer, F.L., Wössner, H. (1981): Algorithmische Sprache und Programmentwicklung. Berlin-Heidelberg-New York: Springer 1981

Bauer, F.L., Broy, M., Dosch, W., Geiselbrechtinger, F., Hesse, W., Gnatz, R., Krieg-Brückner, B., Laut, A., Matzner, T., Möller, B., Partsch, H., Pepper, P., Samelson, K., Wirsing, M., Wössner, H. (1981): Report on a wide spectrum language for program specification and development. Institut für Informatik der TU München, TUM-I8104, 1981

Broy, M., Wirsing, M. (1981): On the algebraic extensions of abstract data types. Int. Coll. on Formalization of Programming Concepts, Peniscola, Spain, 1981, 244-251

Broy, M., Möller, B., Pepper, P., Wirsing, M. (1980): A model-independent approach to implementations of abstract data types. Proc Symp. on Algorithmic Logic and the Programming Language LOGLAN, Poznan, Poland, 1980. Lecture Notes in Computer Science (to appear)

Burstall, R.M., Goguen, J.A. (1979): The semantics of CLEAR, a specification language.
Proc. 1979 Copenhagen Winter School on Abstract Software Specification. Lecture
Notes in Computer Science 86, 292-332 (1980)

Gerhart, S.L., Musser, D.R., Thompson, D.H., Baker, D.A., Bates, R.L., Erickson,
R.W., London, R.L., Taylor, D.G., Wile, D.S. (1980): An overview of AFFIRM: A
specification and verification system. In: Lavington, S.H. (ed.): Information
Processing 80. Amsterdam: North-Holland 1980, 343-347

Goguen, J.A., Tardo, J. (1979): An introduction to OBJ-T. Proc. Int. Conf. on Specifications of Reliable Software, Cambridge, Ma., 1979

Goldman, N., Wile, D. (1980): A relational data base for process specification.
In: Chen (ed.): Entity relationship approach to systems analysis and design.
Amsterdam: North-Holland 1980

Green, C., Barstow, D. (1978): On program synthesis knowledge. Artificial Intelligence
10, 241-279 (1978)

Guttag, J.V., Horning, J.J. (1978): The algebraic specification of abstract data
types. Acta Informatica 10, 27-52 (1978)

Hesse, W. (1981): Methoden und Werkzeuge zur Software-Entwicklung: Einordnung und
Überblick. In: Goos, G. (ed.): Werkzeuge der Programmiertechnik. Informatik-Fachberichte 43, 113-153 (1981)

Knuth, D.E. (1968): The art of computer programming, Vol. 1. Reading, Ma.: Addison-
Wesley 1968

Laut, A. (1980): Safe procedural implementations of algebraic types. Inf. Proc.
Letters 11, 147-151 (1980)

Laut, A. (1981): Developing algebraic specifications of threaded data structure
implementations. In: Goos, G. (ed.): Werkzeuge der Programmiertechnik. Informatik-
Fachberichte 43, 28-40 (1981)

Laut, A., Partsch, H. (1981): Merging algebraic types (in preparation)

Ludewig, J. (1980): Zur Erstellung der Spezifikation von Prozeßrechner-Software.
Fachbereich Mathematik der TU München, Dissertation, 1980

Parnas, D.L. (1972): On the criteria to be used in decomposing systems into modules.
Comm. ACM 15, 1053-1058 (1972)

Partsch, H., Broy, M. (1978): Examples for change of types and object structures.
In: Bauer, F.L., Broy, M. (eds.): Program construction. Lecture Notes in Computer
Science 69, 322-405 (1979)

Partsch, H., Steinbrüggen, R. (1981): A comprehensive survey on program transformation systems. Institut für Informatik der TU München, TUM-I8108, 1981

Riethmayer, H.-O. (1981): Die Entwicklung der Bedienungskomponente des CIP-Systems.
Notizen zur interaktiven Programmierung 6, GI-Fachausschuß 2, 1981

Rosen, B.K. (1973): Tree-manipulating systems and Church-Rosser-theorems. Journal ACM
20, 160-187 (1973)

Steinbrüggen, R. (1980): Pre-algorithmic specifications of the system CIP, Part 1.
Institut für Informatik der TU München, TUM-I8016 (1980)

Wassermann, A.I. (1980): Information system design methodology. Journal of the American Society for Information Science, January 1980, 5-24

Wirsing, M., Broy, M. (1981): An analysis of semantic models for algebraic specifications. Working material for the Int. Summer School on Theoretical Foundations of
Programming Methodology, Marktoberdorf, 1981

Wirsing, M., Pepper, P., Partsch, H., Dosch, W., Broy, M. (1980): On hierarchies of
abstract data types. Institut für Informatik der TU München, TUM-I8007, 1980

Generierung von Programmen für kommerzielle Anwendungen auf Kleinrechnern

Thomas M. Schünemann, Walter Ullmer

Ordinariat für Betriebswirtschaftliche DV
Universität Hamburg

Abstract

In business, small computing systems are used mainly by unexperienced users. Program systems for commercial applications are generally complex, due to the high number of interdependent functions and data. Such software can only be offered economically if it is supplied to several users. Therefore, software for small computing systems requires reliability, robustness, flexibility and user friendliness as well as rentability. Available programming languages do not have sufficient properties to enforce the development and maintenance of programs meeting these requirements.

This report focuses on a programming aid generating complete program systems for commercial applications. The main functions of the generator and the high level programming language for the input are outlined. The application of the generator is demonstrated using detailed examples.

The generator has been applied for the complete generation of a standard accounting-system which is in use in more than seventy companies. The success of the generator is based on the modularity and the consistent administration of the elements as well as on the interactive programming interface.

Inhalt

1. Programmierung kommerzieller Anwendungen

Kommerzielle Anwendungen umfassen Programmsysteme für administrative Aufgaben im betrieblichen Bereich. Typische Beispiele sind Finanzbuchhaltung, Auftragsbearbeitung und Materialwirtschaft. Wesentliche Eigenschaften kommerzieller Anwendungen sind Umfang der Programmsysteme, Einfachheit der Algorithmen und vorwiegend ein-/ausgabeorientierte Verarbeitung, insbesondere Bildschirmdialog und Druckausgabe.

1.1 Anforderungen an kommerzielle Anwendungen

Anforderungen an kommerzielle Anwendungen werden bestimmt durch Komplexität, Qualität und Wirtschaftlichkeit.

Die Komplexität der Programmsysteme resultiert aus dem Umfang und der hohen Integration der Funktionen. Die Komplexität der zu verarbeitenden Daten ergibt sich aus der Abbildung der Anwendungen im Datenmodell und in der Schnittstelle zum Benutzer, der Benutzeroberfläche (1).

Die Qualität der Programmsysteme wird durch die Benutzeroberfläche und die bei der Erstellung und Pflege eingesetzten softwaretechnologischen Methoden bestimmt (2). Die Benutzeroberfläche kommerzieller Anwendungen muss insbesondere den DV-Laien berücksichtigen, der spezifische Anforderungen bezüglich Einheitlichkeit, Einfachheit und Sicherheit stellt. Der Einsatz softwaretechnologischer Methoden zur Erhöhung der Wartungsfreundlichkeit ist bei kommerziellen Anwendungen notwendig, weil die Programme während ihres Einsatzes zahlreichen Änderungen und Erweiterungen unterliegen.

Die Wirtschaftlichkeit wird durch den bei kommerziellen Anwendungen möglichen Mehrfacheinsatz von Programmsystemen und Programmteilen bestimmt. Der Mehrfacheinsatz erfordert Standardisierung, Flexibilität und Portabilität der Software (3).

1.2 Anforderungen an die Programmiersprache

Anforderungen an kommerzielle Anwendungen bestimmen Anforderungen an die Programmiersprache bzgl. Strukturierungsfähigkeit, Mächtigkeit und Dokumentationsfähigkeit.

Die Strukturierungsfähigkeit der Programmiersprache ist Voraussetzung für den Einsatz der Modularen Programmierung, die zur Zeit am besten geeignete Methode zur Strukturierung von Programmen und Programmsystemen (4). Programme und Programmsysteme sollten aus einzelnen Elementen unterschiedlicher Elementtypen bestehen, die automatisch kombiniert werden, wobei keine zusätzliche Information über die Struktur des generierten Programms benötigt wird. Die Strukturierung ermöglicht die unabhängige Erstellung und Pflege einzelner Elemente (5).

Die Mächtigkeit der Programmiersprache wird durch die Verwendung problemorientierter Datenstrukturen und Operationen gewährleistet. Standard-Elemente sollten allgemeine Funktionen abdecken. Innerhalb eines Elementes sind Varianten für unterschiedliche Benutzer und Funktionen vorzusehen.

Die Dokumentationsfähigkeit der Programmiersprache erfordert übersichtliche, selbsterklärende Sprachelemente und umfassende Kommentierungsmöglichkeiten. Namenskonventionen legen Aufbau und Bedeutung von Namen fest. Leerzeilen und Einrücken sind zusätzliche Hilfsmittel. Unabhängig von der Eingabe sollte die Ausgabe von Elementen auf Bildschirm und Liste in einer einheitlichen, aufbereiteten Form erfolgen.

1.3 Programmiersprachen auf Kleinrechnern

Als Kleinrechner werden Systeme mit ein oder zwei Bildschirmen, Disketten und Matrixdrucker bezeichnet. Trotz marktfähiger Weiterentwicklungen, z.B. Plattenspeichern, ist die genannte Konfiguration typisch. Die Entwicklung des DV-Marktes zeigt eine steigende Nachfrage von Erstanwendern nach Kleinrechnern (6). Erstanwender stellen hohe Anforderungen an die Software und gehen von niedrigen Preisobergrenzen aus (7). Das gegenwärtige Marktangebot von Software für Kleinrechner ist hinsichtlich der Qualität unzureichend.

Kleinrechner werden fast ausschließlich in BASIC programmiert (8). BASIC wurde für die interaktive Programmierung auf einem Time-Sharing System als leicht zu erlernende und einfache Programmiersprache entwickelt (9). BASIC eignet sich zur Programmierung einfacher technisch-wissenschaftlicher Anwendungen durch den Anfänger. Zur Realisierung kommerzieller Anwendungen ist BASIC nicht geeignet.

Die Strukturierungsfähigkeit von BASIC ist unzureichend. Programmstrukturen werden durch die Verwendung von Zeilennummern und Referenzen auf diese Zeilennummern realisiert, wobei der Umfang der Zeilennummern eingeschränkt ist. Getrennte Programme sind nur isoliert aufrufbar, dasselbe Programmteil kann nicht in unterschiedlichen Programmen verwendet werden. Unterprogramme sind nicht parametrisierbar, die Verwendung von Funktionen ist für diese Zwecke ungeeignet. Als Kontrollstruktur ist der (bedingte) Sprung auf eine Zeilennummer und die Schleife mit Laufvariable verfügbar.

Die Mächtigkeit von BASIC wird durch den extrem einfachen Sprachumfang bestimmt, insbesondere für E/A-Operationen und zur Aufbereitung der Ausgabe. Als Datenstrukturen stehen nur elementare Standardtypen und indizierte Variable zur Verfügung.

Die Dokumentationsfähigkeit von BASIC beschränkt sich auf die Verwendung programm-
interner Kommentare, die bei interpretierenden DV-Systemen während der Ausführung
den Hauptspeicher belasten. Variablennamen sind in der Regel ein- oder zweistellig.
Strukturen, z.B. Unterprogramme, werden durch Nummern benannt.

Als Alternative zu BASIC wird PASCAL zunehmend auf Kleinrechnern eingesetzt. PASCAL
bietet zwar Möglichkeiten zur Strukturierung, erzwingt aber nicht deren Anwendung.
Die Mächtigkeit von PASCAL ist in dem für kommerzielle Anwendungen wichtigen Bereich
der E/A-Operationen unzureichend.

Aus der Marktsituation für Kleinrechner mit dem überwiegenden Einsatz von BASIC und
dem Mangel an geeigneten Alternativen ergibt sich die Notwendigkeit, Hilfsmittel zur
Erstellung und Pflege von Programmen für kommerzielle Anwendungen zu entwickeln (10).
Im folgenden wird ein System zur Generierung derartiger Programme in der Zielsprache
BASIC vorgestellt.

2.   Beschreibung des Generierungs-Systems

Zur Implementation eines Generierungs-Systems sind Kleinrechner nicht geeignet. Das
Generierungs-System wird daher auf einem Entwicklungsrechner mit höherer Verarbei-
tungsgeschwindigkeit und Speicherkapazität implementiert. Die generierten Programme
werden vom Entwicklungsrechner auf den Kleinrechner übertragen.

Das Generierungs-System ist charakterisiert durch die Funktionen, die dem Programm-
mierer zur Verfügung gestellt werden, und die Programmiersprache, in der der Programmierer Programme erstellt.

2.1 Funktionen

Das Generierungs-System umfasst die Funktionen Edieren, Verwalten und Generieren.
Alle Funktionen greifen auf die Elementdatenbank zu (s. Abb. 1).

Elementdatenbank: Die Elementdatenbank enthält alle Elemente, die zur Generierung
von Programmen und Programmsystemen erforderlich sind. Das Generierungs-System prüft
die Beziehungen zwischen Elementen auf Konsistenz. Es werden Daten- und Verarbeitungselemente unterschieden. Datenelemente sind Datenfelder und daraus gebildete,
komplexe Datenstrukturen. Der Programmierer deklariert neue Datenfelder mit einer
speziellen Funktion und vermeidet dadurch Redundanz. Verarbeitungselemente sind programmspezifische Elemente oder Standard-Elemente. Verarbeitungselemente entsprechen
den Moduln der Modularen Programmierung.

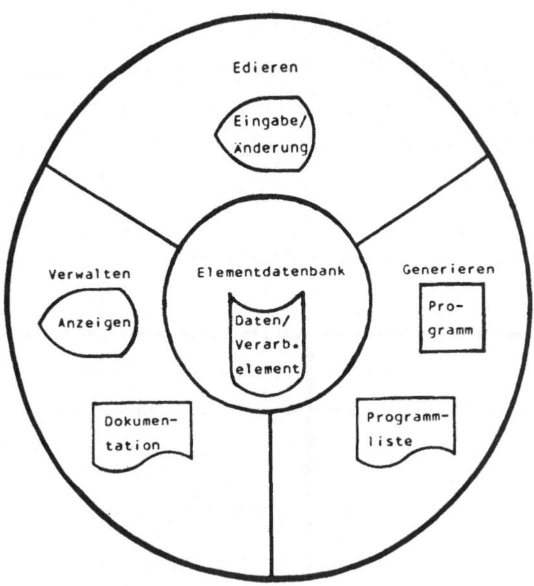

Abb. 1:   Funktionen des Generierungs-Systems

<u>Edieren:</u> Der Programmierer gibt neue Elemente ein und ändert vorhandene Elemente. Für die unterschiedlichen Elementtypen stehen spezifische Eingabeformate zur Verfügung. Das Edieren wird durch zusätzliche Funktionen unterstützt (z.B. Suchen von Textstrings und Anzeigen anderer Elemente). Gleichzeitig erfolgt eine interaktive Syntaxprüfung.

<u>Verwalten:</u> Zur Unterstützung des Programmierers gibt das Generierungs-System gespeicherte Elemente wahlweise auf dem Bildschirm oder in Listenform aus. Der Programmierer kann weitere Auswertungen abrufen (z.B. Inhaltsverzeichnisse und Referenzlisten).

<u>Generieren:</u> Das Generierungs-System generiert Programme und Programmsysteme für den vom Programmierer vorgegebenen Zielrechner in der vorgegebenen Version der Zielsprache. Beim Aufruf der Generierung gibt der Programmierer die Namen der zu generierenden Programme ein.

2.2 Programmiersprache

Die im Generierungs-System verwendete Programmiersprache berücksichtigt die im ersten Abschnitt genannten Anforderungen an die Programmiersprache zur Erstellung von Programmen für kommerzielle Anwendungen. Im folgenden werden wesentliche Merkmale der Programmiersprache des Generierungs-Systems beschrieben.

<u>Namenskonventionen:</u> Namen der Datenfelder umfassen maximal 13 Stellen und werden aus einer vorgegebenen Menge von Präfixen, Infixen und Suffixen aufgebaut. Präfix, Infix und Suffix sind hierarchisch geordnete, mnemotechnische Abkürzungen. Der aus diesen Abkürzungen zusammengesetzte Name kennzeichnet eindeutig Inhalt und Funktion des Datenfeldes (s. Tabelle 1).

Tabelle 1: Namenskonventionen für Datenfeldnamen

Datenfeldname	Beispiel: 'IA.SKT.KTOINT'
Präfix: Funktion	dateispezifische Kennzeichnung IA = Interne Anwenderdatei
Infix : Spezifikation	Bereich in der Datei SKT = Skonto
Suffix: Inhalt	KTO = Konto / INT = intern

Namen aller übrigen Elemente der Elementdatenbank umfassen maximal 8 Stellen und dienen zur Klassifizierung der unterschiedlichen Elementtypen hinsichtlich ihrer Funktion. Tabelle 2 zeigt beispielhaft Namenskonventionen für programmspezifische Verarbeitungselemente und Standard-Verarbeitungselemente.

Tabelle 2: Namenskonventionen für Verarbeitungselemente

prog.sp. Verarbeitungselement	Beispiel: 'B1101H2'
Programmsystem	B = Buchhaltung
Funktionsbereich	1 = tägliche Verarbeitung
Programmnummer	10 = Erfassen
Version	1 = Standard
Funktion im Programm	H = Hauptverarbeitung
Spezifikation	2 = Einlesen Buchungssatz

Standard-Verarbeitungselement	Beispiel: 'XRIAS' - Dateizugriff
Standard-Element	X
Funktion	R = Lesen
Dateiname	IA = Interne Anwenderdatei
Zugriffsart	S = sequentiell

<u>Strukturierung der Verarbeitungselemente:</u> Verarbeitungselemente werden entsprechend der Modularen Programmierung unabhängig erstellt und gepflegt. Ein Programm ist ein Verarbeitungselement. Jedes Verarbeitungselement kann untergeordnete Verarbeitungselemente als Unterprogramme mit Eingabe-/Ausgabe-/Update-Parametern aufrufen oder auf eingebundene Verarbeitungselemente springen. Zusätzliche Sprungmarken innerhalb eines Verarbeitungselements dürfen nur in demselben Verarbeitungselement angesprochen werden. Anfang und Ende des Verarbeitungselements sind implizit deklarierte Sprungmarken. Teile von Verarbeitungselementen werden gekennzeichnet, um bei der Generierung unterschiedlicher Programme Varianten desselben Verarbeitungselements zu erzeugen. Die Erzeugung von Varianten ermöglicht z.B. die Einsparung von Code und die Generierung von Sonderfunktionen. Für bestimmte Klassen von Verarbeitungselementen stehen allgemeine Rahmen zur Verfügung, die der Programmierer beim Edieren kopiert und aufgabenspezifisch ergänzt.

<u>Deklaration von Datenelementen:</u> Datenfelder werden einzeln deklariert. Die Deklaration umfasst Name, Typ, Format und Kommentar. Die übrigen Datenelemente werden für E/A-Operationen benötigt. Datensätze, Listenzeilen und Bildschirmmasken fassen mehrere Datenfelder zusammen und ergänzen sie mit zusätzlichen Attributen. Ein Datensatz umfasst Datenfelder, die beim Zugriff auf eine Datei logisch zusammengehören. Eine Datei kann verschiedene Datensätze enthalten. Eine Listenzeile umfasst Datenfelder und Konstante, die beim Drucken in einer Zeile ausgegeben werden. Für Datenfelder wird die Druckaufbereitung angegeben. Eine Liste beschreibt die Druckausgabe eines Programms und besteht aus dem Listenkopf und verschiedenen Listenzeilen. Eine Bildschirmmaske umfasst Datenfelder und Konstante, die in einem Dialogschritt auf dem Bildschirm ein- bzw. ausgegeben werden. Bei Eingabefeldern werden allgemeine Prüfungen, bei Ausgabefeldern die Aufbereitung spezifiziert. Die zu den Datenelementen gehörenden E/A-Operationen werden durch Parameter ergänzt (s. Tabelle 3). Fehlerbehandlung, Bedienungshilfen für die Hardware und Dialogsteuerung sind Bestandteile der jeweiligen E/A-Operation.

Tabelle 3: Datenelemente und zugehörige E/A-Operationen

Datenelement	E/A-Oper.	Befehl	Parameter
Datensatz	Lesen Schreiben Update	READ WRITE REWRITE	Datei,Zugriffsart, Schlüssel,Datensatz, Fehlerausgang
Listenzeile	Drucken	PRINT	Listenzeile,Zeilenvorschub
	Leerzeile	PRINTL	Anzahl
Bildschirmmaske	Ausgabe	DISPLAY	Bildschirmmaske,Ausgabeart
	Eingabe	ACCEPT	Datenfeld,Bildschirmmaske

<u>Übersichtlichkeit:</u> Zur Strukturierung und besseren Lesbarkeit der Elemente können bei der Eingabe Leerzeilen, Folgezeilen und Einrückungen verwendet werden. Bei der Ausgabe auf dem Bildschirm und in Listenform werden auszugebende Elemente aufbereitet. Elemente können an beliebiger Stelle mit Kommentaren versehen werden. Jedes Element enthält einen Kurzkommentar, der bei Referenzen zusätzlich zum klassifizierenden Elementnamen verwendet wird.

3.   Einsatz des Generierungs-Systems

Der Einsatz des Generierungs-Systems zur Erzeugung von einzelnen Programmen und Programmsystemen wird beispielhaft anhand von Abbildungen dargestellt. Die Abbildungen zeigen Elemente der Programmiersprache und Auswertungen aus der Elementdatenbank.

3.1 Erzeugung eines einzelnen Programms

Die Strukturierungsfähigkeit der Programmiersprache wird in Abb. 2 bis 4 durch zwei programmspezifische Verarbeitungselemente und ein Standard-Verarbeitungselement verdeutlicht.

```
PROGRAMMSPEZIFISCHES VERARBEITUNGSELEMENT      10.09.81  10.56
-------------------------------------------------------------------

***************
*   B6211     *           Pflege Sachkonten              Name/Kurzkommentar
***************

001  /---------------------------------------------------- ( / ) Kommentar
002  /   Vorverarbeitung / Dateieröffnung
003  /----------------------------------------------------
004
005  $XEIA                 /OPEN Interne Anwenderdatei     ( $ ) eingebundenes
006  $XEKK                 /OPEN Kontendatei                     Verarbeitungs-
007                                                              element
008  /---------------------------------------------------
009  /   Hauptverarbeitung
010  /---------------------------------------------------
011
012  $B6211B1I             /Initialisierung Sachkonto
013
014  $B62111A              /Eingabe Schlüsselbegriff
015  $B62111B              /Eingabe Sachkonto
016
017   IF U1.NOKEY-KK = 1  $XWKK    /Neuzugang Konten       ( $ ) Unterprogramm
018   IF U1.NOKEY-KK = 0  $XUKK    /Änderung Konten
019
020   #B6211B1I            /Initialisierung Sachkonto      ( # ) Sprung auf
021                                                              Verarbeitungs-
022  /-----------------------------------------------           element
023  /   Schlussverarbeitung
024  /-----------------------------------------------
025
026  $B6211B1S             /Abschluss Pflege-Sachkonten
027  $XCMM11               /Rücksprung Hauptmenü
```

Abb. 2: Programmspezifisches Verarbeitungselement: Pflege einer Stammdatei

```
PROGRAMMSPEZIFISCHES VERARBEITUNGSELEMENT      10.09.81  10.56
-------------------------------------------------------------


****************
*    B62111A    *              Eingabe Schlüsselbegriff
****************

001    $ACCEPT (W1.KTO.NR,B6211B1)  /Eingabe Kontonummer
002    IF U1.FT = 0   #50          /keine Funktionstaste      ( # ) Sprung auf
003    IF Y1.FTNR = 0  #B6211B1S   /Programmende = FTO              Sprungmarke
004    $AL.MEWS (11)               /Fehlermeldung
005    #00
006
007    /-------------------------------------------------
008    §50 /Prüfung - Satz vorhanden                         ( § ) Deklaration
009    /-------------------------------------------------           Sprungmarke
010
011    $XRKKI (W1.KTO.NR)          /Lesen Konten              ( $ ) Unterprogramm
012    IF U1.NOKEY-KK = 1   #60    /Konto nicht vorhanden           mit aktuellen
013                                                                 Parametern
014    /-------------------------------------------------
015    /   Änderung - Anzeige alten Datensatz
016    /-------------------------------------------------
017
018    $DISPLAY (B6211B1,U)        /Ausgabe vorhandener Daten
019    #99                                                   ( # ) Sprung Ende
020                                                                des Verarbei-
021    /-------------------------------------------------          tungselements
022    §60 /Neuzugang - Initialisierung neuen Datensatz
023    /-------------------------------------------------
024
025    KK.KTO.BEZ,KK.GBL.KZAPW,KK.VKZ.KASBNK,KK.VKZ.STE  =  ' '
```

Abb. 3: Programmspezifisches Verarbeitungselement: Bildschirmeingabe - Datenfeld

Zur Strukturierung des Programms werden Verarbeitungselemente eingebunden (§ <Ver-
arbeitungselement>) oder als Unterprogramm aufgerufen ($ <Verarbeitungselement>).
Auf eingebundene Verarbeitungselemente kann gesprungen werden (# <Verarbeitungsele-
ment>). Analog dazu werden Sprungmarken deklariert (§ <Sprungmarke>) und im gleichen Verarbeitungselement angesprochen (# <Sprungmarke>). Anfang (§00) und Ende
(§99) eines Verarbeitungselements sind implizit deklariert.

```
STANDARD-VERARBEITUNGSELEMENT                  10.09.81  10.56
-------------------------------------------------------------


****************
*    XRKKI      *              Lesen Konten                ( LG ) Länge
****************                                            ( TYP ) alphan./num.
                                                           ( E/U/A ) Eingabe/
 LG  DATENFELD                   TYP E/U/A                          Update/Ausgabe
-------------------------------------------------------------
  7  X1.KTO.NR                   N   E                     formaler Parameter

001    $READ (KK,X1.KTO.NR,DSBKK,NOKEY #20)
002    U1.NOKEY-KK = 0
003    #99
004    §20 /Satz nicht vorhanden
```

Abb. 4: Standard-Verarbeitungselement: Unterprogramm mit Eingabeparameter

Verarbeitungselemente können mit Datenelementen parametrisiert werden. Standard-Verarbeitungselemente übernehmen vorwiegend aufgabenunabhängige Funktionen.

Die Mächtigkeit der Programmiersprache wird in Abb. 5 bis 8 durch Beispiele zur Druckausgabe und zur Bildschirmverarbeitung verdeutlicht.

```
LISTENZEILE                                     10.09.81  10.56
---------------------------------------------------------------

********************
*   B1222LK7    *                    Überschrift Journal
********************
                                                                 ( ST ) Stelle in Li-
                                                                        stenzeile
  ST  LG   DATENFELD/KONSTANTE             TYP  AB                ( AB ) Aufbereitung
---------------------------------------------------------------
   1  40   'Buchung  Beleg----------- Konto---------'            ( ' ' ) Konstante
  41   3 F
  44  26   'Betrag--------------------'
  70   2 F
  72  23   'Steuer-----------------'
  95   2 F
  97  24   'Information-------------'

********************
*   XPLK123     *                    Zeile 3 Standardkopf (120)
********************

  ST  LG   DATENFELD/KONSTANTE             TYP  AB
---------------------------------------------------------------
   1   3 F                                                       ( F ) Leerstellen
   4  26   P1.PLK.31                        A
  30  20 F
  50  20   IA.FIR.NAMKRZ                    A
  70   1   '/'
  71   2   II.FIR.NRALP                     A
  73   1 F
  74  13   P1.PLK.32                        A
  87   1 F
  88   9 F
  97   6   II.PGS.DAT                       N   Y               ( Y ) Aufbereitung
 105   3 F                                                            eines Datums
 108   5   'Seite'                                             ( Z ) Nullenunter-
 113   5   Z1.DRU.SEI                       N   Z                     drückung
```

Abb. 5: Listenzeile

```
-----------------------------------------------------------------------------------------
                                                               Währungseinheit    DM
   Journal                        **  UNTERNEHMUNG  **/01       28/06/80  Seite    1
                                                               - NAME -
-----------------------------------------------------------------------------------------

Buchung  Beleg----------- Konto--------  Betrag--------------- Steuer------------ BS  Buchungstext
  Datum  Nummer    Datum  Soll    Haben     S o l l   H a b e n  Art         Betrag

31/12/79       1 30/06/80   1200             100.00                              SSS bbbbbbbbbbbbbbbbbbbb
31/12/79 1234567 30/06/80           20001               100.00                  SSS bbbbbbbbbbbbbbbbbbbb

S U M M E                                    100.00      100.00
V O R T R A G                                  0.00        0.00
Ü B E R T R A G                              100.00      100.00
```

Abb. 6: Druckausgabe

Ausgehend von der Deklaration der Listenzeile werden spezifische Druckfunktionen automatisch generiert (z.B. Druckaufbereitung, Besetzen der programmspezifischen Texte im Standard-Listenkopf). Allgemeine Druckfunktionen werden standardisiert (z.B. Ausgabe des Listenkopfes, Seiten-/Zeilenzähler).

```
BILDSCHIRMMASKE                              10.09.81  10.56
---------------------------------------------------------------

*****************
*   B6211B1    *                  Sachkonto
*****************                                       ( ZL ) Zeile
                                                       ( SP ) Spalte
ZL SP LG  DATENFELD/KONSTANTE           TYP  AB  ET    ( ET ) Eingabetyp
---------------------------------------------------------------
 4  1 32  'Konto               :  ........'

 5  1 55  'Kontobezeichnung  :  ...............................'
 6  1 48  'Bilanz,GuV        :  ........     (A/P/W/E/ ) : .'

 8  1 24  'Verarbeitungskennzeichen'

10  1 59  'Kasse,Bank  (K/B) : .  OP-Konto        (J/N) : N'  ( 'N' ) Vorbesetzung
11  1 59  'Tagesauszug (J/N) : N  Sammelbuchung   (J/N) : N'
12  1 59  'Kostenkonto (J/N) : N  Umsatzsteuerkonto(J/N): N'
13  1 61  'Steuerart (V/M/*) : .       -Position      : ...'
14  1 27  'Steuerschlüssel   : ..'

 4 26  7  W1.KTO.NR                     N   *   E      ( * ) Aufbereitung
 5 26 30  KK.KTO.BEZ                    A   K   E        Wert > 0
 6 26  7  KK.GBL.POS                    N   *   E      ( K ) Aufbereitung
 6 59  1  KK.GBL.KZAPW                  A                    Gross-, Klein-
10 26  1  KK.VKZ.KASBNK                 A                    schreibung
10 59  1  KK.VKZ.OPKTO                  A       J      ( E ) Eingabetyp
11 26  1  KK.VKZ.TAGAZG                 A       J            Zwangseingabe
11 59  1  KK.VKZ.SAMBCG                 A       J      ( J ) Eingabetyp
12 26  1  KK.VKZ.KOSKTO                 A       J            nur 'J'/'N'
12 59  1  KK.VKZ.UVA                    A       J
```

Abb. 7: Deklaration einer Bildschirmmaske

```
Pflege/Sachkonten          -Konto-                        28/06/80
**  UNTERNEHMUNG  ** / 01   - NAME -
------------------------------------------------------------------
Konto                   :  ........
Kontobezeichnung        :  ...............................
Bilanz,GuV              :  ........          (A/P/W/E/ ) : .
- - - - - - - - - - - - - - - - - - - - - - - - - - - - - - - - -
Verarbeitungskennzeichen

Kasse,Bank      ( /K/B) : .      OP-Konto           (J/N) : N
Tagesauszug     (J/N) : N        Sammelbuchung      (J/N) : N
Kostenkonto     (J/N) : N        Umsatzsteuerkonto(J/N) : N
Steuerart     ( /V/M/*) : .          -Position        : ...
Steuerschlüssel        : ..
```

Abb. 8: Bildschirmmaske

Ausgehend von der Deklaration der Bildschirmmaske werden für Ausgabe und Eingabe
spezifische Funktionen generiert. Generierte Funktionen der Ausgabe umfassen z.B.
Löschen des Bildschirms und Aufbereitung der einzelnen Ausgabefelder. Generierte
Funktionen der Eingabe umfassen z.B. Cursorpositionierung, feldabhängige Standard-
Funktionstasten zur Cursorsteuerung (z.B. Satz-Neueingabe, Satz-Freigabe, Feld-Rück-
sprung), formale Prüfungen (z.B. numerische Eingabe, Zwangseingabe) und logische
Prüfungen (z.B. Datum).

```
GENERIERTES PROGRAMM                              10.09.81  10.56
----------------------------------------------------------------

DATENFELDER

W1.EIN.FRM                    16    1     A$                      alphanum. Variable
II.FIL.IND                    12    1     B$
X1.XDE.FIL                     3    1     C$
C1.TXT.WS∠61                  26    3     §$
W1.AUS                        64   14     #$

II.XDE.IA                      3          A$(1)                   alphanum. Feldgruppe
II.XDE.KK                      3          A$(2)
II.FIL.KZ                      3          A$(3)

II.FRT                                    A0                      num. Variable
X1.XDE.ART                                A1
X1.VRS.FIL                                A2

SPRUNGMARKEN

B6211                        §00         1343
XEIA                         §00         1343
XEIA                         §90         1349
XEIA                         §99         1353
XEKK                         §00         1353
XEKK                         §99         1361
B6211B1I                     §00         1361


B A S I C -------------------------------------------------------

0001 DIM A$3(4),B$2(3),C$26(3),D$1(17),§$26(3),#$64(14)
000∠ DIM A(1),B(30)
1001 E$(5)='000000000000000000000000000000000'          Konstante - §INIT
100∠ E$(4)='.................................'
1003 A8=13
1004 C$(2)='Pflege/Sachkonten'
- - - - - - - - - - - - - - - - - - - - - - - - - - -
1343 B$='IA'                                             Programmanfang
1344 C$=A$(1)
1345 A1=1
1346 GOSUB2005
1347 A3=A∠
1348 GOTO 1353
1349 GOSUB ∠0∠6
1350 GOTO 1346
- - - - - - - - - - - - - - - - - - - - - - - - - - -
1353 B$='KK'
1354 C$=A$(∠)
1355 A1=1
1356 GOSUB202∠
1357 A4=A2
- - - - - - - - - - - - - - - - - - - - - - - - - - -
1361 D$='01000000000'
136∠ READFILEUSING6001,FL3,KEY=D$,§$,MATA
1363 W$=STR(§$,14,20)
```

Abb. 9: Programmausdruck

Die Generierung beinhaltet die Auflösung der Programmstruktur, die Vergabe von Zeilennummern für Unterprogramme und Sprungmarken, die Vergabe von Variablennamen, die Umsetzung der E/A-Operationen und die Abbildung der Syntax der einzelnen Anweisungen. Der Programmausdruck enthält programmspezifische Referenzen für Verarbeitungselemente, Sprungmarken und Datenelemente. Im Normalfall greift der Programmierer nicht auf das generierte Programm zu. Die Generierung unterstützt die Lesbarkeit des generierten Programms nicht, z.B. werden Kommentare nicht übernommen (s. Abb. 9).

3.2 Erzeugung eines Programmsystems

Die Abb. 10 bis 14 zeigen Auswertungen, die aus der Elementdatenbank erstellt werden, um dem Programmierer den aktuellen Entwicklungsstand des Programmsystems zu
zeigen und eine konsistente, redundanzarme Erstellung und Pflege von Programmen zu
ermöglichen. Die Auswertungen sind Auszüge und geben nicht den vollständigen Inhalt
der Elementdatenbank wieder.

```
DATENFELD - PRÄFIX                                10.09.81  10.56
-------------------------------------------------------------------

C1-C9                         Konstante
G1-G9                         Gruppenwechselsteuerung
IA                            Interne Anwenderdatei

DATENFELD - INFIX
-------------------------------------------------------------------

ABS                           Abstimmung
ASB                           Ausbuchen Restsalden
BCG                           Buchung

DATENFELD - SUFFIX
-------------------------------------------------------------------

ABL                           Abschluss
ABR                           Abrechnung
ADR                           Adresse
```

Abb. 10: Präfixe/Infixe/Suffixe

```
DATENFELD - sortiert nach INFIX              10.09.81  10.56
-------------------------------------------------------------------

IA.SKT.KTOFOR      7 N     Skonto - Konto Forderungen        Name, Länge, Typ,
IA.SKT.KTOINT      7 N     Skonto - Konto intern             Kurzkommentar
IA.SKT.KTOVER      7 N     Skonto - Konto Verbindlichkeiten
IA.SKT.PRZ         3 N     Skonto - Prozent
IA.SKT.SL          3 N     Skonto - Schlüssel

IA.STE.KTOINT      7 N     Steuer - internes Konto
IA.STE.KZVM        1 A     Steuer - Kennzeichen Vorst./Mwst
IA.STE.SL          3 N     Steuer - Schlüssel

KA.ADR.ANRSL       3 N     Adresse - Anredeschlüssel
KA.ADR.NAM        30 A     Adresse - Name
KA.ADR.ORT        30 A     Adresse - Ort
KA.ADR.STR        30 A     Adresse - Strasse
```

Abb. 11: Ausgabe vorhandener Datenfelder

Die konsistente Vergabe von Namen ist wesentliche Voraussetzung zur Entwicklung eines
komplexen Programmsystems. Die Namen von Datenfeldern werden aus einer vom Programmierer definierten Menge von Präfixen/Infixen/Suffixen zusammengesetzt, wodurch Dokumentationsfähigkeit und inhaltliche Kontrolle der Programme erleichtert wird.
Die vorhandenen Datenfelder werden nach unterschiedlichen Kriterien geordnet und auf
dem Bildschirm oder in Listenform ausgegeben.

```
┌─────────────────────────────────────────────────────────────────────────────┐
│                                                                             │
│ PROGRAMMSPEZIFISCHE VERARBEITUNGSELEMENTE        10.09.81   10.56            │
│ ----------------------------------------------------------------            │
│                                                                             │
│ B6211                          Pflege - Sachkonten         Name, Kurzkommentar│
│ B62111A                        Eingabe Schlüsselbegriff                      │
│ B62111B                        Eingabe Sachkonto                             │
│ B6211B1I                       Initialisierung Sachkonto                     │
│ B6211B1S                       Abschluss Pflege-Sachkonten                   │
│ B6211B1              B         Sachkonto                    Bildschirmmaske   │
│                                                                             │
└─────────────────────────────────────────────────────────────────────────────┘
```

Abb. 12: Ausgabe vorhandener programmspezifischer Verarbeitungselemente

Die Ausgabe der vorhandenen programmspezifischen Verarbeitungselemente zeigt Struktur und Funktion der Programme. Die verwendeten Datenelemente werden in unterschiedlichem Detaillierungsgrad ausgegeben.

```
┌─────────────────────────────────────────────────────────────────────────────┐
│                                                                             │
│ STANDARD-VERARBEITUNGSELEMENTE                   10.09.81   10.56            │
│ ----------------------------------------------------------------            │
│                                                                             │
│ XCMM11                         Rücksprung Hauptmenü        Name, Kurzkommentar│
│ XEIA                           OPEN Interne Anwenderdatei                    │
│ XEKK                           OPEN Kontendatei                              │
│ XRKKI                          Lesen Konten                                  │
│ XWKK                           Neuzugang Konten                              │
│ XUKK                           Änderung Konten                               │
│                                                                             │
└─────────────────────────────────────────────────────────────────────────────┘
```

Abb. 13: Ausgabe vorhandener Standard-Verarbeitungselemente

Standard-Verarbeitungselemente haben z.B. folgende Funktionen: Menüsteuerung (Auswahl und Rücksprung), Eröffnen von Dateien, Zugriffe auf Dateien (Lesen, Schreiben, Update) mit zusätzlichen Funktionen (z.B. Aufbau einer Verkettung), Druck von Standard-Listenzeilen (z.B. Standard-Listenkopf), umfangreichere Aufbereitung (z.B. Datum, Adresse), Ausgabe einer Fehlermeldung.

```
┌─────────────────────────────────────────────────────────────────────────────┐
│                                                                             │
│ REFERENZ/VERARBEITUNGSELEMENTE                   10.09.81   10.56            │
│ ----------------------------------------------------------------            │
│                                                                             │
│ B6211B1S                  $    B6211                    Art der Beziehung    │
│                           #    B62111A  B62111B         Verarbeitungselement │
│                                                                             │
│ REFERENZ/DATENFELDER                                                         │
│ ----------------------------------------------------------------            │
│                                                                             │
│ IA.SKT.KTOINT                  B1101W2N B1102W2N B6111H52  Verarbeitungselement│
│                           D    DSBIA110                    Datenelement       │
│                                                                             │
└─────────────────────────────────────────────────────────────────────────────┘
```

Abb. 14: Referenzen

Die Elementdatenbank wird in Referenzen ausgewertet. Referenzen geben die Beziehungen zwischen Verarbeitungselementen untereinander bzw. zwischen Datenelementen und Verarbeitungselementen an. Die Referenzen sind für nachträgliche Änderungen und Erweiterungen ein entscheidendes Hilfsmittel.

Die zentrale Verwaltung aller Elemente in der Elementdatenbank ermöglicht weitere
Funktionen, die beispielhaft in Abb. 15 und 16 angegeben sind.

```
STANDARD-VERARBEITUNGSELEMENT                        10.09.81   10.56
-----------------------------------------------------------------

************
*  $INIT     *             Vorbesetzung der Konstanten
************

  C1.NUL                = '000000000000000000000000000000'
  C1.PKT                = '..............................'
  C1.FIL.IND            = '000000000'
  C1.TXT.MONNAM(1)      = 'Januar'
  C1.TXT.MONNAM(2)      = 'Februar'
  C1.TXT.MONNAM(3)      = 'März'
  C1.KLN                = 'abcdefghijklmnopqrstuvwxyzäöü'
  C1.GRS                = 'ABCDEFGHIJKLMNOPQRSTUVWXYZÄÖÜ'
  C1.ZHL.TXT(1)         = 'ein'
  C1.ZHL.TXT(2)         = 'zwei'
  C1.ZHL.TXT(3)         = 'drei'
  C1.TXT.WS21(1)        = '-Zahlungsverkehr-'
  C1.TXT.WS21(2)        = '-Rechnungseingang-'
  C1.TXT.WS21(3)        = '-Rechnungsausgang-'
  C1.PGS.CMM(1,1)       = 'B1101'
```

Abb. 15:   Vorbesetzung allgemeine Konstanten

In einem internen Standard-Verarbeitungselement werden alle Konstanten vorbesetzt.
Bei der Generierung werden die jeweils verwendeten Konstanten übernommen.

```
STANDARD-VERARBEITUNGSELEMENT                        10.09.81   10.56
-----------------------------------------------------------------

***************
*  $ACCEPT    *             Bildschirmeingabe
***************


  001   IF X1.ACC.UMF = 'E' & X1.VAR.NUM = 0   #85
  002
  003
  004 *D---------------------------------------------------- Variante
  005   IF X1.ACC.AFB = 'Y' ! X1.VAR.NUM = 0   #85
  006
  007   $AL.DATPRF (X1.VAR.NUM)       /Datum prüfen
  008
  009   IF U1.ERR = 1   #10           /Rücksprung
  010 *D----------------------------------------------------
  011
  012
  013 §85 /Weitere Prüfung
```

Abb. 16:   Variante für Sonderfunktion

Teile von Verarbeitungselementen können variantenspezifisch gekennzeichnet werden.
Z.B. wird der mit 'D' gekennzeichnete Teil der Einleseroutine nur übernommen, wenn
im Programm mindestens ein Datenfeld eingegeben wird, das als Datum geprüft wird.
Analog dazu können benutzerindividuelle Varianten gekennzeichnet werden.

4.   Beurteilung des Generierungs-Systems

Das vorgestellte Generierungs-System ist auf einem System IBM /34 implementiert. Das Generierungs-System wurde zur Entwicklung eines umfangreichen Standard-Programmsystems für eine integrierte Dialog-Finanzbuchhaltung in BASIC auf dem System IBM 5120 eingesetzt. Die Finanzbuchhaltung ist zur Zeit bei über siebzig Kunden installiert. Alle Programme wurden mit dem Generierungs-System erstellt und werden weiterhin gepflegt. Im folgenden werden die Erfahrungen beim Einsatz des Generierungs-Systems und Weiterentwicklungen dargestellt.

4.1 Erfahrungen beim Einsatz

Der Umfang des Programmsystems ist durch den Umfang der Elementdatenbank und der generierten Programme gekennzeichnet (s. Tabelle 4).

Tabelle 4:   Umfang des Programmsystems Finanzbuchhaltung

Art	Anzahl
Elementdatenbank	
Datenelemente:	
Präfixe/Infixe/Suffixe	272
Datenfelder	1227
Datensätze	65
Listenzeilen	247
Bildschirmmasken	76
Verarbeitungselemente:	
programmspezifische Verarbeitungselemente	464
Standard-Verarbeitungselemente:	
Dateizugriff	113
Bildschirmsteuerung	16
Listensteuerung	12
Aufbereitung	17
Sonstige	32
Statements:	
Datenelemente	ca. 5000
programmspezifische Verarbeitungselemente	ca. 11000
Standard-Verarbeitungselemente	ca. 3000
generierte Programme	
Dateien:	
Stammdateien	5
Bestandsdateien	4
temporäre Dateien	8
Programme:	
Steuerung	5
Dateipflege	11
Datenerfassung	3
Abfrage (Bildschirm)	8
Auswertung (Liste)	19
Reorganisation	6
Statements	ca. 43000

Der Einsatz des Generierungs-Systems auf dem Entwicklungsrechner erbringt gegenüber
der Programmentwicklung auf dem Kleinrechner Zeitvorteile beim Edieren und Verwalten
der Elemente. Der Zeitaufwand zur Generierung beträgt ca. 2 - 9 Minuten je Programm.
Dieser Aufwand fällt nicht ins Gewicht, da die Programme i.d.R. im Hintergrund unabhängig von der aktuellen Arbeit generiert werden. Die Laufzeit der generierten Programme ist im Verhältnis zur Laufzeit herkömmlich erstellter Programme aufgrund des
optimierten Codes niedriger.

Die Entwicklung von Programmsystemen der genannten Grössenordnung erfordert ein hohes Mass an Programmierdisziplin und eine permanente Kontrolle des aktuellen Ent-
wicklungsstandes. Das Generierungs-System bietet dazu die Möglichkeit. Wesentliche
Vorteile sind die rechnergestützte Erstellung und Pflege der Elemente im Dialog sowie die Standardisierung und Konsistenz der Elemente. Damit konnten insbesondere
Fehlerkorrekturen und nachträgliche Erweiterungen problemlos durchgeführt werden.
Ohne ein derartiges Generierungs-System wäre ein erfolgreicher Vertrieb mit der vorliegenden Anzahl von Installationen und Varianten nicht möglich gewesen.

4.2 Weiterentwicklung

Das Generierungs-System wird bezüglich der Funktionen und der Programmiersprache
weiterentwickelt.

Funktionen: Das Generierungs-System erzeugt Programme für unterschiedliche Zielrechner bzw. Sprachversionen. Gegenwärtig werden zusätzlich zum Tischcomputer IBM
5120 für die Systeme IBM /34 und IBM /23 Programme erzeugt. Insbesondere die Erzeugung von Programmen, die auf dem Entwicklungsrechner (IBM /34) lauffähig sind, ermöglicht den Funktionstest der Programme unabhängig vom Zielrechner. Bei der Generierung für einen bestimmten Zielrechner werden charakteristische Merkmale der Hardware zur Optimierung ausgenutzt (z.B. Definition des Arbeitsbereichs für Zugriffe
abhängig vom verfügbaren Hauptspeicher). Die Installation der generierten Programm-
me im nicht-deutschsprachigen Ausland erfordert die Änderung der natursprachlichen
Textkonstanten. Die Verwaltung der Elemente in der Elementdatenbank ermöglicht den
Austausch der Textkonstanten während der Programmgenerierung. Gegenwärtig ist neben
der deutschsprachigen Version eine französischsprachige Version im Einsatz. Das Generierungs-System bietet Schnittstellen zu einem Dokumentations-System, das automatisch Dokumentationsunterlagen (z.B. Erfassungsbelege, Beispielabdrucke von Bild-
schirmmasken und Listen) aus den Informationen der Elementdatenbank erzeugt.

Programmiersprache: Eine naheliegende Erweiterung der Programmiersprache ist die
Aufnahme von Konstrukten der Strukturierten Programmierung. Die bisherige Erfahrung
zeigt, dass eine derartige Erweiterung keine entscheidenden Vorteile bietet, die

nicht auch durch Programmierdisziplin bei der Erstellung und Pflege der Elemente erreicht werden. Grössere Vorteile erbringt die Bereitstellung von funktionsorientierten, standardisierten Programmstrukturen (z.B. Dateiverarbeitung im Sinn der Normierten Programmierung, Dialogstrukturen zur Steuerung oder Dateipflege). Durch zusätzliche Attribute zu Datenelementen können bestimmte Verarbeitungen automatisch gesteuert und geprüft werden (z.B. Angaben zum zulässigen Wertebereich der Datenfelder, semantische Kontrollen aufgrund der Namenskonventionen der Datenfelder).

Das beschriebene Generierungs-System ermöglicht die wirtschaftliche Erstellung und Pflege von Programmen für kommerzielle Anwendungen. Darüber hinaus können weitere softwaretechnologische Methoden integriert werden, um Entwurf, Test und Dokumentation von Programmsystemen zu erleichtern.

Literatur

(1) Pressmar, D.B. Grundlagen und Richtlinien für den Entwurf einer einheit-
     Schünemann, T.M. lichen Benutzeroberfläche von dialogorientierten Bürocom-
     Ullmer, W. putern im administrativen Bereich, Studie im Auftrag der
     SIEMENS AG, München 1981

(2) Shneidermann, B. Software Psychology - Human Factors in Computer and In-
     formation Systems, Cambridge Mass. 1980, S. 94ff.

(3) Kirsch. W. Standardisierte Anwendungssoftware in der Praxis, Berlin
     Börsig, C. 1979, S. 68f.
     Englert, G.

(4) Glass, R.L. Software Reliability Guidebook, Englewood Cliffs N.J.
     1979, S. 78

(5) Turner, J. The Structure of Modular Programs, in: Communications of
     the ACM, Vol. 23 (1980), S. 272-277

(6) Pfeil, G.J. Bürocomputer in der Praxis, Stuttgart 1980, S. 17ff.

(7) Neugebauer, U. Der Markt für Anwendungssoftware in der Bundesrepublik
     et al. Deutschland, München/Wien 1980, S. 137

(8) Diebold Deutsch- Der Markt für Tischcomputer, Frankfurt 1980
     land GmbH (Hrsg.)

(9) Sanderson, P.C. Interactive Computing in BASIC, London 1973, S. 43

     IBM (Hrsg.) IBM 5110, BASIC Reference Manual, SA21-9308

(10) Hauer, K.-H. Einsatzerfahrungen mit Standard-Anwendungssoftware und
     et al. Anforderungen an ein Bausteinkonzept, München/Wien 1980,
     S. 14ff.

LL- AND LR-ATTRIBUTED GRAMMARS

Reinhard Wilhelm

FB 10 - Informatik

Universitaet des Saarlandes

D-6600 Saarbruecken

ABSTRACT
The L-attributed grammars form an attractive subclass of attribute
grammars since the test for L-attributedness is cheap and attribute
evaluation can be done in one left-to-right depth-first traversal of
the syntax tree. Still more attractive are subclasses of L-attributed
grammars which allow parser-directed attribute evaluation. Two such
classes called LL- and LR-attributed grammars, are supported by the
compiler generating system MUG1 (WRC 76,Gan 76). Their implementation
is described in the LR-case based on work by Watt (Wat 74,77). The
concepts of L- and LR-attributed grammar are extended to attributed
grammars with an underlying regular right part grammar.

1. L-attributed grammars

Attribute grammars (Knu 68, Wil 79) in this paper are written in a
notation borrowed from affix grammars (Kos 71). Besides the alphabets
of _terminal_ and _nonterminal symbols_, there is a third alphabet of
semantic action symbols. Semantic action symbols can occur anywhere in
the right side of a production. Associated with each nonterminal, each
terminal, and each semantic action is a list of _attribute positions_.
Any attribute position is either _inherited_ or _derived_ (_synthesized_).
For semantic actions, an inherited position can be thought of as an
input parameter position, and a derived position as an output parameter
position. Inherited positions of a nonterminal allow the transport of
information into the syntax trees rooted with that nonterminal, derived
positions allow the transport of information out of such syntax trees.

Terminals have no inherited positions, and one derived position. This
position receives its values from the scanner. The startsymbol of the
grammar has no inherited positions.

Attribute positions of terminals, nonterminals and semantic actions
occurring in productions are classified as _importing_, i.e. bringing
information into the production, or as _exporting_, i.e. using informa-

tion available from importing positions. Inherited positions on the left side and derived positions on the right side are classified as importing. Inherited positions on the right side and derived positions on the left side are classified as exporting. An occurence of a nonterminal or semantic action in a production is associated with a list of <u>attribute names</u>, one name for each attribute position. A name on an importing position makes (later at compile-time) attribute values available for other symbols in the same production having this name on an exporting position.

Example:
A(↓a↓b↑c) -> B(↓a↓b↑d1) S1(↓a↓d1↑d2) C(↓a↓b↓d2↑d3) S2(↓d3↑c)

Nonterminals A,B and semantic action S1 have two inherited and one derived attribute position.

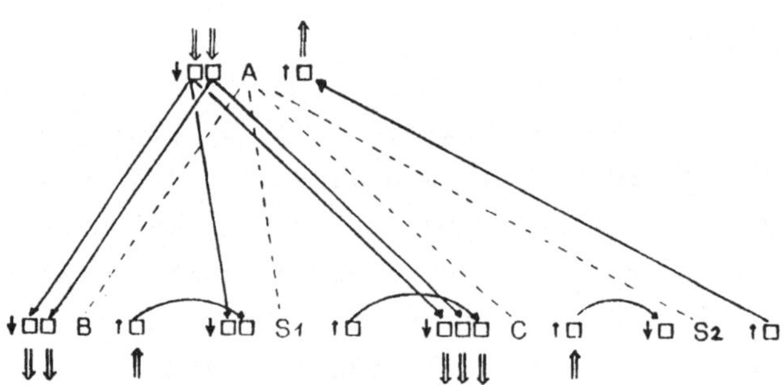

Each attribute name occurring in a production has exactly one importing occurrence, i.e. on an importing attribute position.

Let p: $X_0(...)$ -> $X_1(...)$ ... $X_{np}(...)$ be an attributed production.

inh[p,i] (der[p,i]) denotes the set of attribute names on inherited (derived) position at symbol X_i in production p.

↓[p,i] (↑[p,i]) denotes the list of names on inherited (derived) positions at X_i in p in the order given in the grammar. We assume in the following that each syntactic symbol has at most one occurrence in a production. Hence, we may talk about symbol X and its attribute names meaning names on positions at a particular occurrence of X in production p. Assuming that p is clear from the context, we will write $inh(X_i)$ $(der(X_i))$ instead of $inh(p,i)$ $(der(p,i))$, $\downarrow X_i$ $(\uparrow X_i)$ instead of $\downarrow[p,i]$ $(\uparrow[p,i])$.

If symbol occurrences in productions are not unique, the usual trick of indexing is used.

An attribute grammar is called <u>L-attributed</u> (LRS 73) (well formed (Kos 71)) iff for each production p: $X_0(...)$ -> $X_1(...)$ ... $X_{n_p}(...)$ and for $1 \leq i \leq n_p$:
$$inh(X_i) \subseteq inh(X_0) \ u \bigcup_{1 \leq j \leq i-1} der(X_j)$$
holds.

Attribute evaluation according to an L-attributed grammar can be directed by a left-to-right depth-first traversal of the syntax tree. This canonical attribute evaluation algorithm will be assumed to work correctly. The parser-directed algorithms in what follows will be shown to compute the same translation as this algorithm.

An <u>assignment</u> to a list LN of attribute names is a list of attribute values LV of the same length. A <u>consistent assignment</u> to a list LN of names is an assignment LV such that the same value stands on all positions of LV bearing the same name in LN. An <u>extension</u> of a consistent assignment to a list LN1 by an assignment to a list LN2 is called consistent, iff the result is a consistent assignment to LN1 LN2. A <u>replacement</u> of a consistent assignment lV1 to LN1 by an assignment LV2 to LN2 with names(LN2) $\subseteq$ names(LN1) is called consistent, iff LV1 LV2 is a consistent assignment to LN1 LN2.

A <u>correct assignment</u> to a list of attribute names of an instance of a nonterminal X in a syntax tree is the list of attribute values as computed by the treewalk evaluator for this instance of X.

2. LL-attributed grammars and their implementation

An L-attributed grammar is called <u>LL-attributed</u> iff the underlying context-free grammar is an LL-grammar. In this case, no syntax tree need be built, because attribute evaluation can be driven by an LL-parser(WRC 76). This parser should not be of the predictive parser type (AhU 72) but of the recursive descent type, i.e. it should anounce reductions to as well as expansions of nonterminals.

Attribute values are kept on an attribute stack AS. An attribute stack action is associated with each parser action. An AS-situation is given which is expected to hold before the action is performed. Another situation ("resulting AS-situation") is given, which results if the action is applied to the expected AS-situation.

Given production $p : X_0(\ldots) \rightarrow X_1(\ldots) \ldots X_{np}(\ldots)$.

(1.1) initialization of AS : empty stack

(1.2) parser action:	expansion of nonterminal X_i in p
	(call of semantic action X_i in p)
expected AS-situation:	assignment to $\downarrow X_0 \uparrow X_1 \ldots \uparrow X_{i-1}$
resulting AS-situation:	consistent assigment to $\downarrow X_0 \uparrow X_1 \ldots \uparrow X_{i-1} \downarrow X_i$
action performed:	consistent extension of the assignment to
	$\downarrow X_0 \uparrow X_1 \ldots \uparrow X_{i-1}$ by an assignment to $\downarrow X_i$.

(1.3) parser action:	reduction by production p
expected AS-situation:	assignment to $\downarrow X_0 \uparrow X_1 \ldots \uparrow X_{np}$
resulting AS-situation:	assignment to $\uparrow X_0$
action performed:	consistent replacement of the assignment to
	$\downarrow X_0 \uparrow X_1 \ldots \uparrow X_{np}$
	by the appropriate assignment to $\uparrow X_0$.

(1.4) parser action:	semantic action X_i returns
expected AS-situation:	consistent assignment to
	$\downarrow X_0 \uparrow X_1 \ldots \uparrow X_{i-1} \downarrow X_i$
resulting AS-situation:	consistent assignment to
	$\downarrow X_0 \uparrow X_1 \ldots \uparrow X_{i-1} \uparrow X_i$
action performed:	semantic action overwrites its input parameter
	values by its output parameter values.

(1.5) parser action:	parser reads terminal symbol X_i
expected AS-situation:	assignment to $\downarrow X_0 \uparrow X_1 \ldots \uparrow X_{i-1}$
resulting AS-situation:	assignment to $\downarrow X_0 \uparrow X_1 \ldots \uparrow X_{i-1} \uparrow X_i$
action performed:	attribute value as delivered by the
	scanner is pushed on AS.

Remark:

A simple proof by induction shows that every time the parser is about to perform one of the actions (1.2) - (1.5) a top section of AS is the expected assignment as described in (1.2) - (1.5). In fact, the same proof shows that the assignment formed on the top of the stack for an instance of a production is a correct assignment. Hence, what is described as "expected AS-situation" is an invariant for all instances of the corresponding parser actions.

Implementation

The following implementation lies at hand (Gan 76):

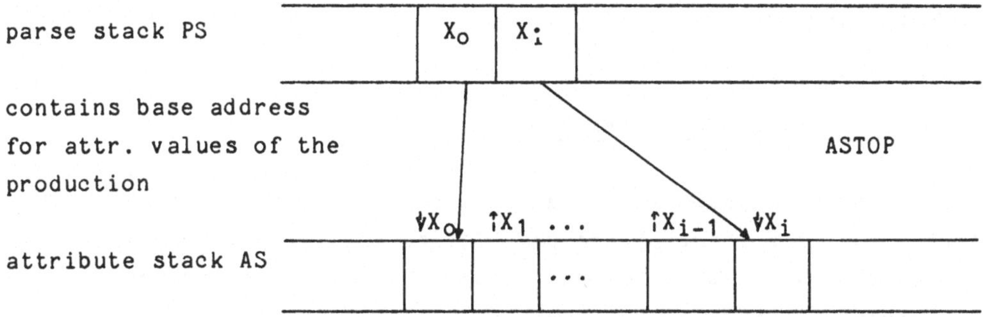

parse stack PS

$$\boxed{X_0} \boxed{X_i}$$

contains base address
for attr. values of the
production   ASTOP

$$\downarrow X_0 \quad \uparrow X_1 \ \ldots \ \uparrow X_{i-1} \quad \downarrow X_i$$

attribute stack AS

consistent extension: copies values of inh. positions to the
                      top of AS using relative addresses known
                      at generation time.

consistent replacement: extends the assignment to $\downarrow X_0 \uparrow X_1 \ldots \uparrow X_{np}$
                      consistently with the values of inh. pos. of X_0
                      (to prevent overwriting), copies the whole
                      block of values of $\downarrow X_0$ down to
                      relative address 0.

3. LR-attributed grammars

While attribute evaluation driven by an LL-parser looks quite natural, there are some obstacles to the cooperation of LR-parsing and attribute evaluation. Only the reduce-actions of an LR-parser are suited for synchronizing parsing and attribute evaluation. Hence, there are the following problems which were not present in the LL-case:

- semantic actions can only be called at the end of a right side of a production ;

- the transferral of values of inherited positions to a nonterminal cannot be done in time;

- an implementation using a base pointer for all attribute values of a production and positive relative addresses is no more possible, since we don`t recognize the beginning of a production when we would have to set this base pointer.

Watt (Wat 77) has proposed a solution to this problem which has been implemented in the compiler generating system MUG1 (WRC 76, Gan 76). This solution will be described next, and in section 4 it is extended to regular right part grammars.

Invariant properties of the attribute stack

We will now formulate invariant properties of top sections of the attribute stack for items of the underlying context-free grammar, i.e. properties that we want to be satisfied everytime the LR-parser is in a state containing the regarded item.

(2.1) Item$[S'\mathord{-}\mathord{>}\cdot S\underline{\downarrow}]$
AS-situation: emptystack

(2.2) Item $[X_0 \mathord{-}\mathord{>} X_1...X_{i-1}\cdot X_i...X_{np}]$
     X_i nonterminal, terminal or sem. action
expected AS-situation: consistent assignment to
$$\downarrow X_0 \downarrow X_1 \uparrow X_1...\downarrow X_{i-1} \uparrow X_{i-1}$$
resulting AS-situation:consistent assignment to
$$\downarrow X_0 \downarrow X_1 \uparrow X_1...\downarrow X_{i-1} \uparrow X_{i-1} \downarrow X_i$$
action performed: X_i terminal   : push attribute value of
                      X_i's synth.position
            X_i nonterminal: consistent extension to
$$\downarrow X_0...\uparrow X_{i-1} \downarrow X_i$$
            X_i sem.action : consistent extension to

$$\downarrow X_0 \ldots \uparrow X_{i-1} \downarrow X_i$$
$$\text{call to } X_i$$
$$\text{push values of } X_i\text{'s}$$
$$\text{synth. positions}$$

(2.3) Item[$X_0 \to X_1 \ldots X_{np}.$]

    expected AS-situation: consistent assignment to
$$\downarrow X_0 \downarrow X_1 \uparrow X_1 \ldots \downarrow X_{np} \uparrow X_{np}$$
    resulting AS-situation: assignment to $\downarrow X_0 \uparrow X_0$

    action performed: consistent replacement

These invariants look different than those in (1), in particular the attribute stack mechanism seems to be more costly in space. But this mechanism will be improved as far as stack space consumption and the class of acceptable grammars are concerned.

Grammar transformation to ensure the invariants

These invariants cannot be guaranteed by a mechanism directed by the LR-parser for the original grammar. Watt (Wat 77) proposed a transformation of the underlying context-free grammar that will guarantee the validity of the invariants. This transformation works as follows:

(3.1) For any occurrence of a nonterminal X in a right side of a production introduce a new nonterminal symbol N (a copysymbol). Insert N in front of this occurrence of X into the production. Add a production N -> e (empty right side) to the grammar. Associate the appropriate consistent extension as required by (2.2) with this new production.

(3.2) For any occurrence of a semantic action S in a right side introduce a new nonterminal M. Replace this occurrence of S by M. Add a new production M -> e. Associate a call to S with this production, using the descriptions of $\downarrow S$ and the actual stack contents to address the actual input parameters. This call should leave its result parameters on top of the stack.

Optimization of the mechanism

The grammar transformation and the attribute stack management described so far have several disadvantages:

(4.1) The grammar transformation might introduce too many copy symbols. This might result in the transformed grammar not being LR(k) any more. Any leftrecursive nonterminal would cause this trouble, since a copysymbol would be inserted at the beginning of the leftrecursive production.

(4.2) The attribute stack management seems to keep to many attribute values on the stack for which there is no use any longer.

Therefore, the following improvements are built into the grammar transformation:

Given production $p : X_0(\ldots) \rightarrow X_1(\ldots)\ldots X_{np}(\ldots)$

(5.1) No copysymbol is introduced in front of the nonterminal symbol X_i if $\downarrow X_i$ is a suffix of $\downarrow X_0 \downarrow X_1 \uparrow X_1 \ldots \downarrow X_{i-1} \uparrow X_{i-1}$, because this would mean that X_i would find its inherited attribute values in the right order on top of the stack.

(5.2) If a proper prefix of $\downarrow X_i$ is a suffix of $\downarrow X_0 \downarrow X_1 \uparrow X_1 \ldots \downarrow X_{i-1} \uparrow X_{i-1}$, the longest such prefix is chosen, and a copysymbol is inserted with a push-action that copies only the smallest necessary rest of X_i's inherited attribute values on top of the stack.

(5.3) Before a new copysymbol is created, it is checked whether a copysymbol with an identical push-action does already exist. If so, this copysymbol is inserted.

<u>Remarks:</u>

(6.1) Optimizations (5.1) and (5.3) increase the class of attribute grammars with underlying LR(k)-grammars which will be still LR(k)-parsable after the grammar transformation. In (PuB 80), positions in grammars were classified as free, forbidden or contingent, depending on whether the insertion of a new e-Nonterminal is allowed, forbidden or depending on insertions in other positions. (5.1) will often suppress the insertion at forbidden positions, e.g. in front of left-recursive productions; (5.3) will sometimes insert the same copysymbol into several contingent positions.

(6.2) Optimizations (5.1), (5.2), (5.3), and (5.4) will all reduce
stack space consumption. In fact, one can easily see, that in the
optimized description $\downarrow X_o \downarrow X_1 \uparrow X_1 \downarrow X_2 \uparrow X_2 \ldots \downarrow X_{np} \uparrow X_{np}$ there will be no
common neighboring nonempty sublists at any border between a
$\downarrow X_o \downarrow X_1 \uparrow X_1 \ldots \uparrow X_{i-1}$ and $\downarrow X_i \ldots \uparrow X_{np}$.

(6.3) Let us call an L-attributed grammar, whose transformed underlying
grammar is still LR(k), <u>LR-attributed</u>. Although LL-parser-driven
attribute evaluation seems to be more natural the class of
LL-attributed grammars is a proper subclass of the class of
LR-attributed grammars (Bro 74), i.e. if the above grammar
transformation produces a non LR(k)-grammar, the original attribute grammar had no underlying LL(k)-grammar.

4. LR-attributed regular right part grammars

Regular right part grammars (rrp-grammars) are a convenient description
mechanism for context-free languages. They allow regular expressions
over terminals and nonterminals as right sides of productions. Their
advantages over conventional context-free grammars are improved reada-
bility, smaller size, presumably smaller parsers (PuB 81). Also,
regular right parts seem to eliminate the need for left-recursive and
right-recursive nonterminals in the description of realistic programming languages.

In this section, LR-attributed rrp-grammars will be defined and a
scheme for their implementation presented. It consists of a stack
mechanism and grammar transformation like the scheme in section 3.

An attributed rrp-grammar has productions of the following form:
The left side consists of an attributed nonterminal, i.e. a nonterminal
together with a list of names for its attribute positions. The right
side is a regular expression over attributed terminal, nonterminal and
semantic action symbols. The usual definition of "instance of a regular
expression" is extended in the following way. Each symbol occurring in
the regular expression takes its list of attribute names over to all
occurrences in the instance of the expression. (We still assume that
occurrences of nonterminals in productions are unique or made unique by
indexing). An instance of a production is an instance of the right
side, preceded by the left side nonterminal with its list of attribute
names.

An <u>item</u> of a rrp-grammar is a production with a dot in the right side. We are interested in the set of attribute names with importing occurrences available for an item of the underlying grammar.

$$\text{avail}([A \rightarrow .a]) = \text{inh}(A) \text{ the set of names on inherited}$$
$$\text{positions at this occurrence of A}$$
$$\text{avail}([A \rightarrow aN.b]) = \text{avail}([A \rightarrow a.Nb]) \cup \text{der}(N)$$
$$\text{avail}([A \rightarrow a(.b_1|b_2)g]) :=$$
$$\text{avail}([A \rightarrow a(b_1|.b_2)g]) := \text{avail}([A \rightarrow a.(b_1|b_2)g])$$
$$\text{avail}([A \rightarrow a(b_1|b_2).g]) :=$$
$$\text{avail}([p:A \rightarrow a(b_1.|b_2)g]) \cap \text{avail}([A \rightarrow a(b_1|b_2.)g])$$
$$\text{avail}([A \rightarrow a(.b)^*g]) :=$$
$$\text{avail}([A \rightarrow a(b)^*.g]) := \text{avail}([A \rightarrow a.(b)^*g])$$

We are also interested in the set of attribute names with exposed uses at an item or one of its successors:

$$\text{use}([A \rightarrow a.]) = \text{der}(A)$$
$$\text{use}([A \rightarrow a.Nb]) = (\text{use}([A \rightarrow aN.b]) - \text{der}(N)) \cup \text{inh}(N)$$
$$\text{use}([A \rightarrow a.(b_1|b_2)g]) = \text{use}([A \rightarrow a(.b_1|b_2)g]) \cup$$
$$\text{use}([A \rightarrow a(b_1|.b_2)g])$$
$$\text{use}([A \rightarrow a(b.)^*g]) = \text{use}([A \rightarrow a(b)^*.g]) \cup$$
$$\text{use}([A \rightarrow a(.b)^*g])$$
$$\text{use}([A \rightarrow a.(b)^*g]) = \text{use}([A \rightarrow a(.b)^*g]) \cup$$
$$\text{use}([A \rightarrow a(b)^*.g])$$

An attributed rrp-grammar is called <u>L-attributed</u> iff for any item i of the grammar use(i) $\subseteq$ avail(i) holds.

This definition ensures, that in every instance of a production, any exporting occurrence of a name is preceded by an importing occurrence, whereby names on derived position of the left side are considered to occur at the right end of an instance.

An attribute name may have several importing occurrences in a production. The importing occurrence corresponding to an exporting occurrence in an instance of the production is the last occurrence preceding this exporting occurrence.

Invariant properties of the attribute stack

We define a list of attribute names for any item of the grammar:

(7.1) $list([A \rightarrow .a]) = \Downarrow A$

(7.2) $list([A \rightarrow aN.b]) = list([A \rightarrow a.Nb])\ \Downarrow N \Uparrow N$

If the parser has reduced by production N->a, a consistent replacement of an assignment to $list([N \rightarrow a.])$ by an assignment to $\Downarrow N$ has to be performed.

(7.3) $list([A \rightarrow a(.b_1|b_2)g]) = list([A \rightarrow a.(b_1|b_2)g])$

(7.4) $list([A \rightarrow a(b_1|.b_2)g] = list([A \rightarrow a.(b_1|b_2)g])$

(7.5) $list([A \rightarrow a(b_1|b_2).g]) =$
$\qquad merge(list([A \rightarrow a(b_1.|b_2)g]), list([A \rightarrow a(b_1|b_2.)g])$

(7.6) $list([A \rightarrow a(.b)^*g]) = list([A \rightarrow a.(b)^*g])$

(7.7) $list([A \rightarrow a(b)^*.g]) = list([A \rightarrow a.(b)^*g])$

$merge(L1,L2)$ constructs a new list L in the following way:
$\qquad$ if L1 and L2 start with a list L_3, i.e.

$\qquad L1 = L_3L_1'$ and $L2 = L_3L_2'$ then $L = L_3L_4$
$\qquad$ where L_4 is a list containing all the names in
$\qquad L_1'$ and L_2' once.

The L-attributedness of a grammar has a consequence for *-expressions in right sides.

<u>Lemma:</u> Let G be a L-attributed grammar, $A \rightarrow a(b)^*g$ a production of G.

Claim: $avail([A \rightarrow a(b.)^*g]) \cap use ([A \rightarrow a(b)^*.g]) \subseteq avail([A \rightarrow a.(b)^*g])$,

i.e. b can not define more names which are used later on, than are already defined in $[A \rightarrow a.(b)^*g]$.

Proof: Since G is L-attributed, we have $use([A \rightarrow a(b)^*.c]) \subseteq avail([A \rightarrow a(b)^*.c]) = avail([A \rightarrow a.(b)^*p])$. This prooves the claim.

The lemma implies that the invariants (7.6) and (7.7) can be guaranteed. This means in particular, that the stack mechanism has no trouble with instances of a production having different lengths. The stack mechanism has only to ensure, that before entering the instance of b and when leaving the last instance of b the value of the most recent definition of any name in $avail([A \rightarrow a.(b)^*c])$ is on top of the stack in the order of $list([A \rightarrow a.(b)^*c])$.

Grammar transformation

The grammar is transformed to guarantee the invariants of (7).

(8.1) Insert a new nonterminal (copysymbol) N in front of any nonterminal X occurring in the right side of a production. Add a production N->e to the grammar. Associate the appropriate consistent extension with this production.

(8.2) Replace any semantic action symbol by a new nonterminal M. Add a production M->e. Associate with this production the appropriate consistent extension action, a call to the semantic action leaving the results on top of the stack.

(8.3) Insert two new nonterminals N_1, N_2 into the production A -> $a(b_1|b_2)c$ after b_1 and b_2, respectively. Add productions N_1 -> e and N_2 -> e. Associate with N_1 -> e the consistent replacement of an assignment to list([A -> $a(b_1.|b_2)c$]) by an assignment to list([A -> $a(b_1|b_2).c$]). Associate with N_2 -> e the consistent replacement of an assignment to list([A -> $a(b_1|b_2.)c$]) by a consistent assignment to list([A -> $a(b_1|b_2).c$]).

(8.4) Insert a new nonterminal N into any production A -> $a(b)^*c$ after b. Add a production N -> e. Associate with this production the consistent replacement of a consistent assignment to list([A -> $a(b.)^*c$]) by a consistent assignment to list([A -> $a.(b)^*c$]).

Remark: Consistent extension and consistent replacement have to be redefined in order to cope with inconsistent assignments due to several importing occurrences of one name in a production or in an instance of a production. They are now supposed to take the value of the last importing occurrence of a name in list([...]).

Optimizations:

Optimizations will enlarge the class of grammar that can be treated, reduce attribute stack space consumption, and speed up the compiler since many e-reductions will be eliminated. Besides the optimizations described in (5), the following additional improvements are possible:

(9.1) Choose a list for the item [A -> a(b_1|b_2).c] that eliminates one
of the copy symbols after b_1 or b_2, or a copysymbol at a
following nonterminal.

(9.2) Insert no copysymbol that has an associated extension by an empty
list, or a replacement of a list by an identical list.

(9.3) Combine if helpful and possible two or more consecutive copysym-
bols by a new one and associate with it an efficient combination
of the associated actions.

Acknowledgements: Thanks go to Cosima Schmauch and Thomas Raeuchle for
critical comments to a preliminary version of this paper.

R e f e r e n c e s

(AhU 72)   Aho,A.V., Ullman,J.D., The Theory of Parsing
                    Translation, and Compiling,
                    Prentice Hall, 1972

(Bro 74)   Brosgol,B.M., Deterministic Translation Grammar,
                    Ph.D. dissertation Harvard University, 1974

(Gan 76)   Ganzinger,H., MUG1-Manual, Bericht Nr. 7608,
                    Fachbereich Mathematik, TU Muenchen, 1976

(GiW. 78)   Giegerich,R., Wilhelm,R., Counter-one-pass
                    features in one-pass compilation,
                    Information Processing Letters, 7(6), 1978

(Knu 68)   Knuth,D.E., Semantics of context-free
                    languages, Math. Systems Theory 2, 1968

(Kos 71)   Koster,C.H.A., Affix grammars, in: J.E.L. Peck, ed.,
                    ALGOL 68 Implementation, North-Holland,
                    Amsterdam, 1971

(LRS 73)   Lewis,P.M., Rosenkrantz,D.J., Stearns,R.E.,
                    Attributed translations, Proc. 5th Annual
                    Symposium on Theory of Computing, 1973

(PuB 80)   Purdom,P., Brown,C.A., Semantic Routines and
            LR(k) Parsers, Acta Informatica, 14(4), 1980

(PuB 81)   Purdom,P., Brown,C.A., Parsing Extended LR(k)-
            Grammars, Acta Informatica, 15(2), 1981

(Wat 74)   Watt,D.A., Analysis Oriented Two-Level Grammars,
            Ph.D. Thesis, Glasgow University, 1974

(Wat 77)   Watt,D.A., The parsing problem for affix
            grammars, Acta Informatica 8, 1977

(Wil 79)   Wilhelm,R., Attributierte Grammatiken,
            Informatik Spektrum 2, 123-130, 1979

(WRC 76)   Wilhelm,R., Ripken,K., Ciesinger,J., Ganzinger,H.,
            Lahner,W., Nollmann,R., Design evaluation
            of the compiler generating system MUG1, Proc.
            2nd International Conference on Software
            Engineering, San Francisco, 1976

Static Semantic Checks of Global Variables
in a Procedural Language

Bernhard Böhringer, Hartmut Feuerhahn

Epsilon GmbH, Berlin

Abstract
A data flow analysis of global variables is described that applies to
recursive procedures and is based on value/result specifications of
parameters. Undefined or unused values of variables are detected,
thereby potential and severe error cases are distinguished.
The method is applicable to complete programs, but by means of path
expressions is extended to separate modules. It has been implemented
for a system implementation language as part of a programming support
environment.

Introduction
Static semantic checking of programs as performed by a compiler may
greatly reduce the time and effort of testing and debugging. Errors can
be detected eraly and completely - for a given class of errors - long
before they would show up in an incidental test run. Besides the confidence put into a program is more justified if its semantics are checked
for all possible cases by a general check algorithm, not only for the
test cases by a programmer.

Of course, the class of errors that can be checked by general algorithms is restricted and depends on properties of the programming
language.
While missing definitions of parameters and global variables are rather
frequent and hard to find semantic errors in programming, not all
languages behave well enough to permit automatic detection of such
errors. If parameters are called by name, or if procedures are admitted
as parameters, the alias problem of variables generally will be unde-
cidable, so that a complete analysis of the data flow is impossible
/4/. Worst case assumptions as proposed by numerous authors (e.g.
/5,8/) for optimization purposes generally can not be applied to error
detecting strategies /3/.

Languages that have a value/result (i.e. copy/restore) parameter mechanism and that do not have procedures as parameters behave better in that they permit full analysis of the data flow between local and global variables as far as simple variables are concerned /1,2/. Simple variables in the sense of this paper are variables not pointed to. Indexed variables (arrays) may be present, but are outside the range of the check algorithm.

In this paper an analysis of the data flow is described, that checks for undefined values of global variables, and distinguishes between severe and potential error cases. Thereby the problem of boolean and of recursive procedures is given special attention. The method is extended to the analysis of separate modules by means of path expressions.

The analysis has been implemented for the programming language CDL2 /9/, which is an open-ended procedural language suitable for system implementation. The implementation is part of a progamming support environment for that language, called the CDL2-LAB /10/. The extension to path expressions is under work.

Approach

To analyse the variable application of a program for each procedure an application vector is computed, that describes the variable usages inside. Especially it is computed which variables must have a value before it is called and which variables obtain a value before the first use.
The application vectors are computed in a bottom-up manner for all procedures of a program, taking special care of iterations inside procedures. Recursion between procedures is handled by an iterative method using a special start value. The application vector of the root procedure (e.g. main program) represents the result of the analysis: if any variables must have a value before the program can be called, there is an error in the program. Information about suspicious cases can be displayed to the user or is subject to deeper local analysis of the suspicious procedures.

Preliminaries

A _program_ consists of a set or procedures P1, ..., Pn, and of a set of variables V1, ..., Vm. Each _procedure_ is represented by a flow graph, which is a directed graph with distinguished _entry_ and _exit_ nodes. Exit nodes do not contain operations. All other nodes are labelled with calls of procedures, the edges connect successive execution steps.

A <u>call</u> of a procedure may have local or global variables and constants as actual <u>parameters</u>. The parameters of a procedure are specified as value and/or result parameters. <u>Value</u> parameters are copied into the procedure before the call, <u>result</u> parameters are restored from the procedure after the call. If a variable V is applied as value parameter of a call its value is <u>used</u>, if it is applied as result parameter its value is <u>set</u>.

In this paper we will first restrict ourselves to procedures with single exit nodes. An extension to Boolean procedures with a <u>true</u> and a <u>false</u> exit is formulated in a natural way. The resultant binary control structure can be used to model any flow of control. Primitive operations of a programming language are modelled by procedures.

<u>Application Tuples</u>

A variable V may be applied differently on the different paths that the execution of a procedure P may take. For each path the sequence of using and setting applications can be represented by a string α of ´U´ and ´S´ letters, $\alpha \in \{U,S\}^*$, called <u>application path</u> of V in P. Let A(V,P) be the set of possible application paths of the variable V in the procedure P, $A(V,P) \subset \{U,S\}^*$.

The set A(V,P) of possible application paths indicates the different application cases of a variable V in a procedure P: the variable V is possibly <u>used</u> (before being set), iff some application path starts with ´U´; it is possibly <u>set</u> (before being used), if some path starts with ´S´; it is possibly <u>neglected</u>, iff some application path is empty; it is possibly <u>forgotten</u>, iff some path ends with ´S´; and it is possibly <u>overwritten</u>, iff some path contains ´SS´.

These properties of the set of application paths form a tuple a(V,P) of logical values, called the <u>application tuple</u> of the variable V in the procedure P; the application tuple belonging to a set A of application paths is denoted a(A), or simply ´a´. The components of ´a´, a=(ux,sx,e,xs,ss), are defined as follows:

$$ux \iff A \cap U \cdot \{U,S\}^* \neq \emptyset$$
$$sx \iff A \cap S \cdot \{U,S\}^* \neq \emptyset$$
$$e \iff A \cap \varepsilon \neq \emptyset \text{ , where } \varepsilon \text{ denotes the empty string}$$
$$xs \iff A \cap \{U,S\}^* \cdot S \neq \emptyset$$
$$ss \iff A \cap \{U,S\}^* \cdot S \cdot S \cdot \{U,S\}^* \neq \emptyset$$

Some combinations of the elements of an application tuple ´a´ have a special meaning. They can be verbalized as follows:

combination	ux,sx, e,xs,ss				
neglected	0	0	1	0	0
used	1	0	0	0	0
set	0	1	0	1	0
used and then set	1	0	0	1	0
possibly used	1	0	1	0	0
possibly set	0	1	1	1	0
possibly used, possibly set	1	1	1	1	0

These tuples are assigned to the primitive operations occuring in a program dependent on their parametrization and semantics.

Operations

To compute the application tuple of a flow graph starting from the application tuples of its nodes, we need operations, that reflect concatenation and union of sets of applications paths. Given such operations the flow graph can be traversed in such a way that the possible application paths are (virtually) rolled out and merged together, while the respective application tuples are (actually) multiplied and added. Since the problem can be restricted to that of one variable and one procedure, the arguments V and P will be omitted where obvious.

Def The empty application tuple w is defined as follows:

$$w = (0,0,0,0,0)$$

The empty application tuple models an empty set of paths. It is used as a start value during the computation.

Def Let a1 and a2 be application tuples. Then the sum a of a1 and a2, a = a1+a2, is defined as follows:

    a = a1 + a2   ai = (uxi,sxi,ei,xsi,ssi)

    ux = ux1 ∨ ux2
    sx = sx1 ∨ sx2
    e = e1 ∨ e2
    xs = xs1 ∨ xs2
    ss = ss1 ∨ ss2

The sum of application tuples models the union of application paths
with the following properties:

    a1 + a2 = a2 + a1
    a1 + w = a1
    (a1 + a2) + a3 = a1 + (a2 + a3)

<u>Def</u> Let a1 and a2 be application tuples. Then the <u>product</u> a of a1 and
a2, a = a1 * a2, is defined as follows:

    a = a1 * a2   ai = (uxi,sxi,ei,xsi,ssi)

    ux = ux1 $\wedge$ (ux2 $\vee$ sx2 $\vee$ e2) $\vee$ e1 $\wedge$ ux2
    sx = sx1 $\wedge$ (ux2 $\vee$ sx2 $\vee$ e2) $\vee$ e1 $\wedge$ sx2
    e = e1 $\wedge$ e2
    xs = xs2 $\wedge$ (ux1 $\vee$ sx1 $\vee$ e1) $\vee$ e2 $\wedge$ xs1
    ss = ss1 $\vee$ ss2 $\vee$ xs1 $\wedge$ sx2

The product of application tuples models the concatenation of paths
with the following properties:

    (a1 * a2) * a3 = a1 * (a2 * a3)
    w * a = a * w = w

<u>Graph traversal</u>
To compute the application tuple of a single exit flow graph P, given
the appication tuples of the calls in P, each node N in P is associated
with an application tuple a(N), that belongs to the set of paths leading from the entry node up to that node (not including it). The application tuple of the flow graph a(P) is that one associated to its exit
node.

Initially, before any paths have been traversed, the empty tuple w is
assigned to each node. Then the graph is traversed recursively, starting with the entry node following the successor links. Thereby at each
node N the associated tuple a(N) is combined with the given tuples of
the call and is added to the tuples of the successor nodes of N.

For each call node N three tuples must be given, one for the value
parameters, named a(N.val), one for the procedure called, named
a(N.proc), and one for the result parameters, named a(N.res). The tuple

a (N.val) indicates "used", iff the variable V is used as value parameter, and the tuple a(N.res) indicates "set", iff V is set as result
parameter of the call. The tuple a(N.proc) is the application tuple of
the respective flow graph.

```
        a(N)                              a(S)
  ───────────────► N ───────────────────────► S ──────────────
   a(N.val)          a(N.res)
            a(N.proc)
```

<u>Def</u> Let P be a flow graph and let the application tuples of calls in P
be given. Then the application tuple a(P) of a flow graph P is computed
as follows:
(0) to each node N of P assign the empty application tuple
    w, a(N)=w
(1) to the entry node assign "neglected"
(i) choose a node N of P, combine its node tuple with its
    call tuples and, for each successor S of N, add the
    result to the tuple a(S)
    a(S) := a(S) + a(N)*a(N.val)*a(N.proc)*a(N.res)
(i+1) repeat step i until n
(n) end if no new (different) tuple can be computed for any
    node of P
(n+1) a(P) is the tuple computed for the exit node.

The computation can be carried out by a recursive traversal of the
graph: starting at the entry node, for each node the application tuple
is combined with the call tuples and is added to all successor tuples,
then the traversal is continued with those successors that have
obtained a new tuple.

Note, that the computation and the traversal do not put any requirements on the structure of a flow graph. Any kind of flow graphs are
admitted, whether reducible or structured or not. Especially branches
or loops do not have to be treated in any special way.

<u>Termination</u>
To proof that the computation terminates, we have to show that the
transformation performed in each step is monotonous (in some sense) and
is restricted to a finite number of cases.
Obviously there are only a finite number of different application
tuples. It is thus sufficient to show that a := a+x is monotonous. This

is true because the "+" operation is defined by a logical "or" for all
components.

<u>Recursion</u>

To compute the application tuples of all procedures Pl, ..., Pn of a
program M, the procedures should be ordered in a bottom-up way (i.e.
definition before application), so that for each procedure Pi the tuple
a(Pi) is calculated before it is applied in some other procedure Pj,
j>i.

However, this ordering is not possible if the program contains recursive procedures. In this case the application tuples of some recursive
procedures will be needed before they can be computed.

At this place it might be helpful to give an example, written in some
bastard notation:

```
VAR V;
PROC P (INT VALUE I):
        IF I = 5
        THEN P(I-1); PRINT(V)
        ELSE V := 999 FI
```

Is the variable V used by the procedure P? In a first analysis, not
looking into the recursive call of P, two execution paths through P can
be seen, one that uses the variable ("PRINT(V)"), one that sets the
variable ("V:=999"). So, together, the variable V is "possibly set and
possibly used" by P. This calculation can be repeated, using the result
for the call "P(I-1)", to yield the same result.
However, this result is wrong. The variable will only be used after the
deepest recursion of the procedure where it is properly set.

A solution to the problem is given by the empty application tuple w
introduced before. Whenever a tuple is needed that has not been computed yet, the empty tuple is assumed. It represents an empty set of
application paths, i.e. it stands for "not yet defined". Products with
w again lead to w.

Now let us analyse the recursive procedure P again, using w as initial
application tuple of P. The procedure body starts with a call that does
not apply V, then one path goes to the recursive call with call vector
w. The product of the tuple with w yields w, which is added to the

succeeding call tuple, resulting again in w. On the other path the
variable is set, and "set"+w = "set".
In a second analysis this preliminary result is used for the recursive
call, which yields "not applied"*"set"*"used"="set" on the first path,
and "set" on the second. The result is again "set" and is a fix point.

Program Traversal

$\underline{Def}$ Let M be a program, consisting of the procedures P1, ..., Pn; then
the application tuples a(p1),...,a(Pn) are computed as follows:
(0)   to each procedure P of M assign the empty application
      tuple w, a(P):=w
(i)   choose a procedure P of M, compute the application tuple
      a´(P) of its flow graph and add it to a(P)
(i+1) repeat step i until n
(n)   stop if no new (different) tuple can be computed for any
      procedure of M.

The termination of this computation can be shown the same way as for
the traversal of flow graphs. In each step of the program traversal a
procedure tuple is changed by addition of another, which results in a
logical "or" for the components. Since there is only a finite number of
different tuples, a fix point is reached.

The computation can be carried out rather efficiently, if the procedures are ordered in an almost bottom-up way (except for some recursive
calls) and if for each (recursive) procedure Pj the first procedure Pi,
i<j, is remembered, that needs a(Pj). Whenever the tuple a(Pj) changes,
the tuples a(Pi),a(Pi+1),...,a(Pj) are computed again. This way the
recomputation of application tuples is greatly reduced.

The result of the variable analysis is represented by the tuple a(Pn)
of the program root Pn. Some values of the application tuple a(Pn)
indicate errors, warnings, or suspicious cases:

$ux \wedge \overline{sx}$	error	V undefined
$ux \wedge sx$	suspicious	V possibly undefined
$\overline{ux} \wedge \overline{sx} \wedge e$	warning	V not applied
$\overline{ux} \wedge \overline{sx} \wedge \overline{e}$	error	program has no termination
ss	suspicious	V possibly overwritten
xs	suspicious	V possibly forgotten

The errors and warnings indicate secure results, while the suspicious

cases need some further analysis. "ux∧sx" indicate that there is some
path, on which the variable is used before being properly set. This
need not be a programming error, since this path may be impossible for
other semantic reasons, if only there exists some setting path to each
using node. Similar statements hold for ss and xs. Overwriting or
forgetting a variable value is often wanted, if only there is some
using node to each setting.
The further analysis of suspicious variables can be left to the programmer, who usually is able to find out quickly, whether the application is correct or wrong.
The result can be refined in a second local scan of suspicious procedures using the results of the analysis described above and taking into
account only the suspicious variables. In this analysis different
setting and using locations are distinguished. The method is described
in /2/, where it has been applied to local variables.

Of course, the variable analysis is not carried out for each variable
separately, but is performed for all variables of a program in parallel. The operations are based on bit operations that can be extended
to bit strings, and the termination condition can be checked for all
variables together.

A further increase in the efficiency is given by the fact, that the
empty application tuple w occurs for all variables simultaneously, if
it occurs for some variable. Therefore the w-case can be checked separately before each operation. This way the complexity of the operations
is reduced.

Boolean Procedures
Boolean procedures play a special rôle in the language CDL2, as they
are used as ´predicates´ that may have an effect and result upon success, but not upon failure. Technically the result parameters of a
boolean procedure are not restored if the call yields ´false´. /9,2/

For the variable analysis this can be taken into account by assigning
two application tuples to each boolean procedure P, namely a(P.true)
and a(P.false), one for the success, one for the failure case. At the
call of a boolean procedure the respective tuple is selected for the
true and for the false successor.

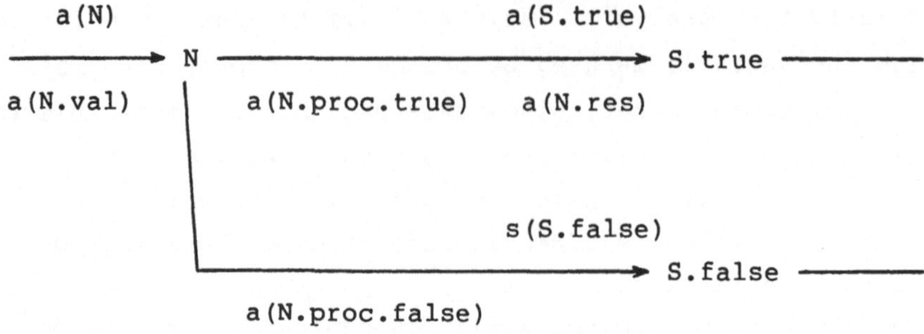

```
a(S.true)   := a(S.true)+a(N)*a(N.val)*a(N.proc.true)*a(N.res)
a(S.false)  := a(S.false)+a(N)*a(N.val)*a(N.proc.false)
```

Path Expressions

For a module there is not a single root for the execution, but there is
a set of exported procedures, that can be called in some order. These
procedures may set and use global variables of the module, in order to
keep information between successive calls of the same or of different
exports.

Such an encapsulation of variables by a number of access algorithms is
often the main purpose of a module. Therefore, exported procedures must
be permitted to use variables that they do not set, or to set variables
that they do not use. For the variable analysis this means that none of
the exported procedures of a module can be expected to behave like a
root.

The idea is to provide an artificial root for a module that substitutes
those parts of the program control, that are outside in one or several
other modules. Or, to say it differently, to describe those paths of
export calls that are admissable for the given module.

These approaches are similar, but may result in quite different expressive means. For a substitution of the missing program control the given
programming language will do, while for a description of paths regular
or context-free expressions may be preferable. In fact, most proposals
for path expressions have come along with special expressive means.

For the language CDL2, such complications are unnecessary: regular and
context-free expressions can be directly mapped onto procedures: procedures are formed like the rules of a grammar, using the ordinary
connectives ´,´ and ´;´ for serial and alternative parts and ´*´ for
iteration of groups.

To give an example of such path expressions let us consider a module
"io" that provides for the input and output of characters and records.
The module exports a number of procedures:

```
EXPORT   init io, open output, out char, out line,
         close output, name output.
```

These exports must be called in a special order. The module must first
be initialized, and before anything is output, the output must be
opened, and must later be closed. Naming can only be done before open-
ing.

```
PATH   use io:
         init io,
            (use output, * ;
             use input, * ;
             use naming, * ;
             ).

PATH   use output:
          open output,
            (out char, * ;
             out line, * ;
             close output).

PATH   use naming:
          name output;
```

Interpreted as a context-free grammar with procedure names as terminals
the path ´use io´ produces the set of admissable paths of export calls
of the module ´io´. Interpreted as procedure the path ´use io´ is the
root of a (pseudo) program, that uses the module ´io´ in admissable
ways.
Note, that the syntax is plain CDL2, except for the symbol ´PATH´. A
path is different from a CDL2-procedure, however, in that it does not
have parameters, and cannot be called, except by other paths.

The admissable paths of export calls can be described by one or by
several path expressions, alternatively. To indicate which paths belong
to the export interface, and which paths are only used as refinements
of other paths, the former ones are exported.

```
EXPORT   use io.
EXPORT   init io, open output, close output, out char,
         out line, name output.
```

For the variable analysis the exported path expressions of a module are
treated like the root procedures of a complete program, having the same
application tuples and calls. Errors are indicated for each path
expression, as if it were a program root.

References

1. Cousot,P., Cousot,R.: Static verification of dynamic type
   properties of variables. Proc. 4th ACM Symposium on Principles of Programming Languages, Sta. Monica, CA, Jan 77

2. Feuerhahn,H., Koster,C.H.A.: Static semantic checks in an
   open-ended language. In: Constructing Quality Software,
   North Holland Publ., Amsterdam 78

3. Fosdick,L.D., Osterweil,L.J.: Data flow analysis in software
   reliability. ACM Computing Surveys 8/3, Sept. 1976

4. Langmaack, H.: On correct procedure parameter transmission
   in higher programming languages. Acta Informatica 2, 1973

5. Killdal, G.A.: A unified approach to global program optimization. Proc. ACM Symposium on Principles of Programming
   Languages, Boston, Oct 73

6. Barth, J.M.: Interprocedural data flow analysis based on
   transitive closure. Proc. 4th ACM Symposium on Principles
   of Programming Languages, Sta. Monica, CA, Jan 77

7. Morel,E., Renvoise,C.: A global algorithm for the elimination
   of partial redundancies. Proc. 2nd International Symposium
   on Programming, Paris, April 76

8. Allen, F.E.: Interprocedural data flow analysis. Proc. IFIP
   Congress 74, North Holland Publ., Amsterdam 74

9. Dehottay,J.P., Feuerhahn,H., Koster,C.H.A., Stahl,H.M.:
   Syntaktische Beschreibung von CDL2. T.U. Berlin, Forschungs-
   gruppe Softwaretechnik, 76

10. Bayer,M., Böhringer,B., Dehottay,J.P., Feuerhahn,H., Jasper,J.,
    Koster,C.H.A., Schmiedecke,U.: Software development in the
    CDL2-Laboratory. In: Software Engineering Environments,
    North Holland Publ., Amsterdam 80

A Formal Model of Instruction Set Semantics[1]

Robert Giegerich

Institut für Informatik
Technische Universität München
Postfach 202420
8000 München 2

Abstract

In order to automate compiler construction beyond
semantic analysis, it is necessary to have a formal
framework wherein the properties of the target machine
may be expressed precisely, such that they become
amenable to automatic treatment. We present a formal
model of instruction sets that defines a precise
semantics to the concepts encountered on the machine
code level: register and storage structure, addressing
modes and side effects, instructions, flag settings and
so on. We give a number of examples to illustrate how
the model can serve in the automatic generation of
target machine dependent compiler parts.

1. Introduction

In the implementation of programming languages, the use of formal mathematical
concepts not only adds to our understanding, but also leads to more reliable compilers
and ultimately to the automatic generation of correct and efficient compiler parts.
This has long been true for the syntactical compiler phases, and is beginning to
emerge for semantic analysis [Gan80], and for program optimization based on flow
analysis methods [CoC79]. For code generation, a number of promising approaches have
been presented [Rip77], [Cat78], [Gla78], but neither of them is capable of modelling
all important aspects of the target machine's instruction set.
The purpose of the present paper is to give a formal model of instruction sets
(section 2). It defines a precise semantics to the concepts encountered on the

---

[1] This research was carried out within the Sonderforschungsbereich 49, Programmiertechnik, Munich

machine code level: register and storage structure, addressing modes and side effects, instructions, flag settings and so on. The appropriateness of the model has been demonstrated in [Gie81], where it was used to develop a method for the automatic generation of machine specific code optimizers. In section 3 we outline applications of our model to instruction set design and automatic generation of code generators and machine code optimizers.

2. A Formal Model of Instruction Set Semantics

2.1. Overall Structure of the Approach

Anyone who has to deal with today's computers on the machine code level knows what it means to make oneself truly familiar with a new processors instruction set. It is not an intellectual challenge at all – and still, it is not easy. On one hand, all processors are alike: there is a small set of functions in the algebraic sense (arithmetic, logical, shift operations and a few more). They all keep the operands to these operations in storage cells of variuos sizes, and they provide a limited number of mechanisms to access these cells. There is really no difference in the basic notions needed to understand traditional instruction sets. The difficulty encountered when studying a new instruction set lies in the way in which these general concepts are combined – how processor storage is arranged, how operations may address their operands, and which operations are combined to form a single instruction.

The approach to be presented reflects this dichotomy of similarity in principle and difference in detail. It comprises a general, abstract model of instruction sets, a notation for the description of a real machine's instruction set, plus a semantics for such descriptions, which is given in terms of the abstract model. As these three components will be introduced in an interleaved fashion, it seems appropriate to make some basic remarks on each of them separately.

Before going into this, let us try to clarify our overall goals further by contrasting them to those of hardware description. The goal of hardware description languages [Su74] is to support the transition from some abstract specification of a processor to its physical implementation. Our interest is in compiler construction, and hence our view is that of using a processor's capabilities. We do not bother which steps comprise the interpretation of a particular instruction word. Rather, we have to answer questions concerning the instruction set as a whole, such as: Are there cases where this instruction is equivalent to some other (in some sense cheaper) instruction? Which groups of instructions have identical operand access capabilities? What is the complete set of machine cells an instruction affects? What can be known about this set at compilation time?

2.1.1. The Abstract Model

The abstract model gives a formal meaning to the notions characteristic to the machine code level. It explains what storage cells, dynamic addresses, addressing modes <u>are</u> in a mathematical setting. It specifies the ways in which these concepts may interact, but of course, it says nothing about a certain feature's presence on a particular machine.

Most of the notions are modelled by functional objects. The abstract model closely relates to the domain definitions of a denotational language definition [Sto77]. However, in denotational semantics the domains also depend on the language to be defined, whereas our abstract model is the same for all machines.

The abstract model will be introduced by a series of definitions, ordered by increasing level of abstraction. We use λ-notation in the form of [Sto77] in order to distinguish these levels. In particular, for $f:X\to Y$ we write fx rather than $f(x)$, and have function application associate from the left.

2.1.2. The Machine Description

For describing instruction sets we could use any notation which can easily be given a semantics in terms of the abstract model. We chose a variant of the ISP-Notation [BeN71], since ISP has been used fairly successfully for expository and hardware design purposes. The notation will be introduced by examples, taken (sometimes simplified) from a MC68000[Mot79]- description. The examples are interspersed with the definitions of the abstract model and illustrate those.

2.1.3. The Semantic Mapping

The semantic mapping interprets a machine description as a particular instance of the abstract model. It extracts the given machine's properties from the description – which classes of cells there are, how they overlap, which addressing modes are available,etc. This mapping is usually straightforward, and hence it is also given by examples.

2.2. Operative Storage Level

We define the structure of a processor's registers and memory not just according to their physical arrangement. Rather, we describe them as an operative storage [Rip77], i.e. according to the way they are operated upon by the instructions. Thus, a physically unique storage cell that can be (part of) a register, half register, or status word will be represented as three operative storage cells with different characteristics. A special relation indicates the physical overlapping of the three.

Definition 1

An operative storage is a tuple

$(\underline{Z}, \underline{V}, v\_range, \underline{A}, a\_range, \underline{C}, overlap)$, where

$\underline{Z}$:   finite set of cell class names,

$\underline{V}$:   set of values, including a special element "<u>undef</u>",

$v\_range: \underline{Z} \to 2^{\underline{V}}$ assigns a set of representable values to each cell class name,

$\underline{A}$:   set of addresses, finite, with $\underline{A} \subseteq \mathbb{N}_o$ and $\underline{A} \subseteq \underline{V}$.

a_range: $\underline{Z}$ --> $2^{\underline{A}}$ assigns a set of addresses to each
                      cell class name,
$\underline{C} \subseteq \underline{Z} \times \underline{A}$, $\underline{C}$ = {(Z,a)|Z $\in \underline{Z}$, a $\in$ a_range(Z)} set of cells,
overlap: $\underline{C} \times \underline{C}$ --> BOOL, a symmetric relation which indicates
                      overlapping of cells.

———

The subset of cells with a given cell class name Z is called the cell class Z. For cells, we write Z[a] rather than (Z,a).
A concrete operative storage is given by a sequence of cell class declarations.

Example (from MC68000 description):
    A,D[0:7]<31:0>   -- 32- bit address/data registers, 8 each
    M8[0:2^{32})<7:0>   -- byte memory
    Z,N,Cy<0:0>   -- zero-, negative- and carry-flag
    program counter PC<31:0>
    These declarations introduce
    $\underline{Z}$ = {A,D,M8,Z,N,Cy,PC},
    a_range(A) = [0:7],
    v_range(A) = set of values representable in 32 bits, etc..
    So far, we have overlap(c,c') = (c=c').

From cell classes already defined, further ones can be built by a set of cell class constructors, such as pairing, subcell selection, concatenation, etc.:
    A16[i]:=A[i]<15:0>   -- low order half register
    M16:=M8 by 2   -- word memory (aligned)
    M32:=M16 by 2 not aligned -- double word memory
Besides augmenting $\underline{Z}$, a_range etc., the semantics of the cell class constructors are such that overlap is extended appropriately. E.g.
    overlap(A16[i],A[j]) = (i=j),
    overlap(M8[a],M16[b] = (b$\leq$a$\leq$b+1),
    overlap(M16[a],M32[b]) = (b$\leq$a$\leq$b+2).
(The overlapping relation we are building up here is tailored to the application in section 3.1. It does not indicate the way in which two cells overlap, but only the fact of overlapping. A more specific overlapping relation could as well be derived from the machine description - the necessary information is there.)
For each declaration, overlapping relations between defined and defining cell classes can be taken immediately from the construction. To determine overlapping with other classes, a kind of transitive closure must be taken. We illustrate the approach by an example:
    overlap(M8[a],M32[b]) = $\exists$c: overlap(M8[a],M16[c]) $\wedge$
                        overlap(M16[c],M32[b])
    = $\exists$c: c$\leq$a$\leq$c+1 $\wedge$ b$\leq$c$\leq$b+2 = b$\leq$a$\leq$b+3.
With the same approach we obtain e.g.
    overlap(A16[i],M16[a]) = false,
    overlap(M32[a],M32[b]) = (b-2$\leq$a$\leq$b+2).
Overlapping of cells within a class is not uncommon on current microprocessors.

2.3. Instruction Execution Level

Execution of instruction modifies the contents of cells. Hence it is modelled by state transformations. The cells an instruction operates on are on this level given explicitly by cell class plus address. Later this address will be seen to be an effective address calculated from some addressing scheme.

Definition 2

$\underline{S} \subseteq \underline{C} \longrightarrow \underline{V}$ set of states, with

$$\forall s \in \underline{S}, \; Z[a] \in \underline{C}: \; s(Z[a]) \in v\_range(Z),$$

$\underline{F} \subseteq \underline{V}^* \longrightarrow \underline{V}$ finite set of algebraic operations,

$\underline{E} \subseteq \underline{S} \longrightarrow \underline{S}$ set of effects, i.e. general state transformations,

$E_e \subseteq \underline{E}$ set of elementary effects, with

$$\forall e \in E_e, \; \forall s \in \underline{S} \; \exists c_{e,s} \in \underline{C}:$$

$$\forall c \in \underline{C}: \; (es)c \neq sc \rightarrow overlap(c, c_{e,s}),$$

$tar: E_e \longrightarrow (\underline{S} \longrightarrow C) := \lambda e. \; \lambda s.c_{e,s}$ assigns a

"target cell" to each elementary effect.

$\underline{F}$ contains algebraic operations like arithmetic and logical operations, shifts, conversions, etc.. Which of those are realized for a given machine can be determined from the descriptions of the instructions (cf. below). Typically, $|\underline{F}| < 60$. Processors do not differ significantly in this respect, but in how these operations are combined to instructions.

Elementary effects implement one such operation, and affect, except for overlapping, exactly one cell. This cell is called the target cell.

Example:

```
Z:=0                       λs.λc. if c=Z then 0 else sc
A16[0]:=A16[0]+M16[122]    λs.λc.if c=A16[0]
                                   then s(A16[0])+s(M16[122])
                                 elsf c=A[0] then  ???
                                 else sc
```

In the second example, since $overlap(A16[0], A[0])$ holds, we must record the change of $A[0]$ that comes along with a modification of $A16[0]$. We model this by a mapping

     $modf: \underline{C} \times \underline{C} \times \underline{S} \times \underline{V} \longrightarrow \underline{V}$, such that

     $modf(c, c', s, b)$ yields the new value of c, if $overlap(c, c')$ and

        in state s, c' is given the new value b.

Clearly, such a function exists, but we shall not specify it here. Rather, we postulate that modf has the following property of identity preservation:

     $sc' = b \rightarrow modf(c, c', s, b) = sc$.

This is the only property of modf we shall use in this paper. We can now formally define the semantics of an elementary effect:

Definition 4

     $Z_0[a_0] := f(Z_1[a_1], \ldots, Z_n[a_n])$ with $Z_i[a_i] \in \underline{C}$, $0 \leq i \leq n$, $f \in \underline{F}$

     denotes the elementary effect

     $\lambda s. \lambda c. \; if \; c = Z_0[a_0] \; then \; b$

$$\underline{elsf} \ overlap(c,Z_0[a_0]) \ \underline{then} \ modf(c,Z_0[a_0],s,b)$$
$$\underline{else} \ sc$$
$$\underline{where} \ b = f(s(Z_1[a_1]),....,s(Z_n[a_n])).$$

Instructions are built from elementary effects by parallel (,) and sequential (;) combination. While the latter is trivially modelled by function composition, parallel combination must handle the case of overlapping target cells.

<u>Definition 5</u>

Let $e,e' \in E_e$, $e = Z_0[a_0]:=f(...)$,
$$e'= Z_0'[a_0']:=f'(...).$$
The semantics of the parallel combination (e,e') is the effect
$\lambda s.\lambda c.\underline{if} \ overlap(Z_0[a_0],Z_0'[a_0']) \ \underline{then} \ \underline{undef}$

$\qquad \underline{elsf} \ c = Z_0[a_0] \ \underline{then} \ f(...)$

$\qquad \underline{elsf} \ c = Z_0'[a_0'] \ \underline{then} \ f'(...)$

$\qquad \underline{elsf} \ overlap(c,Z_0[a_0]) \lor overlap(c,Z_0'[a_0'])$

$\qquad\qquad \underline{then} \ modf(c,(Z_0[a_0],Z_0'[a_0']),s,(f(...),f'(...)))$

$\qquad \underline{else} \ sc$

$\quad \underline{where} \ modf$ is extended correspondingly.

Example:
 a) A[0]:=A[0]+M32[1000], Cy:=<u>carry</u>(A[0]+M32[1000]);
 $\qquad$ Z:=(A[0]=0), N:=(A[0]<0) $\qquad$ --ADD with condition code setting
 b) A[5]:=A[5]+1; PC:= <u>if</u> A[5]=0 <u>then</u> label <u>else</u> PC
 $\qquad\qquad\qquad\qquad\qquad\qquad\qquad$ -- increment and jump
 c) A16[i]:=M16[A[j]],A[j]:=A[j]+2 $\qquad$ -- MOVE with postincrement

The semantics of a) and b) is just what one would expect. The same holds for c) if i $\neq$ j. Otherwise, the target cells overlap, and the whole state becomes <u>undef</u>. Instructions with undefined semantics of this kind are in fact found with many machines, although they must be considered dangerous to programming. Examples are
 MOV -(Ri),-(Ri) -- LSI/PDP 11
 A (Ri)+,(Ri)+ -- TMS 9900
 MOV Ai@+,Ai   -- MC68000
Manufacturer's manuals often do not specify what happens in such cases. The MC68000 in fact delivers an undefined result [Hil80]. Note that our model allows to automatically check an instruction set for instructions with this kind of possibly <u>undef</u>ined semantics.

On the machine operation level, it was correct to consider operand addresses simply to be some $a \in \underline{A}$. The fact that they are "effective addresses", i.e. the result of some address calculation, is irrelevant for the state tranformation achieved by the effect. Now this view becomes relevant, as we turn to how effects are specified in a program.

2.4. Program level

An "instruction" written in some program does not usually denote one specific effect. Rather, it is parameterized with respect to the operand addresses, which may depend on the current state. Thus, on the program level we have to model dynamic addressing.

Definition 5

$D_a \subseteq \underline{S} \longrightarrow \underline{A}$ set of dynamic addresses,

$C_d \subseteq \underline{Z} \times D_a$ set of dynamically addresses cells,

$\mathrm{adc}: D_a \longrightarrow C_d$ assigns a set of address carrier cells
to each dynamic address.

Address carrier cells of a $d \in D_a$ are those whose value is used to calculate the effective address. A $(Z,d) \in C_d$ is again written $Z[d]$. Note that cells in the original sense may be subsumed under dynamically addressed cells by using a constant d. Some examples of dynamic address denotations and their semantics:

d_1: 5 $\qquad\qquad$ $\lambda s.5$

$\qquad\qquad\qquad$ $\mathrm{adc}(d_1) = \emptyset,$

d_2: A[1] $\qquad\qquad$ $\lambda s.s(A[1]),$

$\qquad\qquad\qquad$ $\mathrm{adc}(d_2) = \{A[1]\},$

d_3: A[1]+130 $\qquad\qquad$ $\lambda s.s(A[1])+130,$

$\qquad\qquad\qquad$ $\mathrm{adc}(d_3) = \{A[1]\},$

d_4: M32[A[1]+7] $\qquad\qquad$ $\lambda s.s(M32[s(A[1])+7]),$

$\qquad\qquad\qquad$ $\mathrm{adc}(d_4) = \{A[1], M32[\lambda s.s(A[1])+7]\}$.

These are examples of absolute, indirect, base+displacement and doubly indirect with offset addressing. Examples of dynamically addressed cells would then be

$A[d_1]$, $M8[d_1]$, $M16[d_2]$, $M8[d_4]$.

With these definitions,

$A[d_1] := A[d_1]+M32[d_3]$ denotes the elementary effect

$A[d_1 s] := A[d_1 s]+M32[d_3 s].$

Which dynamic addresses may actually be used by a program is determined by the set of address templates, to be defined on the instruction set level.

2.5. Instruction Set Level

This level embodies all the concepts which structure the machine's addressing and operation capabilities. First, the set of available dynamic addresses is generated from a small set of templates.

Definition 6

$\underline{D} \subseteq \underline{A}^* \longrightarrow D_a$ is the set of address templates.

Logically, address templates are abstractions from dynamic addresses: from $\lambda s.s(A[i])+d$ for given $i,d \in \underline{A}$, we obtain the template $\lambda i,d.\lambda s.s(A[i])+d$. The practical view goes the other direction: The set $\underline{D}$ of address templates is given in the machine description, and D_a is thereby represented implicitly.

Example:

    D_1: a, $a \in [0:2^{32})$

    D_2: A[j], $j \in [0:7]$

    D_3: A[i]+d, $i \in [0:7]$, $d \in [0:2^{16})$

    D_4: M32[A[i]+d], $i \in [0:7]$, $d \in [0:2^{16})$

    Sometimes a template generates only a single dynamic address:

    D_5: HL   denotes $\lambda a.\lambda s.s(HL)$ --implied address, 8080.

Typically, not all address templates may be used to access all cell classes. This leads us to the notion of addressing modes.

<u>Definition 7</u>

    <u>M</u> is the set of addressing modes, where each $m \in \underline{M}$ is a tuple

    (m,cost(m),side(m),sind(m)) with

    $m \in \underline{Z} \times \underline{D}$, a cellclass/address template pair, denoting that the

               cells of this class may be accessed using this template,

    $cost(m) \in \mathbb{N}_0 \times \mathbb{N}_0 \times \mathbb{N}_0$ = <space cost for address,

             time cost for effective address calculation + access,

                time cost for access only>,

    $side(m) \in E_e \lor \{\underline{empty}\}$, an addressing side effect,

    $sind(m) \in \{1,2,3\}$ indicates whether the side effect occurs before,

             simultaneous with or after the use of the addressing mode.

Example:

    <u>addressing modes</u>

    Areg(i): A[i]   <u>cost</u> 0.0.0   -- address register

    Dreg(i): D[i]   <u>cost</u> 0.0.0   -- data register

    ind(j): M8[A[j]]   <u>cost</u> 0.2.2   -- addressing a byte via a

                                               register

    disp(i,d): M32[A[i]+d] <u>cost</u> 2.6.4   -- base+displacement addressing

                                               of a double word

    postinc(j): M32[A[j]], A[j]:=A[j]+4 <u>cost</u> 0.4.4 -- postincrement mode;

                                        here sind = 2, since the side

                                        effect is combined by ",".

    <u>constant</u> im32: $[-2^{31}:2^{31})$<u>cost</u> 4.4.0   -- immediate data

             im3: [1:8]   <u>cost</u> 0.0.0   -- "quick" operands

Instructions may be described as combinations of elementary effects, parameterized by addressing modes as their operands. However, since an operand of an instruction can often be accessed using a variety of addressing modes, we introduce another level of parametrization:

<u>Definition 8</u>

    $\underline{O} \subseteq 2^{\underline{M}}$ is the set of operand classes.

Instructions are now (informally) defined as combinations of elementary effects, parameterized by operand classes and associated with a (space.time) cost.

Example (from MC68000 description, X,V-flags omitted):

<u>operand class</u>
all:={Areg,Dreg,disp,postinc,im32,...};
data:= all\{Areg};
alterable:=all\{im32};
alt_mem:=alterable\{Dreg,Areg};
alt_data:=alterable\{Areg};
<u>instructions</u>

MOV:	alt_data:=all, Cy:=0,Z:=(all=0),N:=(all<0)	<u>cost</u> 2.2;
MOVEA:	Areg:=all	<u>cost</u> 2.2;
ADD_1:	Dreg:=Dreg+all, Cy:=<u>carry</u>(Dreg+all),	
	Z:=(Dreg+all=0),N:=(Dreg+all<0)	<u>cost</u> 2.2;
ADD_2:	alt_mem:=alt_mem+Dreg, Cy:=<u>carry</u>(alt_mem+Dreg),	
	Z:=(alt_mem+Dreg=0),N:=(alt_mem+Dreg<0)	<u>cost</u> 2.2
ADDA:	Areg:=Areg+all	<u>cost</u> 2.2;
ADDI:	alt_data:=alt_data+im32, Cy:=<u>carry</u>(alt_data+im32),	
	Z:=(alt_data+im32=0),N:=(alt_data+im32<0)	<u>cost</u> 2.2
ADDQ:	alterable:=alterable+im3, Cy:=<u>carry</u>(alterable+im3),	
	Z:=(alterable+im3=0),N:=(alterable+im3<0)	<u>cost</u> 2.2;

For each particular instance of an instruction, the cost contributions from the specific addressing modes and their side effects are combined with the cost and effects of the instruction itself.

2.6. Predefined "Loopholes" of the Model

A formal approach intended to model real world instruction sets must pay tribute to the ingenuity of instruction set designers, and be prepared to deal with instructions whose semantics cannot be described properly. Of course, one can always augment the model by some new function, in order to incorporate some special feature of a given machine. For compiler writing, it is often more appropriate to have a means of consistent abstraction in the following sense: If we do not describe the exact semantics of an instruction, we must at least describe it in a way that ensures that no incorrect information is derived from the instruction's description.

An extreme case is the EXECUTE- instruction (e.g. TMS9900), which takes an arbitrary data word, interpretes it as an instruction word and executes it. This could be modelled by the effect λs.<u>undef</u>, indicating that we know nothing about the contents of any cell after this instruction. Similar considerations apply to io-ports or cells that can otherwise be modified from outside the control of a given program.

The need for consistent abstraction from certain details of an instruction set also arises from the purpose of the machine description. For example, a compiler implementor may decide to use some general register only in some restricted fashion, say as a base register. Then the machine description may be written such that only the permitted operations on this register appear to be possible. Thus, code generators or machine code optimizers generated from the machine description (cf.

section 3) will automatically adhere to the implementor's conventions. For a detailed discussion of these and related aspects the reader is again referred to [Gie81].

3. Applications

The purpose for which this model was developed originally was automatic generation of machine specific code optimizers. In section 3.1, we give two examples from this area, where our model has proved to be useful. In 3.2 and 3.3 we outline some potential applications in the areas of instruction set design and automatic generation of code generators.

3.1. Automatic Generation of Machine Specific Code Optimizers

The need for a compiler phase of a-posteriori optimization on the machine code level has first been observed in [McK65], where the term "peephole optimization" was coined. Since then, this compilation subtask has expanded considerably [Wul75],[PQC80]. Optimization on this level includes utilization of special instructions and of side effects, elimination of redundant load/store operations and of jump chains, use of the cheapest addressing modes possible, and the like. Clearly, these optimizations depend on all the "dirty" features of an instruction set. Consequently, this phase has so far been the least understood of all compiler phases, and the least amenable to automation. We present two aspects in which our model was used to handled these problems in [Gie81].

3.1.1. Derivation of Context Information on the Machine Code Level

Although a single optimization on this level typically affects only one or two instructions, it usually depends on information about the context in which the instruction occurs in the program. The most important types of context information are
- constant and copy information, i.e. which cells contain a known constant, or a copy of some other cell's value at a given point in the program.
- dead variable information, i.e. which cells contain a value irrelevant to the further execution of the program from a given point on.

Both kinds of information can be derived from a progam by flow analysis [CoC79] methods. In order to apply these methods to the machine code, we need to know which cells are affected by operations on others. Since instructions, as they appear in the program, take dynamically addressed cells as their operands, we need a relation which specifies overlapping of dynamically addressed cells:

d_overlap:C_d X C_d X $\underline{S}$-->BOOL is defined as

d_overlap(Z[Da],Z'[D'a'],s) := overlap(Z[Das],Z'[D'a's]).

This is useful only as a starting point, since it is not evaluable at optimization time. We need some approximation which indicates potential overlapping only, but is evaluable at optimization time. We may define two alternative abstractions:

    a) total abstraction from program behaviour:

       $t\_overlap: C_d \times C_d \longrightarrow BOOL$ with

       $t\_overlap(Z[Da], Z'[D'a']) := \exists\, s \in \underline{S}: d\_overlap(Z[Da], Z'[D'a'], s)$.

    b) partial abstraction relative to context information:

       Asssume we have some predicate $1 \in (\underline{S} \longrightarrow BOOL)$, restricting the set of possible states. (Context information provides such predicates.) Then we obtain a more precise relation by

       $p\_overlap: C_d \times C_d \times L \longrightarrow BOOL$ with

       $p\_overlap(Z[Da], Z'[D'a'], 1) := \exists\, s \in \underline{S}: 1s \wedge d\_overlap(Z[Da], Z'[D'a'], s)$.

Both a) and b) are evaluable at optimization time. But we can do much better. Considering that $\underline{M}$ is known at generation time and small compared to C_d (or its subset used in a program), we transform e.g. t_overlap into

    $g\_overlap: \underline{M} \times \underline{M} \longrightarrow (A^+ \times A^+ \longrightarrow BOOL)$ with

    $g\_overlap(Z[D], Z'[D']) = \lambda a, a'.t\_overlap(Z[Da], Z'[D'a'])$.

g_overlap is evaluable for each pair of addressing modes at generation time. Thus we have a generator yielding an overlapping condition depending only on the actual a,a' as they occur in the program. For example, $g\_overlap(ind(j), disp(i,d))$ yields

    <u>if</u> i=j <u>then</u> d<0<d+3 <u>else</u> <u>true</u>.

Clearly, this reduces the optimization time effort to a mimimum. By similar methods, we can derive the functions which propagate context information through the machine program.

3.1.2. Generation of Machine Specific Optimization Rules

The general notion of an optimization rule is that one instruction may be replaced by another if their semantics are equivalent relative to the available context. We cannot formally develop this notion here. Rather, we give some examples for its application. For a given pair of instructions, an applicability condition, under which the replacement of one by the other is legal, can be generated automatically. This condition takes care of cell overlapping, inconsistent flag settings and addressing mode side effects, those aspects which make it so hard to produce a correct machine code optimizer when doing it by hand. Some of the machine specific replacement rules obtained for the instructions described in section 2.3 are:

    ADD_1 x,y <-> ADDI x,z : $x \in Dreg \wedge y \in all \wedge y \notin \{predec, postinc\} \wedge y=z \wedge e \in im32$

    ADD_1 x,y -> ADDI x,z : $y \notin \{predec, postinc\} \wedge y=z \wedge z \in im32$

    ADD_1 x,y <- ADDI x,z : $x \in Dreg \wedge y \in all \wedge y \notin \{predec, postinc\} \wedge y=z$

    ADD_1 x,y -> ADDQ x,z : $y \notin \{predec, postinc] \wedge y=z \wedge z \in [1:8]$

    ADDA x,y -> ADDI x,z :   <u>false</u>

    ADDA x,y -> ADDQ x,z : $y \notin \{predec, postinc\} \wedge y=z \wedge z \in [1:8] \wedge \{Cy, Z, N\}$ are dead

    ADD_1 x,postinc -> ADDI x,z: postinc=z $\wedge$ A[j] is dead

The first rule is bidirectional: the direction of the replacement does not enter the applicability condition. Rather, it is determined from the cost functions. For example, for the first rule the replacement will be

    left-to-right, if $y=M32[a]$, $z \in im32$, saving 4 machine cycles if a is a 32-bit absolute address, or

right-to-left, if y=D[i], z $\in$ im32, saving 4 bytes and 4 machine cycles.
However, when a fixed direction of replacement assumed, simplified applicability conditions may be generated. All rules except the first are of this kind. The second and third rules are specializations of the first rule.

The two examples given in this paragraph demonstrate the usefulness of our model in two respects. First, a precise definition of instruction semantics allows to formally capture instruction equivalence, and hence to produce correct machine dependent criteria for our optimization rules. Second, it serves to systematically separate runtime, program and (only) machine dependent aspects. In deriving context information, we could therefore abstract from runtime dependent aspects by the method of abstract interpretation. Furthermore, at generation time we can simplify the optimization criteria by evaluating those subconditions which are only machine dependent. For example, it is determined that for the rules given above, flag usage is critical only for the rule ADDA->ADDQ. Thus we obtain an efficient machine code optimizer, since at translation time it will only test conditions that in fact depend on the given program.

3.2. Instruction Set Design

A formal description of a prospected instruction set can help to point out problematic aspects of the design. The description can be analysed automatically with respect to questions like: Is there redundancy in the sense that differently encoded instructions achieve identical effects? Are there instructions with potentially undefined semantics? Even more important is the question how certain design decisions (e.g. dedicated vs. general purpose registers) affect the complexity of the instruction set. For example, if the set of operand classes needed in the description is small relative the set of addressing modes, and if furthermore each of these classes can be given a reasonable intuitive interpretation (e.g. "all alterable operands"), the machine will be easy to program.
Another kind of desirable support to judge an instruction sets appropriateness would be if one could easily obtain a code generator for it and see how it performs. This leads us to the next area of application.

3.3. Automatic Generation of Code Generators

Code generators, while emitting instructions, often maintain a "machine image" [Wai77], where the current status of register usage, available copies in memory, etc. is recorded. It has been shown that a good part of the functions which manipulate such a machine image are machine independent [Sch79]. It appears to be possible to automatically generate the machine specific data structure which implements the machine image from a machine description.
Recent approaches to automate the code selection process itself [Rip77], [Cat78], [Gla78] are all restricted in the sense that they base the matching of the intermediate form of the program with the instructions on syntactic similarities only. E.g. [Gla78] views instructions as productions of a grammar, the intermediate form as a sentence from this grammar, and selects code by constructing a parse of this

sentence. Here semantic constraints ("this register's value may not be destroyed") still must be incorporated by hand, often in a nontrivial way. [Gnp80] demonstrates that this can be done by specifying a set of attributes and attribute evaluation rules for the instruction set grammar. Thus it should be possible to give a methodology and at least partial automatic support for a derivation of the necessary attribute rules from a machine description in terms of our model, using methods similar to those which exist for the systematic derivation of compiler descriptions by attribute grammars from denotational language definitions [Gan80]. Both approaches sketched above are currently being investigated.

References

[BeN71] C.G.Bell, A.Newell:
  Computer Structures: Readings and Examples,
  McGraw-Hill,1971
[Cat78] R.G.G.Cattell:
  Formalization and Automatic Derivation of Code Generators,
  Report CMU-CS-78-115, Carnegie Mellon University, Pittsburgh 1978
[CoC79] P.Cousot, R.Cousot:
  Systematic Design of Program Analysis Frameworks, Proceedings
  of 6th ACM Symposium on Principles of Programming Languages, 1979,
  pp.269-282
[Gan80] H.Ganzinger:
  Some Principles for the Development of Compiler Descriptions from
  Denotational Language Definitions, TUM-INFO 8006, Institut für
  Informatik, Technical University Munich, 1980
[Gie81] R.Giegerich:
  Automatische Erzeugung von Maschinencode-Optimierern, TUM-I8112,
  Institut für Informatik, Technical University Munich, 1981 (an English
  summary appears in [Gie82])
[Gie82] R.Giegerich:
  Automatic Generation of Machine Specific Code Optimizers, Proceedings
  of 9th ACM Symposium on Principles of Programming Languages, 1982
[Gla78] R.S.Glanville:
  A Machine Independent Algorithm for Code Generation and its
  Use in Retargetable Compilers, Technical report UCB-CS-78-01,
  University of California, Berkeley 1978
[Gnp80] M.Ganapathi:
  Retargetable Code Generation and Optimization Using Attribute
  Grammars, Computer sciences technical report #406,
  University of Wisconsin, Madison, 1980
[Hil80] W. Hilf, Motorola Munich, private communication
[McK65] W.M.McKeeman:
  Peephole Optimization, CACM 8,7, 1965, pp.443-444
[Mot79] Motorola Inc.:
  MC68000 16 Bit Microprocessor, User Manual, 1979
[PQC80] B.W.Leverett, R.G.G.Cattell, S.O.Hobbs, J.M.Newcomer,
  A.H.Reiner, B.R.Schatz, W.A.Wulf: An Overview of the Production
  Quality Compiler-Compiler Project, IEEE Computer, Aug.1980, pp.38-49

[Rip77] K.Ripken:
Formale Beschreibung von Maschinen, Implementierungen und optimie-
render Maschinencodeerzeugung aus attributierten Programm-
graphen, TUM-INFO 7731, Institut für Informatik, Technical
University Munich, 1977

[Sch79] W.Schürer:
Erarbeitung einer Hierarchie von Schnittstellen für die
Codeerzeugung für verschiedene Microcomputer, Diplomarbeit,
Institut für Informatik, Technical University Munich,1979

[Sto77] J.E.Stoy:
Denotational Semantics: The Scott-Strachey Approach to Programming
Language Theory, MIT Press, Cambridge (Mass.), 1977

[Wai77] W.M.Waite:
Code Generation, in:
F.L.Bauer, J.Eickel (eds.):
Compiler Construction - An Advanced Course, Lecture Notes in
Computer Science No. 25, Springer 1974

[Wul75] W.A.Wulf, R.K.Johnsson,C.B.Weinstock, S.O.Hobbs, C.M.Geschke:
The Design of an Optimizing Compiler, American Elsevier,
New York 1975

System- und Sprachentwicklung für die Verfahrenstechnik auf der Basis abstrakter Maschinen

K.H. Sturm

Versuchsanstalt für Datenverarbeitung und Prozeßtechnik in Berlin

Zusammenfassung

Ausgehend von konkreten (Teil-) Aufgaben zur Steuerung und Regelung verfahrenstechnischer Prozesse in Brauereien werden im ersten Teil Prozeß-Strukturen aufgezeigt, analysiert und dazu praktische Bedingungen sowie Vereinbarungen angeführt, die den Lösungsansatz bestimmen. Als Hilfsmittel zur Formalisierung der Systemstruktur werden abstrakte Maschinenmodelle verwendet.
Im zweiten Teil werden aus einer Menge partieller Prozeßaufgaben resourcen- und programmorientierte Module definiert, die mit einer gewissen Variabilität durch Parameter und Optionen für den vorgegebenen Aufgabenbereich eingesetzt werden können. Diese Module sind in die Systemstruktur als interpretative Funktionen eingebettet und bilden die terminalen Sprachelemente des Brauerei Interpreter SYstems (BISY).
Abschließend werden an einem einfachen Beispiel die Systemgenerierung und die Anwenderprogrammierung erläutert sowie auf neuere Ansätze hingewiesen.

Einleitung

Mit einer technisch wirtschaftlichen Zielsetzung startete 1974 an der TU-Berlin im Verbund mit der Versuchs- und Lehranstalt für Brauerei (VLB) das Forschungsprogramm "Automatische Führung des Mälzungs- und Brauprozesses" (11).

Neben dem ersten PEARL-Sudhausprojekt würden bis 1980 über 10 Pilotsysteme mit dem interpretativen System BISY installiert, getestet und inbetriebgenommen. Während in dem angeführten PEARL-Projekt (3) die statische Grundfließbildbeschreibung durch ein zugeordnetes Petri-Netz überdeckt und damit aufgezeigt wurde, daß diese erweiterte dynamische Beschreibungsmethode geeignet ist, um daraus die zugeordneten Programmstrukturen abzubilden,

Grundverfahren   ⟶   Tasks (parallele Prozesse)

partielle Verfeinerungen   ⟶   Echtzeitelemente

ging es in dem BISY-Projekt schwerpunktsmäßig darum, Strukturen und Operationen aus den funktionellen und logischen Abläufen verfahrenstechnischer Prozesse herauszuarbeiten, zu formalisieren, um sie dann durch konforme Abbildungen in ein Rechnersystem zu überführen.
Der folgende Bericht skizziert Lösungsansätze zu dieser verfahrenstechnisch orientierten System- und Sprachentwicklung.

1. Analyse, Beschreibung und Strukturierung verfahrenstechnischer Prozesse

Im Ablauf der Projektierung verfahrenstechnischer Anlagen entsteht eine Vielfalt von Dokumenten (14), wovon eine ausgezeichnete Menge notwendig ist, um das Verfahren – die Gesamtheit aller Operationen zum Erreichen eines vorgegebenen Produktionszieles – zu beschreiben.

Es wird davon ausgegangen, daß der Verfahrensablauf einer Anlage durch die Dokumente Fließbild und verbale Beschreibung ausreichend spezifiziert ist, und daß für die im Grundfließbild (z. B. Abb. 1) dargestellten Grundverfahren sowie für die Dualitätsbeziehung zwischen Anlage und Verfahren gilt:

- Ein Grundverfahren ist ein Verfahren, bei dem die Stoffumwandlungsvorgänge funktionell definiert sind.

- Eine Apparatur ist ein Apparat – eine reale Maschine – bzw. zusammenhängende benachbarte Apparate, auf denen ein oder mehrere Grundverfahren ablaufen können.

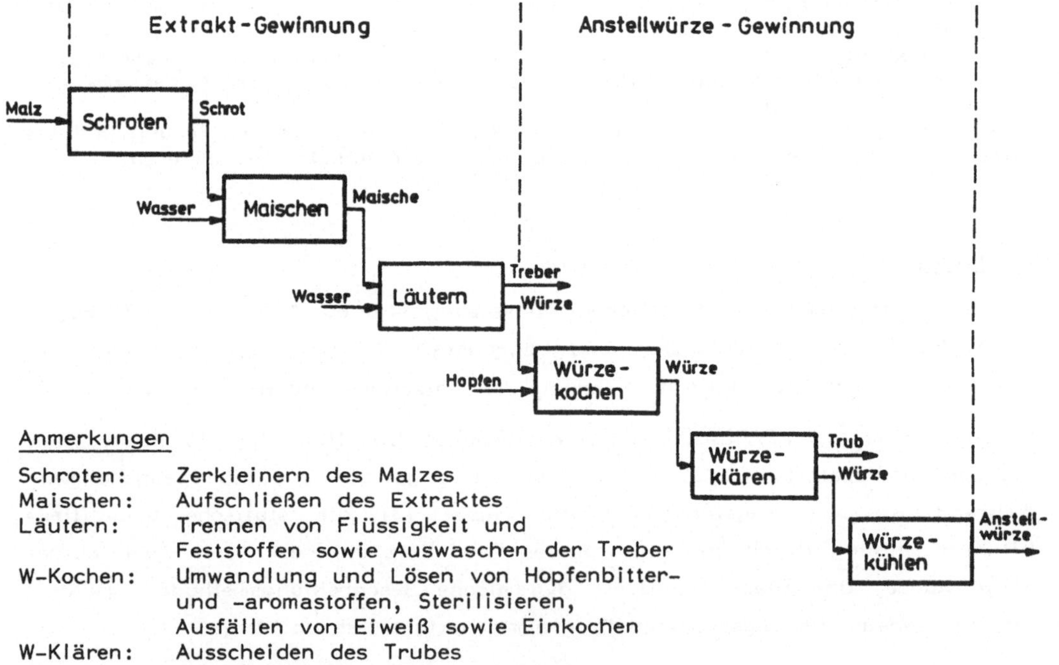

Anmerkungen

Schroten: Zerkleinern des Malzes
Maischen: Aufschließen des Extraktes
Läutern: Trennen von Flüssigkeit und
    Feststoffen sowie Auswaschen der Treber
W–Kochen: Umwandlung und Lösen von Hopfenbitter-
    und –aromastoffen, Sterilisieren,
    Ausfällen von Eiweiß sowie Einkochen
W–Klären: Ausscheiden des Trubes
W–Kühlen: Abkühlen der Würze auf Anstelltemperatur

Abb. 1 Grundfließbild (Beispiel aus dem Bier-Herstellungsprozeß)

Ein erster begrifflicher Übergang erfolgt durch die Verwendung der mehr abstrakten Prozeßbegriffe nach DIN 66 201:

- ein Prozeß ist die Umformung und/oder Transport von Materie, Energie und/oder Informationen

- ein technischer Prozeß ist ein Prozeß, dessen Zustandsgrößen mit technischen Mitteln gemessen und/oder geregelt werden können,

die den Begriff "Verfahren" als einen technischen Stoffumwandlungsprozeß ein-
schließen.

Nachfolgend werden einige Charakteristiken technischer Prozesse beschrieben,
wobei vorrangig von diskontinuierlichen Betriebsformen (9) ausgegangen wird,
die für eine Rechnersteuerung allgemein aufwendiger, um nicht zu sagen
schwieriger sind als kontinuierliche Verfahren.

1.1 Informelle Beschreibung

Vorerst unabhängig davon, daß jeder technische Prozeß beschrieben werden
kann durch Zustandswerte bzw. im Sinne von Petri (8) als ein Zustandsraum
mit Kausalgefüge, sei der Vorstellungsablauf einer verfahrenstechnischen Anlage
dadurch charakterisiert, daß diese Anlage, simpel ausgedrückt, "eingeschaltet"
bzw. - aktiv ist, so daß diese Anlagen-Aktivität durch das folgende Diagramm
(Abb. 2) dargestellt werden kann.

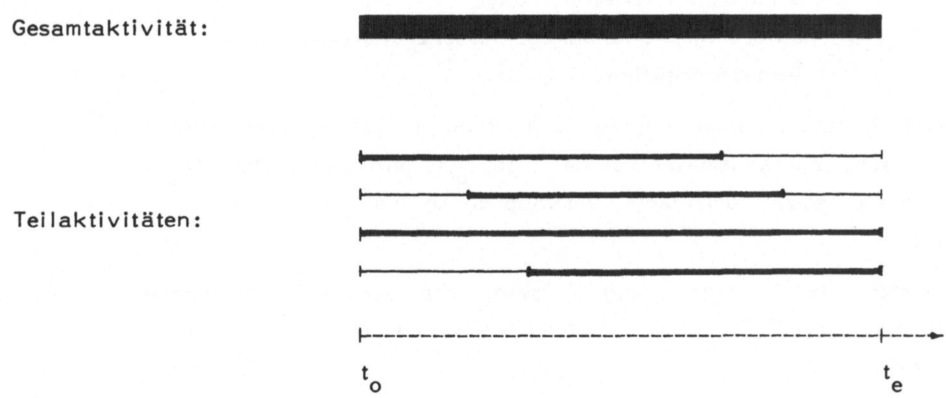

Abb. 2   Aktivität der Anlage

In diesem Zusammenhang wird zum Ausdruck gebracht, daß für eine
rechnergesteuerte Anlage im Echtzeitbetrieb für den gesamten Zeitraum $< t_o, t_e >$,
während die Anlage bzw. der Prozeß läuft - aktiv ist - Rechenzeit zur
Verfügung gestellt werden muß.

Im ersten Schritt kann nun die Gesamtaktivität - der Prozeß - durch die
apparative Zuordnung (jedes Grundverfahren läuft auf einer Apparatur) in n
Teilprozesse zerlegt werden, die nicht notwendigerweise im gesamten Bereich von
t_o bis t_e <u>aktiv</u> sind aber <u>bekannt</u> sein sollen (s. Abb. 2).

Diese Darstellung entspricht auch der intuitiven Vorstellung einer Schar
<u>paralleler Prozesse</u> - Merkmale auf parallelen Linien - mit einem gemeinsamen
Zeitmaßstab, so daß die Beziehung der <u>Gleichzeitigkeit</u> durch orthogonale Linien
festgestellt werden kann.

In einem zweiten Schritt werden die Teilprozesse P_i zerlegt in eine Folge abgegrenzt beschreibbarer Prozeßblöcke P_{ij}, wobei jeder Block aufgelöst wird in sequentielle Prozesse durch:

1. zugeordnete partielle Prozesse p_{ij}
2. eine notwendige Anzahl von ereignisgesteuerten Nebenprozessen mit folgenden Gültigkeitsbereichen:

    a) lokal dem partiellen Prozeß p_{ij} untergeordnet

    b) global dem aktiven Bereich des Teilprozesses P_i untergeordnet.

1.2 Maschinenmodelle

Ausgehend von speziellen Problemstellungen gibt es eine Anzahl formaler Methoden, die in der definierten Abstraktion besonders "gut geeignet" sind, ein vorgegebenes Problem zu beschreiben bzw. zu lösen.

Gut geeignet ist hier zu interpretieren als

        - problemnahe Beschreibung

        - eindeutiger und abgeschlossener Formalismus

        - lesbare Notation.

In diesem Kontext haben Hornig und Randell (4) bereits aufgezeigt, daß deterministische Zustandsmaschinen $M = (S, s_o, f)$ ein geeignetes Mittel sind, um reale Prozesse sowie definierte Verknüpfungen von Subprozessen $p_1 \circ p_2$ zu beschreiben.

Ebenso sollte die Methode geeignet sein, die abstrahierten Prozesse durch zugeordnete "Module" in einem Rechnersystem zu steuern, zu regeln und zu überwachen.

Der Begriff Modul wird hierbei im Sinne von Dennis (1) benutzt:

    "Die externe Verwendung eines Moduls wird lediglich bestimmt durch eine definierte Schnittstelle mit der Außenwelt",

so daß die formale Methode insbesondere Auskunft geben soll zu Fragen der

- Modulhierarchie   (Ordnungsrelation von Modulen),
- Aufgabenverteilung   (prozeßorientierte Zuordnungen),
- Datenflußrelation   (:=,=: ausgezeichneter Daten),
- Beschränkungen   (Anschlußbedingungen für Prozeßoperationen).

1.2.1 Definitionen

Unter diesen vorausgegangenen Aspekten wurden als Hilfsmittel zur Formalisierung Input-Output-Maschinen und zu deren graphischer Darstellung markierte Zustandsgraphen verwendet.

Definition 1.2.1,1

Eine Input-Output-Maschine M ist ein Fünftupel

$$M = (I,O,S,f,h)$$

I eine endliche Menge von Eingangstupeln $i=(i_1,\ldots,i_n)$
O eine endliche Menge von Ausgangstupeln $o=(o_1,\ldots,o_n)$
S eine endliche Menge von Zustandstupeln $s=(s_1,\ldots,s_n)$
f: $S \times I \longrightarrow S$ Überführungsfunktion
h: $S \times I \longrightarrow O$ Ausgabefunktion

Anmerkung:

Wenn nicht anders definiert ist, wird zur einfacheren Darstellung der Zustandsgraphen davon ausgegangen, daß h die Projektion auf S ist, so daß O=S gilt.

Definition 1.2.1,2

Ein eingabemarkierter Zustandsgraph ist ein Viertupel

$$Z = (S,E,I,m) \quad \text{mit}$$

(S,E) Graph, $E \subset S \times S$
m: $E \longrightarrow I$ Markierungsfunktion
$E_m := \{\,[e,i]\,|\ e \in E,\ i \in I,\ i=m(e)\,\}$

S eine endliche Menge von Zustandsknoten
I eine endliche Menge von Eingabemarkierungen
E_m eine endliche Menge von eingabemarkierten Kanten

Anmerkung:

In einigen Fällen wird nachfolgend ein Verschmelzungs-Homomorphismus (7) verwendet, der es ermöglicht, zusammenhängende Teilgraphen in einer einfachen
Weise zu einem Grobknoten zu verschmelzen (s. Beispiel Abb. 3).

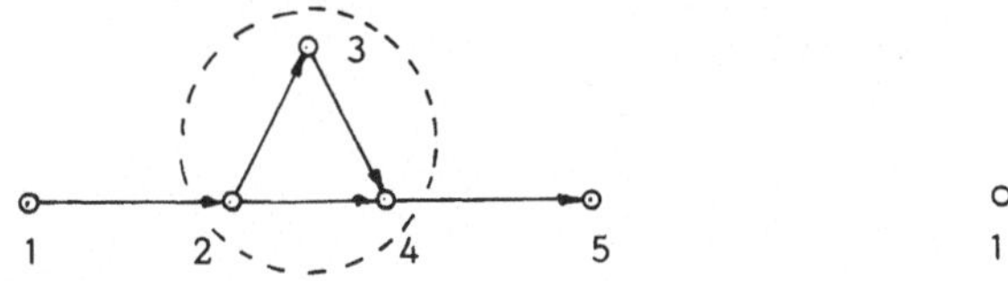

Abb. 3 Verschmelzungsbeispiel

1.2.2 Grundstrukturen

Im Zusammenhang mit dem BISY-Projekt wurden einige Prozeßstrukturen:
sequentielle Prozesse, wiederholbare Prozesse, alternative Prozesse, parallele
Prozesse, ereignisgesteuerte Prozesse, analysiert und ihnen abstrakte Maschinen
zugeordnet, die diese Prozesse beschreiben (12).

Ausgehend von einer mehr umfassenden Klassifizierung in <u>sequentielle</u> und <u>nichtsequentielle</u> Prozesse und von der Voraussetzung, daß nichtsequentielle Prozesse nach Petri (8) in einer vielfältigen Weise durch sequentielle Prozesse überdeckt werden können, werden nachfolgend die für das BISY-Prozeßkonzept notwendigen Grundstrukturen beschrieben und aufgezeigt, daß für das zugeordnete Rechnersystem im wesentlichen nur zwei Maschinenkonstrukte erforderlich sind.

Während Dijkstra (2) einen sequentiellen Prozeß durch eine 'before-after' Relation beschreibt und am Beispiel einer Relaisschaltung zeigt, daß im sequentiellen Fall ein Kontaktzustand bzw. eine Folge von Kontaktzuständen bestimmt werden kann, bevor der zugeordnete Strom durch die Magnetspule fließt, wird im folgenden die Maschinendefinition unmittelbar genutzt.

<u>Definition: 1.2.2,1</u>

Ein Prozeß P heißt <u>sequentiell</u>, wenn die diskreten Zustände von P definiert sind durch eine Maschine $M = (I,O,S,f,h)$.

Im Kontext zu der vorangegangenen informellen Beschreibung der Prozeßaktivitäten werden folgende Vereinbarungen getroffen:

Vereinbarung 1.2.2,1

1. Jede Maschine M hat zwei ausgezeichnete Zustände

   s_o bezeichnet den Anfangszustand

   s_e bezeichnet den Endzustand

2. Jede Maschine M hat einige ausgezeichnete I/O-Komponenten

   jedes $i \in I$ enthält eine Startkomponente $i_{(S)}$,

   jedes $o \in O$ eine Aktivitätskomponente $o_{(A)}$

3. Eine Maschine ist <u>aktiv</u> bzw. <u>inaktiv</u>, wenn sie sich in einem Zustand $s \neq s_e$ bzw. s_e befindet, so daß gilt:

$$f(s,i) \begin{cases} \neq s_e \iff o_{(A)} = 1 \iff M \text{ ist "aktiv"} \\ = s_e \iff o_{(A)} = 0 \iff M \text{ ist "inaktiv"} \end{cases}$$

4. Eine Maschine M wird aus dem <u>inaktiven</u> Zustand s_e in den <u>aktiven</u> Zustand s_o überführt durch die Startkomponente $i_{(S)}$:

$$f(s_e,i) = s_o \implies i \text{ enthält } i_{(S)} \text{ mit } i_{(S)} = 1$$

Die letzte Vereinbarung berücksichtigt insbesondere den häufigen Fall in der Verfahrenstechnik beim Chargenbetrieb, daß (Teil-) Prozesse wiederholt ausgeführt werden.

Ein __wiederholbarer__ Prozeß P ist durch den folgenden Zustandsgraphen Z dargestellt, wobei P' die Verschmelzung aller Zustände $S - \{s_o, s_e\}$ von P repräsentiert.

$$s_o \qquad\qquad P' \qquad\qquad s_e \qquad i_{(S)} = 0$$

$$i_{(S)} = 1$$

Abb. 4   Wiederholbarer Prozeß

Wie in der informalen Darstellung bereits aufgezeigt wurde, kann ein Prozeß in abgegrenzte Prozeßabschnitte aufgeteilt werden.

Definition 1.2.2,2

   Eine __serielle Folge__ sequentieller Prozesse p_j ist ein zusammenhängender sequentieller Prozeß P

$$P = (p_1, \ldots, p_n)$$

so daß gilt:

Jeder Endzustand s_e^j eines Prozesses p_j mit $j<n$ liefert ein Startereignis für den folgenden Prozeß p_{j+1} (z. B. für die Überführung in den Zustand s_o^{j+1}).

Diese Zerlegung in eine serielle Folge sequentieller Prozesse führt zu einer Familie von Maschinen, in der jedem partiellen Prozeß p_j eine entsprechende indizierte Maschine M_j zugeordnet wird.

Definition 1.2.2,3

   FM ist eine Familie von Maschinen M_j mit der Indexmenge $J \subset |N$, so daß für ein beliebiges aber festes $j \in J$ gilt:

$$M_j = (I,O,S,f_j,h_j)$$
$$f_j : S \times I \longrightarrow S$$
$$h_j : S \times I \longrightarrow O$$

Als Beispiel kann nun ein Prozeß $P = (p_1, \ldots, p_n)$ durch zugeordnete Maschinen M_j wie folgt algorithmisch beschrieben werden.

```
PROC serielle Prozeßfolge (M1,...,Mn)
    starte Maschine (M1);
        .
        .
        .
    starte Maschine (Mn);
END PROC;
```

Da die Prozedur "serielle Prozeßfolge" auf einem höheren Level abläuft als die Prozedur "starte Maschine", liegt es nahe, auch für die maschinenorientierte Beschreibung eine ähnliche Konstruktion zu wählen.

Ausgehend von einer Serienschaltung (10) wird eine Master-Slave (MS-) Maschine mit synchronisiertem wechselseitigem Ausschluß vereinbart, so daß die

Master-Maschine M_M in einer Art Warteposition steht, solange die Slave-Maschine M_S aktiviert ist.

Vereinbarung 1.2.2,2

1. für die MS-Kommunikation sind folgende I/O-Komponenten reserviert:

Start:	$^o(S)$Master	$=:$	$^i(S)$Slave
Index:	$^o(J)$Master	$=:$	$^i(J)$Slave
Rückmeldung:	$^i(R)$Master	$:=$	$^o(A)$Slave

2. für die Synchronisation gilt:

   a) M_M startet M_S

   b) M_M wartet auf Aktivierung von M_S

   c) M_M wartet auf Ende von M_S

   d) Die zugeordneten Synchronisationszustände $\{s_a, s_b, s_c\} \subset S_M$ werden durch die Verschmelzung W repräsentiert.

Der 2. Teil dieser Vereinbarung kann für die Master-Maschine M_M durch den folgenden (Teil-) Zustandsgraphen Z bzw. Z' dargestellt werden.

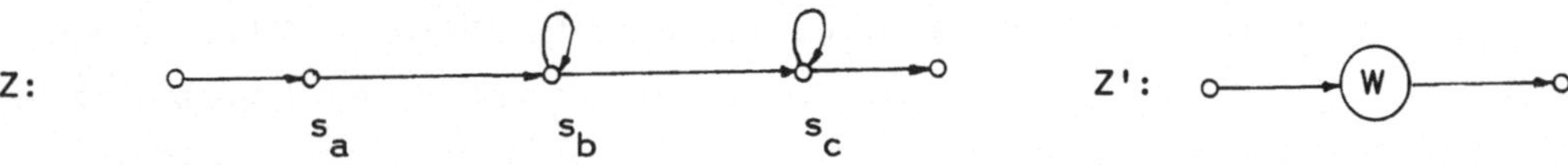

Definition 1.2.2,4

Eine <u>Typ I</u> MS-Maschine ist die Verknüpfung einer übergeordneten Master-Maschine M_M mit einer untergeordneten Slave-Maschine M_S

$$M = (I,O,S,f,h) := M_M \circ M_S$$

$$I := I_M$$

$$O := O_S$$

$$S := S_M \times S_S$$

$$f : S \times I \longrightarrow S : ((s_M, s_S), i_M) \longmapsto (s'_M, s'_S) := (f_M(s_M, i_M), f_S(s_S, h_M(s_M, i_M)))$$

$$h : S \times I \longrightarrow O : ((s_M, s_S), i_M) \longmapsto o := h_S(s_S, h_M(s_M, i_M)),$$

und für den wechselseitigen Ausschluß nach Vereinbarung 1.2.2,2, so daß für die Zustandsüberführung unter f gilt:

$$((s_M, s_S), i_M) \xmapsto{f} \begin{cases} (f_M(s_M, i_M), s_{Se}), & \text{wenn } M_M \underline{\text{ aktiv}} \text{ und } M_S \underline{\text{ inaktiv}} \\ (W, f_S(s_S, W)), & \text{wenn } M_S \underline{\text{ aktiv}} \\ (s_{Me}, s_{Se}), & \text{wenn } M_M, M_S \underline{\text{ inaktiv}} \end{cases}$$

Somit kann eine Folge sequentieller Prozesse $P = (p_1, \ldots, p_n)$ beschrieben werden durch eine MS-Maschine von Typ I, wobei die Mastermaschine zugeordnete Slave-Maschinen $(M_{S1}, \ldots, M_{Sn})$ aufruft.

Graphisch kann dieses Beispiel dargestellt werden durch einen Master-zustandgraphen Z_M mit einer Folge von Slave-Zustandsgraphen Z_S

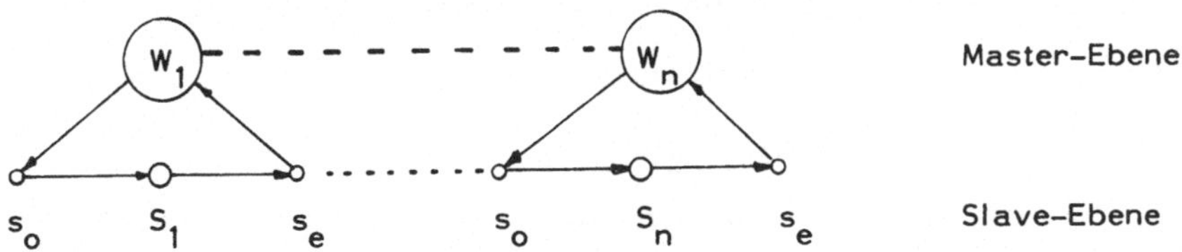

Wie in der vorangegangenen informellen Darstellung bereits aufgezeigt und von Petri in seinem Papier über nichtsequentielle Prozesse dargelegt wurde, gilt:

"Reale Prozesse sind im allgemeinen nichtsequentiell (8)".

Ausgehend von einer den Parallelismus erzeugenden Relation der Nebenläufigkeit, die als einzige empirische Beziehung nach Petri bereits ausreicht, eine genügend umfassende Prozeß- und Systemtheorie zu begründen, weil aus ihr sich insbesondere "die Beziehungen der Koinzidenz, der faktischen Äquivalenz, der Zeitordnung und der Verhaltens-Alternative" ableiten lassen, werden nachfolgend nebenläufige Maschinenkonstrukte dargestellt, die die aufgezeigte Problemstellung beschreiben.

Definition 1.2.2,5

Eine zweigliedrige Parallelschaltung M ist die Verknüpfung zweier Maschinen M_1, M_2 als kartesisches Produkt, so daß gilt:

$M = (I, O, S, f, h) := M_1 \circ M_2$
$I := I_1 \times I_2$
$O := O_1 \times O_2$
$S := S_1 \times S_2$
$f : S \times I \longrightarrow S$
$h : S \times I \longrightarrow O$

Anmerkung:

Der Begriff "parallel" bezieht sich in diesem Zusammenhang auf die Verknüpfung der Objekte $I_1 \times I_2$, $O_1 \times O_2$ und $S_1 \times S_2$, so daß deren Elemente als Paare auftreten.

Unter der Voraussetzung, daß beide Maschinen M_1, M_2 initialisiert sind (koexistieren), erhält man per Definition

$f: S \times I \longrightarrow S: ((s_1, s_2), (i_1, i_2)) \longmapsto (s_1', s_2') := (f_1(s_1, i_1), f_2(s_2, i_2))$

zwei nebenläufige Maschinen.

Ebenso ist klar, daß es sich im speziellen Fall um eine nichtsequentielle Maschinenkonstruktion handelt:

Da reale Prozesse Vorgänge – Zustandsänderungen – in der Zeit sind und für die Überführung f_1, f_2 beliebige Zeitmaßstäbe T gewählt werden können, ist zwar jede partielle Überführung von M

$$(s_1, i_1) \xrightarrow{T1} f_1(s_1, i_1) \quad \text{und} \quad (s_2, i_2) \xrightarrow{T2} f_2(s_2, i_2)$$

berechenbar; aber es ist nicht allgemein durch

$$((s_1, s_2), (i_1, i_2)) \longmapsto f((s_1, s_2), (i_1, i_2)) := \ldots$$

ein Nachfolgezustand (s_1', s_2') berechenbar, so daß die Bedingung der "before-after Relation" von Dijkstra (2) nicht erfüllt ist, und es sich in diesem Fall um eine nichtsequentielle Zustandsüberführung handelt.

Im Zusammenhang mit technischen Prozessen wird dieses Maschinenkonstrukt durch eine Vielzahl von Apparaten realisiert, so daß der Prozeß auf der untersten Ebene definiert werden kann durch eine endliche Anzahl nebenläufiger terminaler Maschinen M_j:

$$M = \mathop{\times}_{j=1}^{n} M_j$$

Ausgehend davon, daß diese terminalen Maschinen von einem hierarchischen Rechnersystem gesteuert werden, kann nachfolgend eine ähnliche MS-Konstruktion vom Typ I vereinbart werden, die im Übergangsbereich zwischen Rechner und Anlage nicht auf das Beenden jeder aktivierten terminalen Maschine warten muß, da der Anlage im Gegensatz zum Rechner ausreichende reale Maschinen – Prozessoren – zur Verfügung stehen.

Somit kann die Vereinbarung 1.2.2,2-2 wie folgt vereinfacht werden:

Vereinbarung 1.2.2,3

   a) M_M <u>weist</u> einer zugeordneten M_S neue Eingangswerte <u>zu</u>

   b) M_M <u>wartet nicht</u> notwendigerweise auf Quittierung bzw. Ende von M_S

Dadurch entfällt der wechselseitige Ausschluß und es gilt die Ausgangsform der Überführungsfunktion von Definition 1.2.2,4

$$f : S \times I \longrightarrow S : ((s_M, s_S), i_M) \longmapsto (s_M', s_S') := (f_M(s_M, i_M), f_S(s_S, h_M(s_M, i_M))),$$

   die zwei nebenläufige Prozesse beschreibt:

   1. $f_M(s_M, i_M)$

   2. $f_S(s_S, h_M(s_M, i_M))$, wobei M_M über die Ausgabe $h_M(s_M, i_M) =: i_S$ zugeordnete Slave-Maschinen partiell steuert.

Nachfolgend wird diese Grundform der MS-Maschine als <u>Typ O</u> bezeichnet.

1.3 Maschinenstruktur

Aufgrund der vorliegenden Untersuchungen wurde ein vierschichtiges Maschinen-
modell (Abb. 5) entwickelt, wobei die zugeordneten Levels wie folgt definiert
sind:

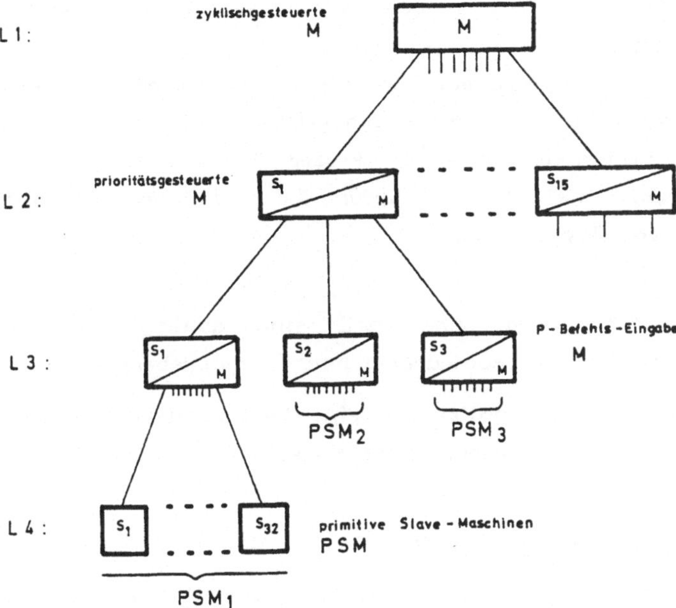

Abb. 5 Hierarchische Maschinenstruktur

<u>Level 1 und 2</u> := zyklisch gesteuerte MS-Maschine vom Typ I

Ausgehend davon, daß ein komplexer Prozeß sinnvoll zerlegt werden kann in
eine Anzahl nebenläufiger Prozesse $P = (P_1, \ldots, P_n)$, ist auf dem Level 1 eine
zyklisch gesteuerte Master-Maschine realisiert, die die auf dem Level 2
liegenden Slave-Maschinen steuert. Jeder Slave-Maschine M_j kann ein Prozeß P_j
zugeordnet werden, so daß die zugeordneten Prozesse parallel ablaufen können.

<u>Level 2 und 3</u> := ereignisgesteuerte MS-Maschine vom Typ I

Ausgehend davon, daß ein nichtsequentieller Prozeß durch ereignisgesteuerte
sequentielle Prozesse überdeckt werden kann, sind auf dem Level 2 prioritäts-
gesteuerte Slave-Master-Maschinen realisiert, die als Slave vom Level 1
gesteuert werden und ihrerseits als Master die auf dem Level 3 zugeordneten
Slave-Maschinen ereignis- und prioritätsabhängig steuern.
Jedem Master sind dabei drei Slave-Maschinen für folgende Prozesse zugeordnet:

        Slave 1:   Hauptprozeß

        Slave 2:   prozeßgesteuerte Nebenprozesse

        Slave 3:   bedienergesteuerte Nebenprozesse

<u>Level 3 und 4</u> := befehlsgesteuerte MS-Maschine vom Typ I

Auf dem Level 3 sind Slave-Master-Maschinen realisiert, die aus zugeordneten Programmspeichern als serielle Prozeßfolge indizierbare Slave-Maschinen vom Level 4 aufrufen. Die auf dem Level 4 hinterlegten Slave-Maschinen sind die eigentlichen Steuermechanismen, die die zugeordneten Aktionen im technischen Prozeß realisieren.

In Bezug auf ein zugeordnetes Rechnersystem werden die Maschinen auf der untersten Systemebene als primitive Slave-Maschinen (PSM) bezeichnet.

In Richtung verfahrenstechnischer Prozeß handelt es sich hier jedoch um Mastermaschinen, die in Verknüpfung mit Anlagen-Resourcen (Apparaten) MS-Maschinen vom Typ 0 bilden.

Anmerkungen:

Die Klassen PSM_1, PSM_2 und PSM_3 sind abhängig von prozeßbedingten Einschränkungen für die zugeordneten Haupt- und Nebenprozesse.

Nachfolgend werden im Hinblick auf eine Implementierung zu diesen primitiven Slave(Master)-Maschinen interpretative Funktionsmodule spezifiziert.

2. Interpretative Funktions-Module

Nicht nur um die bekannten Effizienznachteile in der Ausführungszeit konventioneller Interpreter (15) zu umgehen, sondern mehr, um die primitiven Slave-Maschinen durch eine Menge von Funktionsmoduln konform für den technischen Prozeß abzubilden, wird die von Knuth (5) angegebene Technik interpretativer Routinen angewandt.

Unter dieser Voraussetzung ist der Interpreter eine einfache Aufruf-Maschine, die das durch F indizierte Modul mit Daten D versorgt, so daß F angewandt auf D einen Wert liefert (Abb. 6).

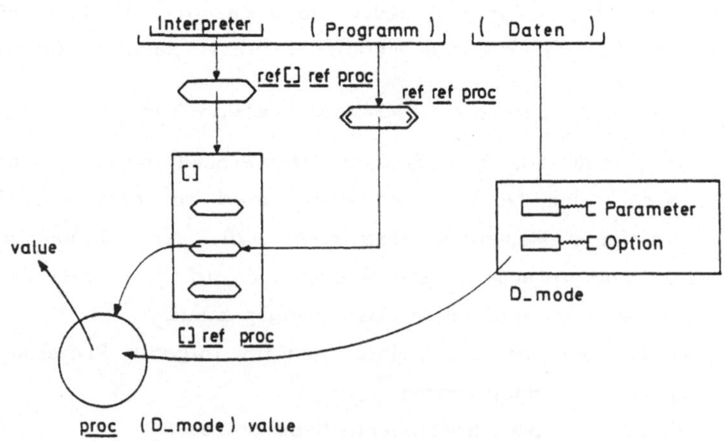

Abb. 6 Interpreter

2.1 Resourcenorientierte Module

Um diese Module konform aus dem verfahrenstechnischen Prozeß zu entwickeln, wurden elementare Prozesse P mit zugeordneten Resourcen r (z. B. Ventile, Antriebe, Sonden usw. aus dem RI-Fließbild) analysiert, für die gilt:

Definition 2.1,1

Eine <u>Prozeßeinheit</u> P_E ist ein nach Aufgabe und Wirkung abgegrenztes Objekt:

$$P_E = (p,r) \quad \text{mit} \quad p := \text{elementarer Prozeß}$$
$$r \in \text{Potenzmenge (Menge der Resourcen)}$$

Nachfolgend wird jeder P_E ein Controller C zugeordnet, über den der elementare Prozeß überwacht und über entsprechende Funktionsmodule F_M gesteuert werden kann (Abb. 7).

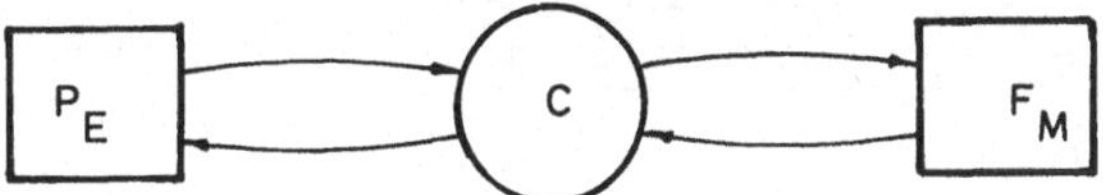

Abb. 7 Prozeßeinheit, Controller und Funktionsmodul

Der erste Schritt zu einer Entwurfsmethode liegt in einer geeigneten Interpretation einer Menge PE von Prozeßeinheiten, die den gemeinsamen Prozeß p' abstrahiert, der auf den zugeordneten Objekten abläuft, so daß zu jeder Prozeßeinheit ein entsprechendes Zustandsmodell (Controller) im Rechner implementiert werden kann.

Eine <u>geeignete Interpretation</u> ist gegeben durch eine Auswahlfunktion f_a, die die zur Realisierung der Prozesse erforderlichen Zustände der betrachteten PE auswählt, so daß die ausgewählten Zustände S' eine Maschine M bilden und es gilt:

$$f_{a1}: \quad S(PE) \longrightarrow S' \iff M$$

Analog dazu verläuft dann der zweite Schritt für die zugeordneten Funktionsmodule, die Aktionen im technischen Prozeß auslösen:

$$f_{a2}: \quad S' \longrightarrow S'' \iff M_j \in PSM$$

2.2 Programmorientierte Module

Neben der Klasse resourcenorientierter Module bestehen in einem Prozeßrechensystem noch Anforderungen für den Ablauf von Anwenderprogrammen, die nur indirekt bzw. gar nicht den Prozeßresourcen zugeordnet werden können (z. B. Blockstruktur, Synchronisation, Verzweigungen, Texte, ...).

Für diese Probleme wurde eine notwendige und hinreichende Anzahl programmorientierter Module entwickelt, die ebenso in anderen objektorientierten Programmiersprachen auftreten.

2.3 System-Struktur

Die entwickelten Funktionsmodule sind auf der untersten Ebene der Systemstruktur (Abb. 8) angeordnet und bilden die terminalen Sprachelemente von BISY.

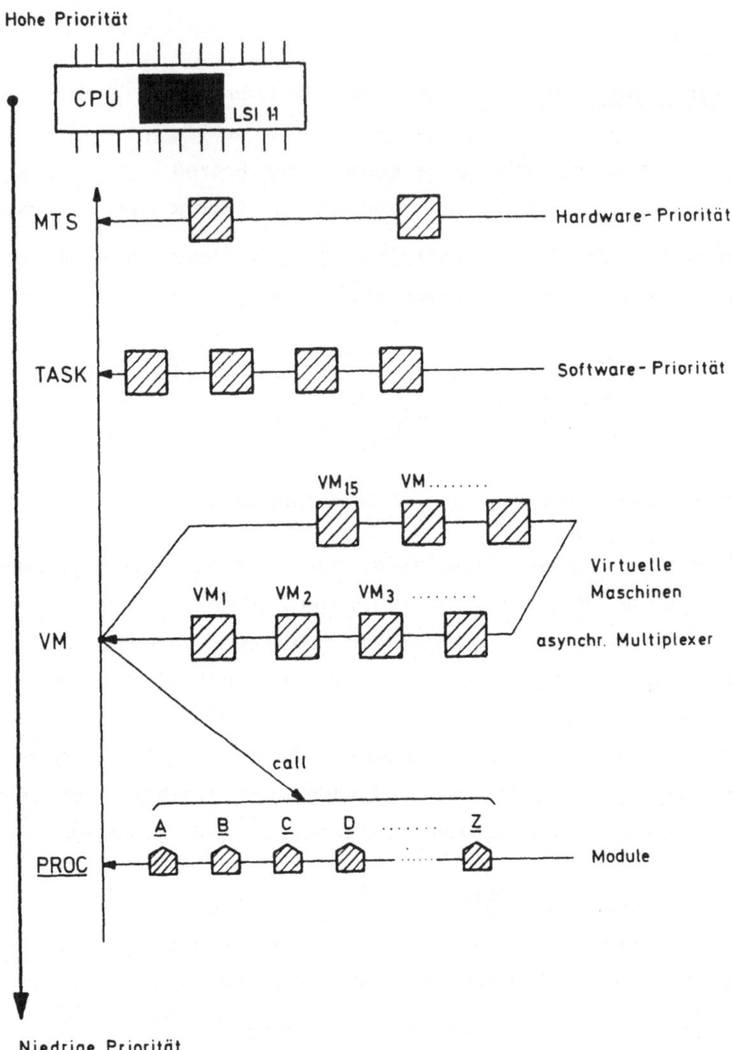

Abb. 8 System-Struktur

Das Konstrukt für die Sprachelemente (A, B, C, ...) wurde dabei wie folgt definiert:

```
mode sprachelement = struct  (ref ref proc modulindex,
                              amode parameterlist,
                              bmode option,
                              bit sequenzende);
```

Anmerkung:

Mit "modulindex" werden zugeordnete Funktionsmodule adressiert, mit "para-
meterlist" können variable Daten (z. B. Resourcenadressen, Sollwerte, ...) der
Funktion übergeben werden, mit "option" können zugeordnete Programmsegmente
innerhalb eines Moduls ausgewählt und mit "sequenzende" kann ein time-out
Mechanismus für die vorangegangene Befehlsfolge aktiviert werden.

Die vollständige Sprachbeschreibung ist in einem PDV-Bericht (13) veröffent-
licht.

3. Systemgenerierung und Anwenderprogrammierung

Ausgangspunkt für die Generiertechnik sind Module, die für eine vorgegebene
Problemstellung flexibel angepaßt werden können durch:

- Auswahl der Module
- Initialisierung von Listen.

In dem vorliegenden Anwendungsbereich geht es schwerpunktsmäßig um die
Einbettung (Initialisierung, Adressierung, Deklarierung und Überwachung) der
Prozeßresourcen in die vordefinierte Systemstruktur (Abb. 8).

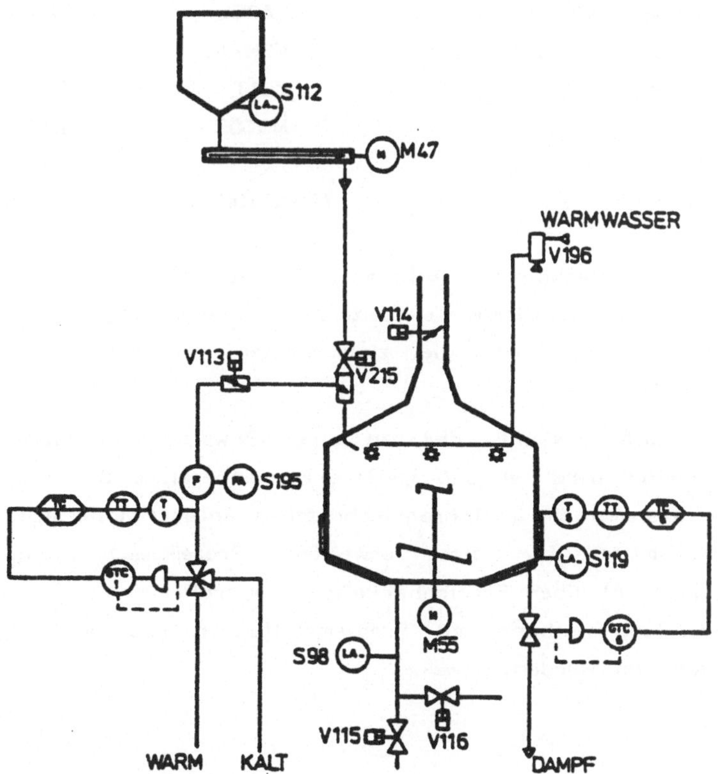

Abb.9 RI-Fließbild für Maischebereitung

Für die Anwenderprogrammierung ist ein simples Beispiel aus dem Maischprozeß (Abb. 1), das "Einmaischen", angeführt.
Die Resourcenbezeichnungen werden dabei identisch aus dem Rohrleitungs- und Instrumenten (RI)-Fließbild (s. Abb. 9) übertragen, so daß eine einfache verfahrenstechnische Fließbild-Beschreibung (sequentieller Prozeß) unmittelbar in ein Anwenderprogramm überführt werden kann.

Verfahrensbeschreibung	Programm	Daten
Maischen:		
Teil 1 "Einmaischen"	FUNKTION	1 EINTRITT;
...		
Ventil Verriegelung	BLOCKIERUNG	115 AUS,
Ventil Verriegelung	BLOCKIERUNG	116 AUS;
Einmaischwasser zuführen	VENTIL	113 EIN;
Rührwerk einschalten	MOTOR	55 SCHNELL;
max. Sonden-Wartezeit	ZEIT	10 MINUTEN,
Wasservorlage abwarten	SONDE	119 EIN;
Halt, (wenn Sonde Aus)	LABEL	31 ALARM;
Schrotschieber Auf (wenn Sonde Ein)	VENTIL	215 EIN,
max. Ventil-Wartezeit	ZEIT	50 SEKUNDEN;
Schrot zuführen	MOTOR	47 LANGSAM,
...		
Teil 1 Ende	FUNKTION	1 AUSTRITT;

Bei komplexen verfahrenstechnischen Anlagen muß natürlich der Prozeß aufgrund einer Prozeßanalyse in definierte Teilprozesse und ereignisgesteuerte Nebenprozesse zerlegt werden, bevor die zugeordneten sequentiellen Programme geschrieben werden können.

Abschließend sei noch erwähnt, daß an einer Erweiterung prozeßkonformer Abbildungen gearbeitet wird, so daß größere Phasenbereiche der Projektierung von Prozeßrechnersystemen in verfahrenstechnischen Anlagen unterstützt werden können. Als Hilfsmittel für diese erweiterte Prozeßbeschreibung werden Ergebnisse von Perl (6) über Erreichbarkeits-Homomorphismen auf Petri-Netzen genutzt, die im Zusammenhang mit Problemstellungen aus den angeführten Pilotprojekten erarbeitet wurden.

Literaturverzeichnis:

1. Dennis, J.B.: Modularity in: Advanced Course on Software Engineering, ed. Bauer, F.L., Springer-Verlag 1973, S.128-182
2. Dijkstra, E.W.: Co-operating sequential processes, Programming languages, F. Genueys (Ed.), Academic Press., New York, (1968), 43-112
3. Eggert, H.: Eine Anwendung von Petri-Netzen für eine partielle Prozeßbeschreibung und deren Abbildung auf Echtzeitelemente von PEARL. Diss. TU-Berlin Fachb. 20, Nov. 1978
4. Horning, J.; Randell, B.: Process structuring. ACM Computing Surveys 5, No. 1, March 1973, S.5-29
5. Knuth, D.E.: The Art of Computer Programming, vol. 1, Fundamental Algorithms, Addison-Wesley, Reading Mass., 1968
6. Perl, J.: Übertragung des Markierungsbegriffes auf vergröberte Petri-Netze. Uni Osnabrück, Fachb. Math. Reihe P, Heft 15
7. Perl, J.: Graphentheorie. Akademische Verlagsgesellschaft, Wiesbaden 1981
8. Petri, C.A.: Nichtsequentielle Prozesse. GMD Interner Bericht 76-6, 2. Auflage 1976
9. Philipp, H.W.: Einführung in die Verfahrenstechnik. Salle + Sauerländer Verlag, 1980
10. Pichler, F.: Mathematische Systemtheorie. De Gruyter Lehrbuch, 1975
11. Runkel, U.D.: Forschungsschwerpunkte der Prozeßautomatisierung im Brauwesen. Monatsschrift für Brauerei 31, Nr. 8, S. 286-293
12. Sturm, K.H.: Hierarchisches Interpretatives Virtuelles Objektorientiertes Maschinen-System zur Steuerung verfahrenstechnischer Prozesse. Diss. TU-Berlin Fachb. 20, 1979
13. Sturm, K.H.: Konzeptionelle Methoden, Richtlinien und Empfehlungen zur Prozeßautomatisierung in Brauereien. KFK-PDV Bericht, voraussichtlich Dez. 1981
14. Ullrich, H.J.: Mechanische Verfahrenstechnik: Berechnung und Projektierung. Springer-Verlag 1967
15. Wegner, P.: The Vienna Definition Language. Computing Surveys, vol. 4, No. 1, March 1972, S. 5-63

Modularer Mustervergleich im Rahmen prozeduraler Programmierung

Eberhard Bertsch

FB Mathematik und Informatik
Fernuniversität 5800 Hagen

Abstract

We discuss recent criticism against the pattern concept of SNOBOL and
similar languages. It is felt that the objections are basically justified.
On the other hand, the pure concept of pattern does have some undoub-
ted virtues which are apparently hampered by the rest of the SNOBOL
language. The present paper contains a new approach to representing
the results of a pattern match, which can be implemented efficiently.
In particular, the bothersome detour via side effects as necessitated
by SNOBOL is avoided.
The implementation is sketched in some detail. Several examples of
applying the proposed ideas conclude the article.

1. Einführung

Eingabedaten, die einem Programm vom menschlichen Benutzer oder einem
anderen Programm übergeben werden, lassen sich grob in formatierte und
unformatierte Daten einteilen.

Aus der Sicht des Programmierers zeichnen sich formatierte Daten dadurch aus, daß ihre Zuweisung an Variablen des Programms wenig oder
gar keine Mühe bereitet. Für unformatierte Daten sind hingegen nicht-
triviale Verarbeitungsphasen im unmittelbaren Zusammenhang mit der Eingabe notwendig. Das Interesse an Sprachen wie SNOBOL, SL 5, MACRO
[5,6,4] und anderen Spezialsprachen mit Mustervergleichsmöglichkeiten
beruht im wesentlichen darauf, daß in diesen Sprachen der Programmier-
aufwand für Erkennung und Zerlegung von Zeichenketten spürbar reduziert
wird. Standard-Anwendungsfall für Erkennung und Zerlegung ist gerade
die Eingabe unformatierter Daten.
In der Literatur über Programmiersprachen und Programmiermethodik bis
Mitte der siebziger Jahre fällt auf, daß von seiten der Informatik De-
tailfragen von ALGOL 60 und dessen Nachfolgern große Aufmerksamkeit gewidmet wird, daß die industriellen Hauptsprachen COBOL, FORTRAN und
PL/1 kaum mehr als ein müdes Lächeln ernten, daß jedoch SNOBOL und man-

che andere Spezialsprachen von Kritik weitgehend verschont bleiben. Es mutet seltsam an, daß die erste ausführlich zu Papier gebrachte Kritik an SNOBOL von dessen Erfindern stammt [7]. Im nächsten Abschnitt sollen diese Aussagen dargelegt werden. Andererseits ist das Prinzip des Mustervergleichs durchaus wert, als programmiersprachliches Mittel berücksichtigt zu werden. Wir wollen deshalb in diesem Beitrag sprachliche und implementierungsmäßige Ansätze vorstellen, die Mustervergleiche ermöglichen, ohne von der Kritik an SNOBOL substantiell betroffen zu sein. Eine ausführliche Beschreibung ist in [2] enthalten.

2. Die neueren Aussagen der SNOBOL-Entwickler

Nachdem R. Griswold und Mitarbeiter mit der Sprache SNOBOL in verschiedenen Versionen und Dialekten sowie mit der Nachfolgesprache SL 5 etwa fünfzehn Jahre lang für die Verwendung des Pattern Matching eingetreten waren, setzen sie sich seit 1978 in massiver Weise dafür ein, explizite Rücksetzmechanismen auf Sprachebene _anstelle_ der früheren Konzepte zu verwenden [7,8]. Worin besteht ihre Kritik an SNOBOL? Zunächst weisen sie darauf hin, daß die Sprache SNOBOL ein nahezu unüberschaubares Vokabular an bedeutungstragenden Sprachelementen besitzt. Dies trägt insofern zur unübersichtlichen Programmierung bei, als zwei verschiedene Programmierer ihre Virtuosität möglicherweise an unterschiedlichen Teilmengen der Gesamtsprache erwerben und somit beim Verständnis der Konstruktionsverfahren des jeweils anderen ihre Mühe haben. Zweitens erkennt Griswold, daß die versteckten Feinheiten des Mustervergleichsverfahrens, die bei SNOBOL bis zur Benutzerschnittstelle durchschlagen, die Fehlersuche erschweren. In der Tat kann der Vergleichsprozeß in raffinierter Weise beeinflußt werden. Hier lohnt sich ein Zitat der Originalaussage:

> "Some aspects of pattern matching are so obscure that even the designers and implementors of the language (womit Herr Griswold sich selbst gemeint haben dürfte) are forced to resort to listings of the system for answers."

Weiterhin wird auf die potentielle Ineffizienz des Mustervergleichsverfahrens hingewiesen. Dieser Punkt bleibt bei Griswold recht pauschal. In [2] zeigten wir, daß in gewissen Fällen die Laufzeit exponentiell von der Länge des Eingabewortes abhängt. Die Strukturiertheit und Verstehbarkeit ist hiervon nicht betroffen. Allerdings liegt es nahe, daß ein Programmierer in Kenntnis dieser Zeitverschwendung zu

selbstgestrickten Tricks greifen wird, um das Problem zu lindern.
Extreme Effizienzprobleme entstehen auch dadurch, daß Muster während
des Programmlaufs erzeugt werden müssen. Dies führt zu einem ähnlichen
Dilemma wie den unter dem vorigen Punkt erwähnten. Da Mustervergleiche
im Sinne von SNOBOL nur die Ausgabe "Erfolg" oder "Mißerfolg" erzeugen,
müssen alle sonstigen während des Vergleichsvorgangs gewonnenen Ergebnisse auf dem Wege des Seiteneffekts übergeben werden. Muster werden
in der Regel nicht am Platz ihrer Verwendung deklariert. Der ernsthaf-
teste Defekt von SNOBOL ist nach der Meinung von Griswold die
grundsätzliche Trennung in eine Mustervergleichs-Teilsprache und eine
funktionell ähnliche, anders geartete Grundsprache. Beide sind in ihren
Ausdrucksmöglichkeiten stark beschränkt. Dennoch sind viele Aufgaben
mit Hilfe beider Teilsprachen formulierbar. Wenn ein Programmierer mit
keiner der beiden Teilsprachen zurecht kommt, greift er zum Mittel der
sogenannten 'unevaluated expressions', also Teilmustern, deren Konstruktion bis zur Anwendungszeit aufgeschoben wird. Griswold hierzu:

"This interface is awkward at best."

Zusammenfassend läßt sich feststellen, daß Griswold einen vollständigen
Zerriß aller Merkmale von SNOBOL 4 formuliert.
Die von Griswold vorgeschlagene Alternative [7] besteht im wesentlichen
darin, Suchoperationen in Zeichenketten und entsprechende Rücksetzmechanismen als Sprachelemente zu verwenden. Der zumindest partiell
deskriptive und statische Charakter von SNOBOL-Mustern wird damit zu-
gunsten zweifelhafter dynamischer Möglichkeiten aufgegeben. Es ist
allerdings nicht Gegenstand dieses Aufsatzes, eine Stellungnahme zur
Nützlichkeit expliziter Backtracking-Sprachmittel vorzulegen [8]. Nach
unserer Ansicht war der Erfolg von SNOBOL durch das Angebot an Formu-
lierungsmöglichkeiten für syntaktische Sachverhalte bedingt. Eine Re-
form sollte also diesen Punkt festhalten. Im folgenden wird ein Muster-
konzept vorgestellt, das die bekannten Probleme von SNOBOL bei der Darstellung von Vergleichsergebnissen nicht aufweist.

3. Das Muster-Konzept und seine Verwendung auf programmiersprachlicher
   Ebene

Informell ist jedes Muster ein regulärer Ausdruck. Zur Abkürzung und
aus Gründen, die unten näher erläutert werden, ist es zulässig, Muster-
bezeichnungen in anderen Mustern zu verwenden.
Die folgende Meta-Syntax definiert die Form von Musterdeklarationen.
Es ist vorzusehen, daß jede Prozedur der Wirts-Sprache (Host language)

solche Deklarationen enthalten kann.

$$patterndec ::= (r\text{-}pattern\ \underline{;})^{*}$$
$$r\text{-}pattern\ \ ::= Sname\ \underline{::=}\ patexpr$$
$$patexpr\ \ \ ::= patterm\ (\ \underline{|}\ patterm)^{*}$$
$$patterm\ \ \ ::= patfact\ (\ \underline{+}\ patfact)^{*}$$
$$patfact\ \ \ ::= patprim\ [\ \underline{*}\ |\ \underline{!}\ ]$$
$$patprim\ \ \ ::= \underline{(}\ patexpr\ \underline{)}\ |$$
$$stringcon\ |$$
$$ANY\ \underline{(}\ stringcon\ \underline{)}\ |$$
$$NONE\ \underline{(}\ stringcon\ \underline{)}\ |$$
$$LETTER\ |\ DIGIT\ |$$
$$Sname$$
$$stringcon\ \ ::= \underline{'}\ Char^{*}\ \underline{'}$$

Die unterstrichenen Symbole und Großbuchstaben sind Terminalzeichen
der Metasyntax. Sname repräsentiert die Menge der möglichen Bezeichner
der Wirts-Sprache, Char einen (möglicherweise rechner-abhängigen) Zeichenvorrat. Um eindeutige, <u>nichtrekursive</u> Deklarationen von Musternamen
zu gewährleisten, fordern wir:

Für jedes r-pattern der Form

$$name_2\ ::= \ldots\ name_1\ \ldots;$$

(mit $name_1$, $name_2 \in$ Sname) existiert genau ein und zwar ein <u>zuvor</u> auf-
tretendes r-pattern der Form

$$name_1\ ::= \ldots;$$

<u>Beispiel</u>:

$$A ::= \text{'\$'} + DIGIT\ !;$$
$$B ::= A\ |\ \text{'no cash'};$$

(Die Unterstreichungszeichen können hier unterdrückt werden.)

Wir wenden uns nun einer begrifflichen Beschreibung der <u>Sprache</u> eines
Musters zu (vgl. auch [3]). Im üblichen Sprachgebrauch handelt es sich
dabei um eine Menge von Ableitungsbäumen.

Zunächst sei $Char_{kla} := Char \cup \{(_p, _p) \mid p \in Sname\}$, wobei alle $(_p, _p)$
neue Zeichen seien.

Wir definieren die Sprache $L(k)$ für gewisse Teile k von Musterdeklarationen.

Für jedes patexpr der Form

$$k = k_1 \underline{|} k_2 \underline{|} \ldots \underline{|} k_n$$

ist $\quad L(k) = L(k_1) \cup \ldots \cup L(k_n)$.

Für jedes patterm

$$k = k_1 \pm k_2 \pm \ldots \pm k_n$$

ist $\quad L(k) = L(k_1) + \ldots + L(k_n)$.

$+$ sei die übliche Verkettung von Mengen von Zeichenketten.

Für jedes patfact

$$k = k_1 \,\underline{*}$$

ist $\quad L(k) = \{\varepsilon\} \cup L(k_1) \cup L(k_1) + L(k_1) \cup \ldots$

$$= (L(k_1))^*$$

Für jedes patfact

$$k = k_1 \,\underline{!}$$

ist $\quad L(k) = (L(k_1))^* \setminus \{\varepsilon\}$.

Für jedes patprim

$$k = \underline{(k_1)}$$

ist $\quad L(k) = L(k_1)$.

Für $\quad k = {}'a_1 \ldots a_n{}'$, wobei $a_1, \ldots, a_n$ einzelne Zeichen sind,

ist $\quad L(k) = \{a_1 \ldots a_n\}$.

Für $\quad k = \text{ANY } ({}'a_1 \ldots a_n{}')$

ist $\quad L(k) = \{a_1, a_2, \ldots, a_n\}$.

Für $\quad k = \text{NONE } ({}'a_1 \ldots a_n{}')$

ist $\quad L(k) = \text{Char} \setminus \{a_1, \ldots, a_n\}$.

Für $\quad k = N$ mit $N \in \text{Sname}$ und einer Deklaration $N ::= k_1$

ist $\quad L(k) = \{ (_N\} + L(k_1) + \{_N) \}$.

Anders ausgedrückt

$$L(k) = \{ (_N \, s \, _N) \mid s \in L(k_1) \}.$$

Für $k = \text{LETTER}$ oder $k = \text{DIGIT}$ ist $L(k)$ die entsprechende Untermenge von Char.

<u>Beispiel</u>:

    Für $A ::= {}'a{}' \mid {}'b{}'$;

       $B ::= {}'cd{}' + A + {}'ef{}'$;

    ist $L(A) = \{ (_A \, a \, _A), \ (_A \, b \, _A) \}$

       $L(B) = \{ (_B \, c \, d \, (_A \, a \, _A) \, e \, f \, _B), \ (_B \, c \, d \, (_A \, b \, _A) \, e \, f \, _B) \}$

Wir sagen nun, daß ein String s zu einem Muster N <u>paßt</u>, wenn

$s \in$ Terminals $(L(N))$.

<u>Terminals</u> ist eine Funktion, die in Wörtern über dem Alphabet $Char_{kla}$ alle Klammern löscht.

Also   Terminals $(\ (_A \ ) = \varepsilon$ für $A \in$ Sname
        Terminals $(\ _A) \ ) = \varepsilon$
        Terminals $(\ a \ ) = a$ für $a \in$ Char
        Terminals $(wv) =$ Terminals (w) Terminals (v) für $wv \in Char_{kla}^{*}$

Damit passen im vorigen Beispiel

c d a e f und c d b e f zum Muster B.

Als Resultat eines Vergleichs zwischen einem String s und einem Muster M soll nun nicht nur eine Ja-Nein-Antwort geliefert werden, sondern eine strukturelle Beschreibung des Strings: Der Funktions-Aufruf match (M,s) soll gerade <u>das</u> Wort $w \in L(M)$ liefern, für das Terminals (w) = s gilt, sofern genau ein Wort mit dieser Eigenschaft existiert. Andernfalls ist eine Fehlermeldung zu geben. (Der Differenzierungsgrad solcher Meldungen ist von keiner geringen Bedeutung. Dieser Problemkreis soll hier dennoch offen bleiben.) Um dieser Anforderung auf sprachlicher Ebene zu genügen, erweitern wir die Wirtssprache um einen Datentyp <u>parse</u>, zu dem alle Wörter aus L(M) für beliebiges M gehören.
Die eigentlich entscheidende Frage bei der programmiersprachlichen Verwendung von Mustervergleichen ist die Zerlegungsmöglichkeit von Werten vom Typ <u>parse</u>. Für den Sprachentwerfer sind hierbei verschiedene Lösungsmöglichkeiten vorhanden. Bei SNOBOL wurde das Problem im wesentlichen ignoriert bzw. auf unelegante Seiteneffekte abgewälzt. Eine einfache Lösung wäre die unmittelbare Umformung von Werten vom Typ <u>parse</u> in Zeichenketten. Dann müßte der Benutzer aber komplizierte Bearbeitungsroutinen in eigener Verantwortung erstellen. Eine andere Lösung wären externe Unterprogramme für Zeichenketten oder Bäume; man hätte Werte vom Typ <u>parse</u> nun als Zeichenketten bzw. Bäume zu übergeben.
Wir haben uns dafür entschieden, auf Kosten einer Implementierungstechnik, die in [2] beschrieben wurde, die Zerlegung eines Strings als Resultat des Vergleichs anzubieten.

Zunächst definieren wir

count (b,p) als die Anzahl der Vorkommen des Klammerpaars $(_p \ ... \ _p)$ in einem Parse b.
Für den Fall, daß count $(b,p) \geq j$, ist $b[p,j]$ derjenige Teil von b, der

von dem von links her j-ten Vorkommen von $($_p und dem darauf folgenden
Vorkommen von _p$)$ umfaßt wird.

Etwas formaler:

Sei $\quad b = v_1\,(_p\,w_1\,_p)\,v_2\,\ldots v_j\,(_p\,w_j\,_p)\,v_{j+1}$

wobei $\quad v_1,\ldots,v_j,w_1,\ldots,w_j \in (\text{Char}_{kla} \setminus \{(_p\,,\,_p)\})$

und $\quad v_{j+1} \in \text{Char}_{kla}^*$.

Dann ist $b[p,j] := w_j$.

Weiterhin ist term $(b[p,j])$ die Zeichenkette Terminals $(b[p,j])$, und
pos $(b[p,j])$ ist die Anfangsposition von $b[p,j]$ in s,
d.h.: $\quad$ pos $(b[p,j]) =$
$\qquad$ Länge (Terminals $(v_1 w_1 \ldots w_{j-1} v_j)) + 1$

Wir stellen fest, daß die Zugriffsfunktionen <u>count</u>, <u>term</u> und <u>pos</u> die
für weitere Zeichenkettenverarbeitung relevanten Daten aus einem durch
Mustervergleich entstandenen Parse zu liefern vermögen. Für undefinierte count- und pos-Angaben legen wir den Wert 0 fest, für undefinierte
term-Angaben die leere Kette.

<u>Beispiel</u>:

Seien die Muster deklariert:

```
        lat  ::= ANY ('abcd...ABCD...')!;
        grie ::= ANY ('αβγ...ω')!;
        phil ::= ((lat | grie) + ' ')!
```

Dann liefert

```
        b := match (phil,s);
```

für den String

```
        s = 'Zenon nennt es πυρ τεχνικον'
```

einen Parse b mit den Werten

```
        count ( b,grie) = 2,    count (b, lat) = 3
        pos   ( b[lat,2]) = 7,
        term  ( b[lat,3]) = 'es',
        term  ( b[grie,2]) = 'τεχνικον'
```

u.a.,
die abgefragt werden können.
Für SNOBOL-Kenner sei angemerkt, daß die hier verwendeten Muster-<u>Dekla-
rationen</u> in SNOBOL ganz analog vorgenommen werden können, daß aber die
count-, pos- und term-Werte nur durch eine komplizierte Ablaufsteuerung
gewonnen werden.

4. Einige Bemerkungen zur Implementierung

Aus Platzgründen können wir in diesem Aufsatz nur ganz beiläufig auf Implementierungsfragen eingehen.

Eine ausführliche verbale Beschreibung der Verfahren sowie eine Präzisierung in Form von PASCAL-Prozeduren findet sich in [2].

Zur Übersetzungszeit sind für die vorhandenen Musterdeklarationen entsprechende Muster-Graphen zu erstellen. Dies geschieht nach der naheliegenden Methode, Verkettungen von Mustern durch Hintereinandersetzen, Alternativen durch Nebeneinandersetzen, Sternoperationen durch Rückkoppeln von Teilgraphen mit Hilfe entsprechender Verweise darzustellen.

Zur Laufzeit werden diese Graphen mit dem vorliegenden String verglichen. Grob gesagt werden dabei an jeder Stelle im Graphen, an der mehr als eine Kante verfolgt werden kann, die nicht verfolgten Möglichkeiten auf einem LIFO-Stack abgelegt. Bei Mißerfolg des weiteren Vergleichs wird auf solche früheren Möglichkeiten zurückgegriffen.

Das Verfahren ist prinzipiell analog zum üblichen Depth-First-Search, wobei hier nicht nur ein Knoten, sondern der ganze Weg bis dorthin einschließlich eventueller Schleifen eine Rolle spielt. Auf Effizienzüberlegungen für diese Phase kommen wir weiter unten nochmals zurück.

Die sprachliche Gegebenheit, daß für den Benutzer nur die Werte von count, pos und term zugänglich sein müssen, läßt sich implementierungsmäßig für die Effizienz des Zugriffs ausnutzen. Als abschließendes Resultat jedes erfolgreichen Mustervergleichs liefern wir eine Datenstruktur, die für jedes direkt oder indirekt aufgerufene Muster p den count-Wert sowie eine Tafel der pos-Werte enthält, genauer: der Positionen von $($_p$ und $_p)$ bezüglich des Vergleichsstrings in dem erzeugten Parse.

Beispiel:

Für   big ::= 'AB' | 'CD';
        seq ::= (ANY ('abcd')| big)*;
produziert b := match (seq,'abABCDcdAB');
ein Parse der Form

$$(_{seq}\ ab\ (_{big}\ AB\ _{big})(_{big}\ CD\ _{big})\ cd\ (_{big}\ AB\ _{big})\ seq)\cdot$$

Die für den Benutzer zugänglichen Werte lassen sich durch

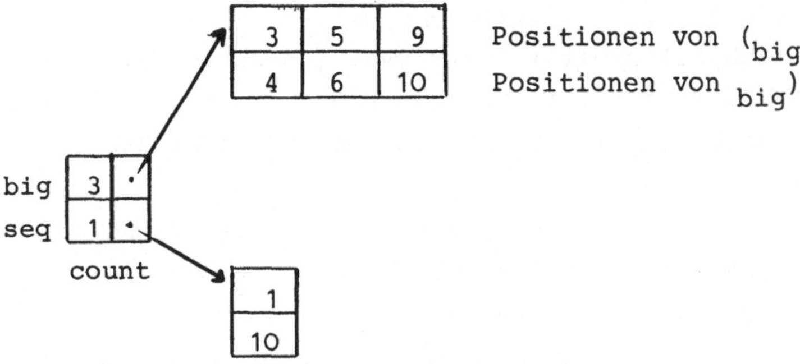

darstellen.

Wegen der Möglichkeit, innerhalb eines Musters andere Muster aufzurufen, muß weiterhin eine Art Prozedurverwaltung für Mustergraphen betrieben werden. Diese gestaltet sich recht kompliziert, da der Aufrufmechanismus und der Backtrackingmechanismus für die Suche voneinander völlig unabhängig sind [8]. Insbesondere wird es vorkommen, daß bei Auftreten einer Sackgasse <u>nach</u> Verlassen eines aufgerufenen Graphen noch Alternativen innerhalb dieses Graphen zu berücksichtigen sind. Es muß also eine Restaurierungsmöglichkeit für früher einmal aktuelle Aufrufketten geben. Unsere Implementierung verwaltet deshalb alte Aufrufketten, die durch Verweise im Such-Stack wieder aktiviert werden können. Für diese Ketten muß darüber hinaus eine Garbage Collection nach dem Mustervergleich möglich sein.

Wir übergehen hier die Zwischenstadien, die eine Positionstafel vor ihrer Fertigstellung durchlaufen muß. Es leuchtet ein, daß alle mutmaßlichen Positionen linker und rechter Klammern vor ihrer Ablage in der Tafel zunächst einmal linear verkettet werden. Solche Positionen, die bei weiterem Fortgang des Mustervergleichs als inkorrekt erkannt werden, lassen sich am Ende der Kette leicht abhängen.

Besonders interessant ist die Frage nach dem größenordnungsmäßigen Zeitbedarf für Mustervergleiche. SNOBOL braucht schlimmstenfalls exponentielle Zeit in Abhängigkeit von der Eingabelänge. Auf unser bisher skizziertes Verfahren trifft dies ebenfalls zu. Allerdings läßt sich zeigen, daß bei Hinzunahme einer weiteren Datenstruktur, die die früheren Such-Zustände enthält, eine schlimmstenfalls <u>lineare</u> Zeitkomplexität erreicht wird. Versuche, von früher bereits erfolglosen Suchzuständen auszugehen, sind nämlich in gewisser Hinsicht wiederum zum Scheitern verurteilt. Diese Beobachtung läßt sich für unser Verfahren ausnutzen. Eine wichtige Voraussetzung hierfür ist die anfangs gefor-

derte Nichtrekursivität des Aufrufs der Muster untereinander. (Naheliegende Ausnahmen von dieser Einschränkung ergäben sich, wenn man zur
Übersetzungszeit einen LL(1)-Test durchführte.)

Der Preis für diese Schnelligkeit ist der zwar lineare, aber nicht ver-
nachlässigbare Platzbedarf für alte Suchzustände. Unsere Implementierung verwendet eine Methode, die pro Suchzustand nur zwei Zahlen benötigt.

Die soweit erläuterte Implementierung funktioniert weitgehend unabhängig vom Laufzeit-System der Wirts-Sprache.

Zu beachten ist, daß bei blockstrukturierten Wirtssprachen [1] eine ver-
nünftige Konvention für die Lebensdauer der Musterdeklarationen und der
Parse-Variablen benötigt wird. Wir schlagen vor, daß die (zur Übersetzungszeit konstruierten) Mustergraphen für alle diejenigen Prozeduren
zugänglich sein sollen, die zu einer an gleicher textlicher Stelle ste-
henden Prozedurdeklarationen Zugang hätten. Parse-Variablen sind wie
Variablen einfachen Typs zu behandeln. Seiteneffekt-Probleme können sich
wegen der sauberen Schnittstelle nicht ergeben.

Wir meinen, daß die von uns im Hinblick auf einfache Textzerlegungen verwendete Sprachenentwurfsmethode auch für viele andere Datenverarbeitungs-
probleme sinnvoll sein kann: Eine sprachlich und möglichst auch implementierungsmäßig isoliert erfaßbare Problematik ist zu modellieren. Dabei ist auf eine saubere und einfache Schnittstelle zu einer problemo-
rientierten Wirts-Sprache zu achten.

5. Beispiele

a) Prosatext:

```
    Wort         ::= (LETTER | DIGIT)!;
    Wortgebilde  ::= Wort + ('-' + Wort)*;
    Fügung       ::= Wortgebilde + (' ' + Wortgebilde)*;
    Satz         ::= Fügung + ((',' | ';' | '-') + Fügung)*;
    Absatz       ::= (Satz + ANY ('.?!:'))!;
```

b) Griechisch-deutsches Wörterbuch:

```
    Deuwort      ::= LETTER!;
    Griewort     ::= ANY ('αβγ...ω')!;
    Wortgruppe   ::= Deuwort + (',' + Deuwort)*;
    Übersetzung  ::= Wortgruppe + (';' + Wortgruppe)* + '.';
    Eintrag      ::= Griewort + ' ' + Übersetzung;
    Wörterbuch   ::= Eintrag!;
```

c) Adressenliste:

    Vorname   ::= LETTER + ('.' | LETTER*);
    Nachname   ::= LETTER!;
    Name   ::= Vorname + ('-' + Vorname | ' ') + Nachname;
    Straße   ::= (LETTER! + ' ')! + LETTER! + ('.' | ") + DIGIT*;
    Stadt   ::= DIGIT! + LETTER! + ('-' + LETTER! | ");
    Adresse   ::= Name + ' '* + ',' + ' '* + Straße +' '* +','+ ' '* + Stadt;
    Liste   ::= Adresse + (' '* +',' + ' '* + Adresse)*;

d) Zahlen:

    Digseq   ::= DIGIT!;
    Expo   ::= 'E' + ('+'|'-'|") + Digseq;
    Zahl   ::= ('+'|'-'|") + Digseq + ('.' + Digseq|") + (Expo | ");

e) Zeichenketten, nach Ketten von Blanks und Ketten von anderen Zei-
    chen getrennt:

    A ::= ' '!;
    B ::= NONE (' ')!;
    Z ::= ((A + B)! + (A|")) | ((B + A)! + (B|"));

Zu diesem Muster geben wir mögliche Verarbeitungsanweisungen an,
wobei COMSKEE als Wirtssprache angenommen wird:

```
        read (line);
        t := match (line,Z);
```

Hierdurch wird eine Textzeile eingelesen und mit dem Muster verglichen.

```
        sumblank := O;
        for i := 1 to count (t,A)
        loop sumblank := sumblank + # term (t[A,i])
        pool;
        average := sumblank / count (t,A);
```

Diese Anweisungen ermitteln die durchschnittliche Länge der Blankketten innerhalb der Zeile.

```
        outstring := term (t[B,1]);
        for i := 2 to count (t,B)
        loop outstring := outstring + average *' ' + term (t[B,i])
        pool;
        write (outstring);
```

Hierdurch wird eine Zeichenkette erstellt und ausgegeben, deren
Blankketten gleichmäßige Länge haben.

6. Literatur

[1]   Bertsch, E. und Mueller-von Brochowski, A.:
String and File Handling in COMSKEE, Sprache und Datenverarbeitung 3, 1-9 (1979/80)

[2]   Bertsch, E.:
Regular Expression Matching - Language Concepts and Efficient
Implementation, Informatik-Berichte Nr. 11, Fernuniversität Hagen
(1980)

[3]   Gimpel, J.F.:
A Theory of Discrete Structures and Their Implementation in SNOBOL 4,
Comm. ACM, 91-100 (1973)

[4]   Greenwood, S.R.:
MACRO - A Programming Language, Sigplan Notices 14, 80-91 (Dec.1979)

[5]   Griswold, R.E., Poage, J.F. und Polonsky, L.P.:
The SNOBOL 4 Programming Language, Prentice-Hall (1971)

[6]   Griswold, R.E. und Hanson, D.R.:
An Overview of SL 5, Sigplan Notices, 40-50 (Apr.1977)

[7]   Griswold, R.E. und Hanson, D.R.:
An Alternative to the Use of Patterns in String Processing,
ACM Trans. Programm. Lang. Syst. 2, 153-172 (1980)

[8]   Lindstrom, G.:
Backtracking in a Generalized Control Setting, ACM Trans. Programm.
Lang. Syst.1,8-26 (1979)

A Language for Set-Theoretic Concepts
Implemented by Microprogrammed Associative Memory Instructions

Josef Grosch

Lehrstuhl für Programmiersprachen
Universität Erlangen-Nürnberg

Abstract

Within the research project EGPA a programming language was developed
which includes among other things elements for set-theoretic concepts:
declarations of the data types SET and SUBSET, the corresponding set-
-theoretic operations and some useful intrinsic functions. These language elements are presented here in a PASCAL-like notation. The compilation maps the set-operations and the intrinsic functions into procedure calls, which are the instructions of an abstract "set-machine".
Some details of the implementation of this "set-machine" are discussed.
For efficient access the sets are stored in a vertical mode in a conventional memory and the set-operations are based on microprogrammed
associative memory instructions. The subsets are implemented as bit-
-vectors. Therefore the subset-operations can use the conventional
logical machine instructions and thus are executed fast. In this way
all the set-theoretic operations can be implemented efficiently. A
special language construct within the intrinsic functions allows the
comfortable specification of a subset through conditions. The computation of this subset is evidently an associative operation where we can
fully use the capabilities of the microprogrammed associative memory
instructions.

1. Introduction

The research project EGPA (Erlangen General Purpose Array) [5] investi-
gates

- the hardware of a hierarchical array structure (pyramid like),
- the operating system to organize the array structure for parallel
  or pipeline processing,
- an associative memory approach (vertical mode) using conventional
  storage modules and a special set of microprogrammed instructions,
  and
- a compiler to support programming of the associative memory capabilities and the synchronization of parallel tasks.

The above concept is implemented on a structure of 5 conventional
ATM 80-60 processors. We will only take a closer look at the use of

the associative memory and the corresponding higher level language constructs.

In an associative memory it is not relevant where the information is stored, because one can access it by its contents. There is a close analogy to sets where one also doesn't care about the order of the elements of the set. Furthermore the question whether an element is contained in a set is closely related to the mode of access in an associative memory, where one virtually looks at all information in parallel in order to either find the desired information or not. Thus we found implementing sets in a programming language would be a very natural way to use the capabilities of our associative hardware. There are a few programming languages allowing sets as language constructs, for example SETL and PASCAL. SETL [8] allows dynamic building of sets and provides the usual set-theoretic operations. The implementation uses hash tables. However the quantifiers (existential $\exists$, universal $\forall$) are translated into loops which cannot considered to be an efficient implemention. PASCAL [6] on the contrary has only a subset concept where the base set must be fixed at compile time. Then, of course, all the subsets can be implemented as bit vectors and the set operations are reduced to boolean instructions. Other disadvantages of the PASCAL sets are the limitation of the set size to a few multiples of the wordlength and the restriction of the possible element types to a subrange of the integers and characters or of an enumeration type. This reduces the range of application of the sets in PASCAL drastically. Our goal was to combine the advantages of dynamic set construction with an efficient implementation [7].

2.   The Language

The language constructs for the set-theoretic concepts follow the PASCAL style. An informal syntax of the language is given in appendix A. We give a brief overview using examples and referring to the production numbers of appendix A.

2.1.   Set-Declarations

A set is an unordered collection of different elements of the same type. In contrast to PASCAL the elements are entered into the sets during runtime and their number can dynamically vary between zero and a maximum limit. This maximum size of a set has to be specified at com-

pile time like the array bounds in PASCAL because of the static storage
management. For the syntax of the declarations refer to productions
1 - 6. Subsets are declared in relation to a base set. Not all data
types are allowed to be used as element types. We didn't implement sets
of sets, because we can 't handle them efficiently with our associative
memory approach (see chapter 4). Arrays and records of sets are not implemented because of too much effort in a pilot implementation. There
is one predefined set or subset constant, $\emptyset$, for the empty set.

Example:
```
    TYPE
        DATE: RECORD
                    YEAR, MONTH, DAY: INTEGER
                END
    VAR
        CALENDAR: SET 365 OF DATE
        WORKINGDAYS, WEEKENDS, HOLIDAYS, VACATION: SUBSET OF CALENDAR
```


2.2. Set-Expressions

With the declared variables for sets and subsets we can construct expressions using set-operators and brackets and regarding the priority
rules like usual (productions 7 - 14). These expressions can be used
for example in assignment statements or as procedure parameters like
other expressions. The set operators are:

-	(unary)	complement
*		intersection
+		union
-	(binary)	difference
=		equality
<>		inequality
<=		inclusion
>=		inclusion
IN		set membership

They may be used for sets of the same element type or for subsets of the
same base set. The complement operation is only defined for subsets of
a given base set. The operator IN checks whether an element is contained
in a set or subset or not.

Example:
```
    WORKINGDAYS := - (WEEKENDS + HOLIDAYS + VACATION)
```

2.3. Set-Statements

Of course one can use set- and subset-expressions in assignment statements. For the universal quantifier we have a loop statement (production 15). The existential quantifier is realized by an intrinsic function (SELECT, see chapter 2.4.), where we can fully use the advantage
of our associative hardware device.

Example:

    FOR X IN SET1 DO WRITE (X)

2.4. Set-Intrinsics

For constructing sets or subsets and for some other useful operations
we provide intrinsic functions. The calls of these functions can be used
instead of variables in an expression. There are intrinsics that allow
the construction of sets or subsets by specifying the elements. Subsets
can also be constructed by restricting the elements of a base set by a
condition (productions 16, 17, 21 - 23).

Examples:

    S := FORMSET (2,A,B+C,(D[I]:VARY I FROM 1 TO N))
    SS := FORMSUBSET (S,(D[I]:VARY I FROM 1 TO N) WITH ELEMENTS > K)
    SS := SUBSET (S WITH ELEMENTS > Ø AND ELEMENTS < K)

The semantics of the keyword ELEMENTS is described in chapter 4.3.. To
convert a set or a subset back to conventional data (array) we have the
intrinsic procedure FORMARRAY (production 18, 24):

    FORMARRAY (ARRAY1, SET1)

A single element can be randomly chosen from a set or subset by the
intrinsic SELECT (production 19):

    X := SELECT (SET1)

Additionally, some intrinsics are provided to obtain general information
about sets and subsets. They yield the maximum, the actual number of
elements in the set, or whether the set has elements at all (production
19, 20).

Examples:

    MAXSIZE := SIZE (SET1)
    ACTSIZE := CARD (SET1)
    IF EMPTY (SET1) THEN BREAK

3. Compilation - Abstract Set-Machine

The set expressions and the use of the intrinsics are compiled in conventional manner and are translated simply into procedure calls.

Examples:

source statement	set-machine instructions
S := S1 + S2 * S3	LOAD (S1)
	LOAD (S2)
	LOAD (S3)
	INTERSECTION ()
	UNION ()
	STORE (S)
S := FORMSET (A,B,(C[I]:	CREATESET ()
VARY I FROM 1 TO N))	ENTERSET (A)
	ENTERSET (B)
	FOR I := 1 TO N DO
	ENTERSET (C[I])
	FINISHSET ()
	STORE (S)

Every operand, operator, or intrinsic function corresponds to one or more procedure calls, which are the instructions of an abstract "set-machine". This machine is stack-oriented and is able to process sets and subsets. It includes a dynamic storage allocation facility for the intermediate results of the set-operations, because in most cases the size of a set yielded by a FORMSET call is not known at compile time. The procedures CREATESET and FINISHSET of the example allocate respectively free memory for a potential infinite set. The sequence of procedure calls for the intrinsic FORMSET has the same effect on the stack as the procedure LOAD. The instructions of the abstract set-machine are listed in appendix B. Sets and subsets are handled by the same procedure calls.

4. Implementation

4.1. Storage of Sets

In a conventional computer memory data is stored in consecutive words. For this let us use the notion horizontal mode. In our memory device the sets are stored in a vertical mode, that means that one element of a set is stored in the same bits of consecutive computer words [4]. The length of an element is theoretically not limited and we can store

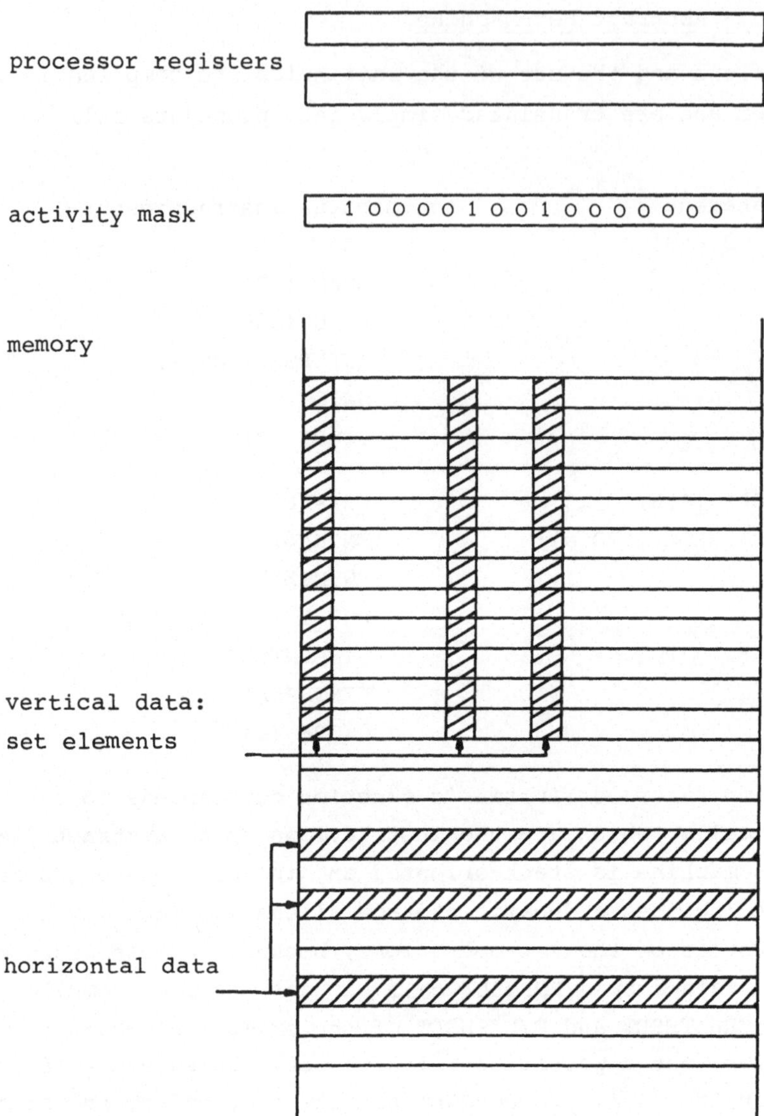

Fig. 1: Horizontal and vertical data in a conventional memory

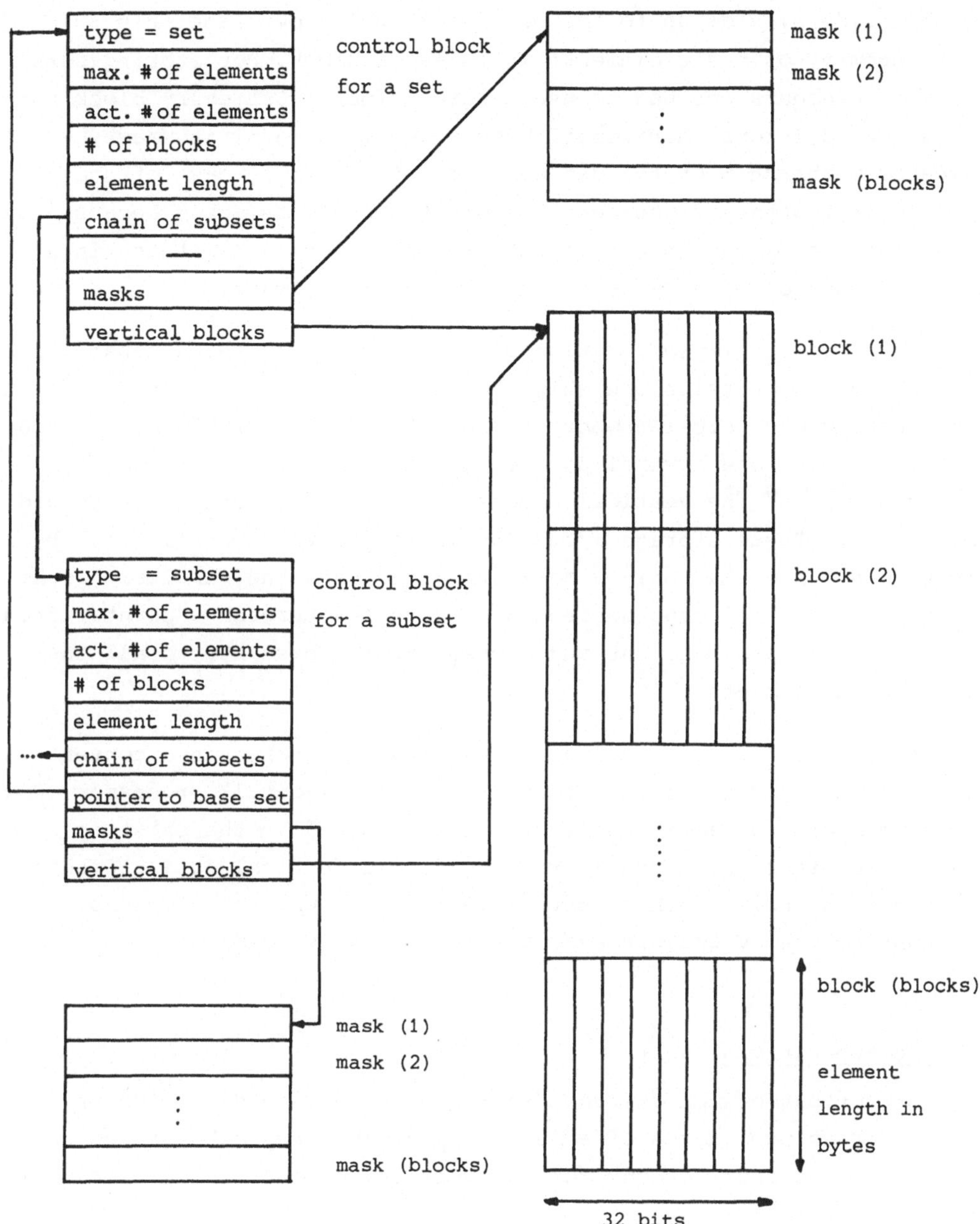

Fig. 2: Implementation structure of sets and subsets

elements side by side up to the wordlength n (in our case: n = 32).
An arrangement of n set elements is called a block. For storing sets
with more elements one has to use several blocks. For every block there
exists one additional horizontal memory word, the activity mask, which
indicates membership of the set elements (Fig. 1). In case of subsets
it would be a waste of storage to store the elements again because they
are already contained in a base set. So an element's existence in a
subset is controlled only by the related activity mask.

Figure 2 shows the implementation structure of a set and a subset. For
both we have a control block which holds the following information:
type, maximum and actual number of elements, number of blocks, element
length in bytes, and several pointers. Besides the control block
a set consists of the vertical blocks containing the set elements and
a mask array. These storage areas are linked to the control block by
pointers. A subset has only a mask array and uses the vertical blocks
of the base set. Sets and subsets are connected through a pointer from
every subset to its base set and a chain from a base set to all the
corresponding subsets.

In this way all the data including the sets are stored in a conventional
memory and are processed by a conventional (horizontal) processor. However some microprogrammed instructions were added to the existing hardware instructions which can operate on single vertical data elements
and even on a whole block of set elements. This unites the capabilities
of a conventional processor and of an assocciative memory.

4.2. Set-Operations

The instructions of the abstract "set-machine" mentioned earlier are
implemented as procedures of a runtime package. They make use of the
microprogrammed instructions for the vertical data [3]. The microprograms used are:

INSERT	inserts an element into a block
EXTRACT	extracts an element from a block
SEARCH	searches for a given element in a block
COMPARE	compares all elements of a block with a given element
FINDMIN	looks for the minimal element in a block
FINDMAX	looks for the maximal element in a block

The first two microprograms handle only one element. All the others
process a whole block and their result is a mask, indicating all the

elements which were found or for which the given condition holds. The microprograms for searching yield a speedup from 3 to 40 compared to conventional high level language programming [1,2].

Unfortunately these microprograms can't be used directly, because they work only on one block. So we had to construct loops around all those microprograms which lead to a layer of procedures with the same purpose as the bare microprograms, but which enable us to process whole sets. Let us call them:

INSERTS

EXTRACTS

SEARCHS

COMPARES

FINDMINS

FINDMAXS

Figure 3 gives an example of the procedure SEARCHS (ELEMENT, SET).

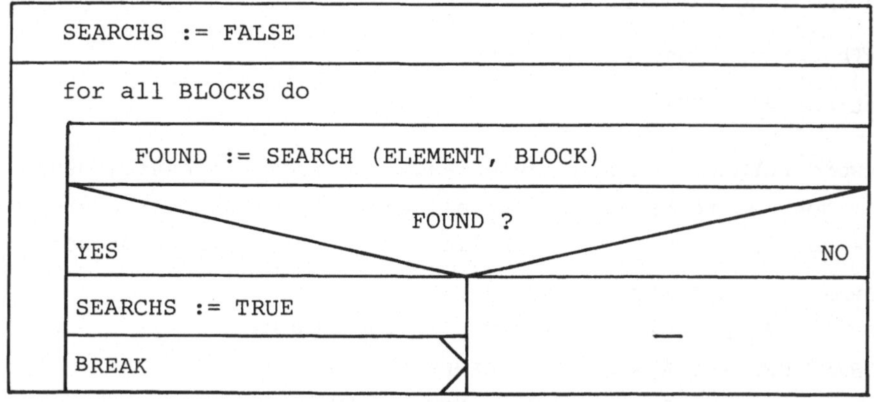

Fig. 3: The procedure SEARCHS (ELEMENT, SET)

With these procedures the set operations can easily be implemented. An example for the operation + is given in Fig. 4.

The same operation on subsets is a simple loop over a boolean instruction:

```
┌─────────────────────────────────────────────────────────────┐
│ RESULT := SET1     // Dynamic allocation of the inter-        │
│                    // mediate result                         │
├─────────────────────────────────────────────────────────────┤
│ for all ELEMENTS in SET2 do                                  │
│  ┌──────────────────────────────────────────────────────┐   │
│  │ ELEMENT := EXTRACTS(SET2)                             │   │
│  ├──────────────────────────────────────────────────────┤   │
│  │            SEARCHS(ELEMENT,RESULT)                    │   │
│  │ FOUND                              NOT FOUND          │   │
│  ├──────────────────────┬───────────────────────────────┤   │
│  │          —           │ INSERTS(ELEMENT,RESULT)       │   │
│  └──────────────────────┴───────────────────────────────┘   │
└─────────────────────────────────────────────────────────────┘
```

<u>Fig. 4:</u> The set-operation union (SET1 + SET2)

4.3. Set-Intrinsics

The set-intrinsics are implemented using the same layer of procedures
as the set-operations. Another aspect of associative processing arises
through the language construct:

    WITH *extended_boolean_expression*

(productions 25 - 29).

The keyword ELEMENTS within the *extended_boolean_expression* means that
a comparison has to be applied to all elements of a set. Some examples
may give an impression of the application of the WITH-construct:

```
FORMSET (A,B,C WITH ELEMENTS > -K)
FORMSET (A,B,C WITH ELEMENTS > -K AND ELEMENTS < K)
FORMSUBSET (S,(A,B,C WITH ELEMENTS > -K),
                (D,E,F WITH ELEMENTS < K))
FORMSUBSET (S, ((A,B,C WITH ELEMENTS > -K),
                D,E,F WITH ELEMENTS < K))
SUBSET (S WITH MIN ELEMENTS.PRICE)
SUBSET (S WITH ELEMENTS [I,J] = ∅)
SELECT (S WITH MIN ELEMENTS.PRICE OR ELEMENTS.YEAR >= 1980)
```

The semantics of WITH is defined such that some action is performed only
on those elements for which the condition following WITH holds. The
implementation of WITH can be derived from the intrinsics SUBSET and
SELECT, where one has a given set, which is restricted by a WITH-condition yielding a subset. SELECT then picks out an arbitrary element of
this subset. The construction of this subset is an associative opera-

tion. It can be performed on all the set elements in parallel. The
intrinsics FORMSET and FORMSUBSET are treated in the same way. First
all the listed elements are inserted into the set and then this set is
associatively restricted by the WITH condition.

As the condition can be combined out of several *elements_expressions*
the computation of the resulting subset leads to another stack processing. Each of the above expressions is one associative operation yielding
an intermediate subset result. These expressions are connected by the
boolean operators AND, OR, and NOT which are mapped to the subset operations intersection (*), union (+), and complement (-).

Let us have a closer look at the implementation of an example of an
intrinsic call:

$$\text{FORMSET } (\underset{1}{A},\underset{2}{B},\underset{3}{C} \underset{4}{\text{WITH}} \underset{5}{\underbrace{\text{ELEMENTS} > -K}_{6}} \underset{8}{\text{AND}} \underbrace{\text{ELEMENTS} < K}_{7})_{9,10}$$

This intrinsic is translated into the following sequence of procedure
calls:

```
        1       CREATESET      ( )
        2       ENTERSET       (A)
        3       ENTERSET       (B)
        4       ENTERSET       (C)
        5       BEGINWITH      ( )
        6       RESTRICT       (GREATER, -K)
        7       RESTRICT       (LESS,     K)
        8       INTERSECTION   ( )
        9       ENDWITH        ( )
       10       FINISHSET      ( )
```

The numbers show the correspondence between the elements of the language
and the generated procedures. The actions of the procedures on the stack
proceed in the following steps:

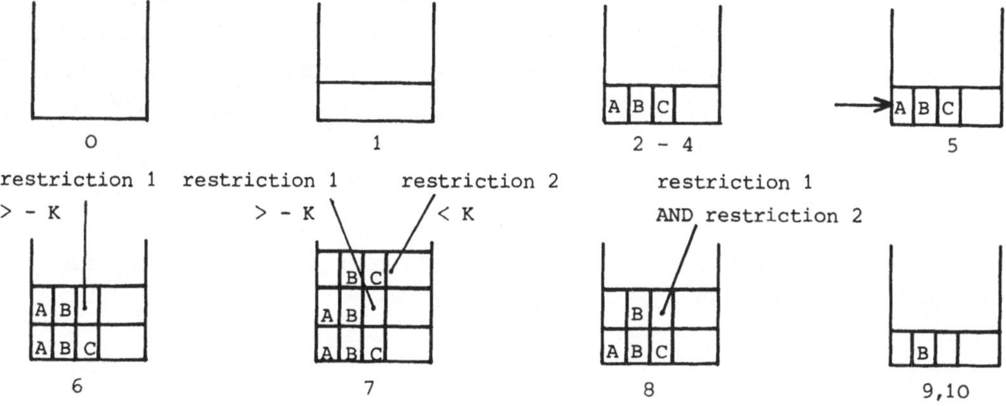

Ø   Assume the stack is empty in the beginning.

1   An empty set is created and pushed on the stack.

2 - 4   The elements A, B, C are inserted into the set.

5   The stack pointer is saved for further references to this set.

6   The first restriction is computed in 3 steps:
- the set whose pointer was saved in step 5 is transformed into a subset (this is only a duplication of the masks)
- this subset is pushed on the stack
- this subset gets restricted

7   The second restriction is computed like the first one, resulting in another push operation.

8   The two restrictions are combined through the intersection operation according to the operator AND. This leaves the resulting restriction on the stack.

9   The resulting restriction takes effect on the constructed set. The restriction is popped from the stack.

10   Some final actions take place. Now the result of the FORMSET call remains on the stack just like after a call of LOAD.

5. Conclusion

The compiler for the described language including the data type set and the corresponding operations is presently (November 1981) under construction. The runtime system to execute the set operations is completed except the FOR loop. We provide the users of our language with the powerful constructs of set expressions and especially the WITH-condition. The set operations are implemented efficiently because up to n (n = 32) elements are processed at a time and the full loop over all blocks of a set is only necessary in the worst case. Like in PASCAL the efficiency of the subset implementation is evident. As our first implementation showed the performance of the set-operations could be improved by some more suitable microprograms. For example the operation EXTRACTS in Fig. 4 would not be necessary if SEARCHS could look for a vertically given element. The whole concept would become fully efficient through the use of a real associative memory where you can process much more then 32 elements at a time.

References

[1] Albert, B., Bode, A., Händler, W.: "A case study in vertical mi-
     gration: The implementation of a dedicated associative instruc-
     tion set", to appear in: Euromicro Journal 12/81, North Holland
     Publ. Comp.

[2] Albert, B., Bode, A., Jacob, R., Kilgenstein, R., Rathke, M.:
     "Vertiaklverarbeitung: Beschleunigung von Anwenderprogrammen durch
     mikroprogrammierte Assoziativbefehle", Hauer, Seeger (Eds.),
     Hardware für Software, Conference of the German Chapter of the
     ACM, Konstanz, p. 114 - 123, Stuttgart: Teubner, 1980

[3] Bode, A.: "Probleme der Emulation unkonventioneller Rechnerarchi-
     tekturen: Pseudoassoziative Verarbeitung im Projekt EGPA", Proc.
     GI-NTG-Fachtagung Struktur und Betrieb von Rechensystemen (Kiel,
     March 1980) = Informatik-Fachberichte, Vol. 27, p. 138 - 148,
     Berlin: Springer, 1980

[4] Händler, W.: "On classification schemes for computer systems in
     the post-Von-Neumann-era", Lect. Notes Computer Sc., Vol. 26,
     p. 439 - 452, Berlin: Springer, 1975

[5] Händler, W., Hofmann, F., Schneider, H.J.: "A General Purpose
     Array with a Broad Spectrum of Applications", Workshop of the
     GI, Computer Architecture, Informatik-Fachberichte, Vol. 4,
     Berlin: Springer, 1976

[6] Jensen, K., Wirth, N.: "PASCAL user manual and report", New York:
     Springer, 1978 (2nd ed.)

[7] Schneider, H.J.: "Set-theoretic concepts in programming languages
     and their implementation", Proc. Workshop on graph-theoretic con-
     cepts in computer science, Bad Honnef, 1980

[8] Schwartz, J.: "Optimization of very high level languages",
     J. Computer Languages 1, 2 (1975), p. 161 - 194, and 1, 3 (1975),
     p. 197 - 218

Appendix A: The Syntax of the Language

1. Declarations

```
1   set_declaration :
        identifier_list : SET size_specification OF element_type

2   subset_declaration :
        identifier_list : SUBSET OF base_set_identifier

3   element_type :
        INTEGER
        REAL
        BOOLEAN
        CHARACTER
        STRING
        array_type_identifier
        record_type_identifier

4   array_type_declaration :
        identifier : ARRAY dimension_specification OF element_type
```

```
5   record_type_declaration :
        identifier : RECORD field_list END

6   field :
        identifier_list : element_type
```

2. Expressions

```
7   set_expression :
        set_term
        set_expression + set_term                                        // union
        set_expression - set_term                                        // difference

8   set_term :
        set_factor
        set_term * set_factor                                            // intersection

9   set_factor :
        ∅                                                                // empty set
        set_identifier
        (set_expression)
        FORMSET (element_specification)

10  boolean_factor :
        ...
        set_expression       = set_expression                           // equality
        set_expression       <> set_expression                          // inequality
        set_expression       <= set_expression                          // inclusion
        set_expression       >= set_expression                          // inclusion
        element_expression IN set_expression                            // set membership

11  subset_expression :
        subset_term
        subset_expression + subset_term                                 // union
        subset_expression - subset_term                                 // difference

12  subset_term :
        subset_factor
        subset_term * subset_factor                                     // intersection

13  subset_factor :
        ∅                                                                // empty set
        subset_identifier
        (subset_expression)
        - subset_factor                                                  // complement
        FORMSUBSET (base_set_identifier, element_specification)
        SUBSET (   set_identifier WITH extended_boolean_expression)
        SUBSET (subset_identifier WITH extended_boolean_expression)

14  boolean_factor :
        ...
        subset_expression    = subset_expression                        // equality
        subset_expression   <> subset_expression                        // inequality
        subset_expression   <= subset_expression                        // inclusion
        subset_expression   >= subset_expression                        // inclusion
        element_expression IN subset_expression                         // set membership
```

3. Statements

```
15  statement :
        ...
        set_identifier     := set_expression
        set_identifier     := subset_expression
        subset_identifier := subset_expression
        FOR identifier IN    set_expression DO statement
        FOR identifier IN subset_expression DO statement
```

<u>4. Intrinsics</u>

16   set_factor :
          FORMSET (element_specification)

17   subset_factor :
          FORMSUBSET (base_set_identifier, element_specification)
          SUBSET (set_identifier WITH extended_boolean_expression)
          SUBSET (subset_identifier WITH extended_boolean_expression)

18   statement :
          FORMARRAY (array_identifier, conditional_set_expression)

19   expression :
          SELECT (conditional_set_expression)
          SIZE   (conditional_set_expression)
          CARD   (conditional_set_expression)

2Ø   boolean_factor :
          EMPTY   (conditional_set_expression)

21   element_specification :
          element_list
          element_list : generator
          element_list WITH extended_boolean_expression

22   element :
          expression
          (element_specification)

23   generator :
          VARY identifier FROM expression TO expression BY expression

24   conditional_set_expression :
          set_expression
          subset_expression
          set_expression   WITH extended_boolean_expression
          subset_expression WITH extended_boolean_expression

25   extended_boolean_expression :
          ...   // like boolean_expression

26   extended_boolean_factor :
          boolean_factor
          elements_expression

27   elements_expression :
          elements_operand
          elements_operand comparison_operator arithmetic_expression
          elements_operand comparison_operator   string_expression
          MIN elements_operand
          MAX elements_operand

28   elements_operand :
          ELEMENTS
          ELEMENTS selector_list

29   selector :
          array_selector
          record_selector

Appendix B: The Instructions of the Abstract Set-Machine

set-machine instruction		language construct
LOAD	(set)	operand
STORE	(set)	:=
COMPLEMENT	( )	- (unary)
INTERSECTION	( )	*
UNION	( )	+
DIFFERENCE	( )	- (binary)
EQUAL	( ) : BOOLEAN	=
NOTEQUAL	( ) : BOOLEAN	<>
INCLUSION	( ) : BOOLEAN	<=
ELEMENT	(element) : BOOLEAN	IN
CREATESET	( )	FORMSET
ENTERSET	(element)	FORMSET
FINISHSET	( )	FORMSET
CREATESUBSET	( )	FORMSUBSET
ENTERSUBSET	(element)	FORMSUBSET
FINISHSUBSET	( )	FORMSUBSET
SUBSET	( )	SUBSET
FORMARRAY	(array)	FORMARRAY
SELECT	( ) : element	SELECT
SIZE	( ) : INTEGER	SIZE
CARD	( ) : INTEGER	CARD
EMPTY	( ) : BOOLEAN	EMPTY
BEGINWITH	( )	WITH
RESTRICT	(operation, expression)	WITH
ENDWITH	( )	WITH

<u>Anschriften der Autoren</u>

Prof. Dr. E. B E R T S C H
Fachbereich Mathematik und Informatik
Fernuniversität Hagen - Gesamthochschule
Fleyer Straße 204
Postfach 940
5800 Hagen 1

B. B Ö H R I N G E R
H. F E U E R H A H N
Epsilon GmbH
Otto-Suhr-Allee 22
1000 Berlin 10

Dr. R. G I E G E R I C H
Institut für Informatik
Technische Universität München
Postfach 20 24 20
8000 München 2

Dr. R. G N A T Z
Institut für Informatik
Technische Universität München
Postfach 20 24 20
8000 München 2

R. G O T Z H E I N
Dr. S. K E R A M I D I S
M. R E I T E N S P I E S S
Institut für Mathematische Maschinen
und Datenverarbeitung
Universität Erlangen-Nürnberg
Martensstraße 3
8520 Erlangen

J. G R O S C H
Lehrstuhl für Programmiersprachen
Universität Erlangen-Nürnberg
Martensstraße 3
8520 Erlangen

L. H I R S C H M A N N
mbp Mathematischer Beratungs-
und Programmierungsdienst GmbH
Semerteichstraße 47
4600 Dortmund 1

H. H U N K E
Commission des Communautés Européennes
25, Rue Archimède
B-1049 Bruxelles

Prof. Dr. H. M Ü L L E R - M E R B A C H
Institut für Betriebswirtschaftslehre
Technische Hochschule Darmstadt
Hochschulstraße 1
6100 Darmstadt

Dr. H. P A R T S C H
A. L A U T
Institut für Informatik
Technische Universität München
Postfach 20 24 20
8000 München 2

G. P A U L, Jr.
Manager, Architecture and Languages
513 System Technology Department
40-239 T.J. Watson Research Center
P.O.B. 218
Yorktown Heights, NY 10598
U S A

Dr. T. M. S C H U N E M A N N
Ordinariat für Betriebswirtschaftlich
Datenverarbeitung
Universität Hamburg
Von-Melle-Park 5
2000 Hamburg 13

W. U L L M E R
Hamburger Software GmbH
Langwisch 10
2000 Hamburg 65

H.-E. S E N G L E R
URW Unternehmensberatung
Harksheider Straße 102
2000 Hamburg 65

Dr. K.-H. S T U R M
Versuchsanstalt für Datenverarbeitung
und Prozeßtechnik
Seestraße 13
1000 Berlin 65

Dr. P. C. T R E L E A V E N
Computing Laboratory
University of Newcastle upon Tyne
Newcastle upon Tyne   NE1 7RU
England

Prof. Dr. W. M. T U R S K I
Institute of Informatics
Warsaw University
PKiN, pok. 850
00-901 Warsaw
Poland

Prof. Dr. R. W I L H E L M
Universität des Saarlandes
FB 10-Informatik
Im Stadtwald
6600 Saarbrücken

Band 44: Organisation informationstechnik-gestützter öffentlicher Verwaltungen. Fachtagung, Speyer, Oktober 1980. Herausgegeben von H. Reinermann, H. Fiedler, K. Grimmer und K. Lenk. 1981.

Band 45: R. Marty, PISA – A Programming System for Interactive Production of Application Software. VII, 297 Seiten. 1981.

Band 46: F. Wolf, Organisation und Betrieb von Rechenzentren. Fachgespräch der GI, Erlangen, März 1981. VII, 244 Seiten. 1981.

Band 47: GWAI – 81 German Workshop on Artificial Intelligence. Bad Honnef, January 1981. Herausgegeben von J. H. Siekmann. XII, 317 Seiten. 1981.

Band 48: W. Wahlster, Natürlichsprachliche Argumentation in Dialogsystemen. KI-Verfahren zur Rekonstruktion und Erklärung approximativer Inferenzprozesse. XI, 194 Seiten. 1981.

Band 49: Modelle und Strukturen. DAG 11 Symposium, Hamburg, Oktober 1981. Herausgegeben von B. Radig. XII, 404 Seiten. 1981.

Band 50: GI – 11. Jahrestagung. Herausgegeben von W. Brauer. XIV, 617 Seiten. 1981.

Band 51: G. Pfeiffer, Erzeugung interaktiver Bildverarbeitungs- systeme im Dialog. X, 154 Seiten. 1982.

Band 52: Application and Theory of Petri Nets. Proceedings, Stras- bourg 1980, Bad Honnef 1981. Edited by C. Girault and W. Reisig. X, 337 pages. 1982.

Band 53: Programmiersprachen und Programmentwicklung. Fach- tagung der GI, München, März 1982. Herausgegeben von H. Wössner. VIII, 237 Seiten. 1982.